The Danube
A river guide

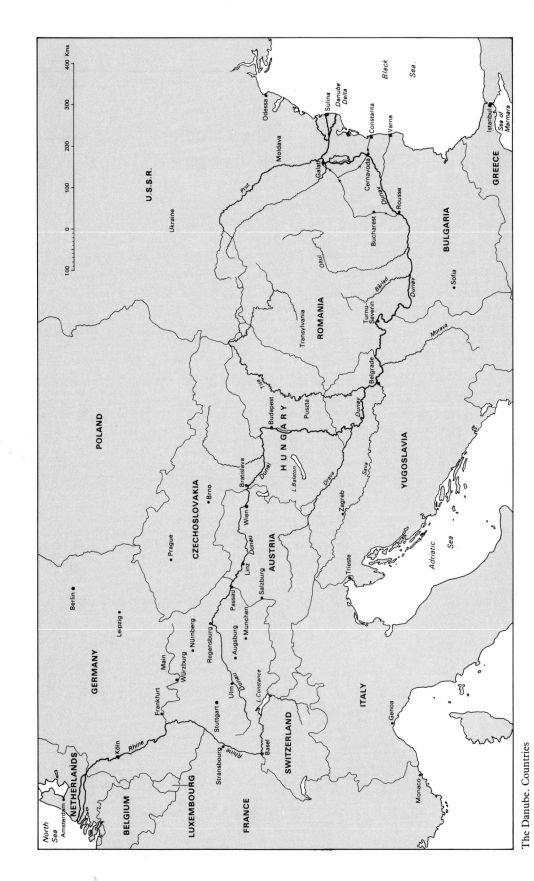

The Danube. Countries

The Danube

A river guide

ROD HEIKELL

Imray Laurie Norie & Wilson Ltd
St Ives Cambridgeshire England

Published by
Imray, Laurie, Norie & Wilson Ltd
Wych House, St Ives, Huntingdon,
Cambridgeshire, PE17 4BT, England.

British Library Cataloguing in Publication Data

Heikell, Rod
   The Danube. A river guide
   1. Danube. Rivers. Boating
   I. Title
   914.9604

   ISBN 0 85288 147 9

CAUTION
Whilst every care has been taken to ensure accuracy, neither the Publishers nor the Author will hold themselves responsible for errors, omissions or alterations in this publication. They will at all times be grateful to receive information which tends to the improvement of the work.

PLANS
The plans in this guide are not to be used for navigation. They are designed to support the text .

Printed at The Bath Press, Avon

Contents

Preface

Johann Strauss is responsible for most people's knowledge of the Danube. When he was casting around for a title for his waltz, probably the most well known in the world, he labelled it, for some unknown reason, the *Blue Danube Waltz*. As anyone who has gazed into the waters of the Danube will tell you, it is not blue, but the same muddy brown that characterises most large rivers in the world. Apart from Strauss' waltz most people know little of the Danube. I was shocked on my first trip down the Danube to be asked by a German which countries it flows through. For the Germans the Rhine is the German river, their *Schicksalsfluss*, the 'river of destiny', the river where the major events of the *Nibelungen* take place, the major German water-road. The Danube has no popular literature associated with it and in Europe it is ironic that many people will feel they know the Mississippi through the *Adventures of Huckleberry Finn* or the Amazon, from innumerable television documentaries, but not the Danube. Once the Danube gets to the Eastern Bloc countries, knowledge of it reaches a dead-end. The Iron Curtain brought down a veil over these separate and very individual countries, lumping them into the category of the Eastern Bloc, and my response to enquiries about life in the Eastern Bloc was always to ask why we never talk about the Western Bloc in the same way, lumping all of Western Europe into a homogeneous title.

This superficial idea of Central and Eastern Europe fell apart in the second half of 1989 when the world's media was concentrated on the devastating changes and the revolution that swept through the Eastern Bloc, changing not only the politics of these countries, but also our perception of them. Television screens that had carried perhaps ten or fifteen minutes on a country like Bulgaria or Hungary in past years were suddenly filled with images from them. Newspaper editors who hadn't a clue where Romania or Czechoslovakia were, apart from a vague 'over there in the Eastern Bloc somewhere', were forced to drag out an atlas and brush up on their geography. All of us became sixty second experts on Central and Eastern Europe and consequently there was a lot of myth created by the media and by politicians in the west. There still is. There is no doubt that the events of 1989 have radically changed the face of Europe and that this wave of revolution can be compared to other events which had a similar cataclysmic effect on Europe: 1945 and the settlement after Second World War; 1918 and the ensuing harsh terms of Versailles and Trianon; and a fact that was not lost on anyone is that 1989 was the bi-centenary of the French Revolution. But amongst it all there is much that has not changed despite the euphoric claims of journalists and politicians in the west who somehow feel they have been vindicated not only in their politics, but in a wider moral sense also.

To put things in perspective I have assembled the following chronological table of the principal events of 1989 which must, without the benefit of an additional hundred pages, brush briefly over many of the changes that occurred in that year, let alone the events leading up to them in previous years.

1989

26 January – *Hungary* The Government announces that Imre Nagy and his colleagues, hanged after the 1956 uprising was crushed by the Soviets, are to be reburied as heroes of the Hungarian state.

10 February – *Hungary* The Communist Party accepts the need for multi-party democracy and frees the way for independent political parties.

April 4 – *Poland* Solidarity and the Government agree to hold free elections.

Mid-April – *Romania* Veteran Communists put their names to an open letter accusing Nicolai Ceausescu of the destruction of the economy and terrorising the population. He arrests them and their families.

May – *Bulgaria* Ethnic Turks demonstrate against a law to change their surnames to a Bulgarian patronymic. Sixty killed.

2 May – *Hungary* Hungarian troops begin dismantling the barbed wire fence between Hungary and Austria.

8 May – *Hungary* Janos Kadar, in power since the 1956 uprising, is forced out of office.

June – *Bulgaria* Exodus of ethnic Turks to Turkey.

4 June – *Poland* First round of free elections gives an overwhelming success to Solidarity and discredits the Communist Party.

16 June – *Hungary* Nagy and his colleagues are reburied.

6 July – *Hungary* Janos Kadar dies. The Supreme Court rules that Imre Nagy was innocent of the crimes the pro-Soviet Government convicted him of.

24 August – *Poland* Tadeusz Mazowiecki is made the first non-Communist Prime Minister in the Soviet bloc since the Second World War.

11 September – *Hungary* East Germans are allowed to pass unhindered across the border to Austria despite protests from the East German government.

2 October – *East Germany* 20,000 people march in Leipzig in opposition to the Government, the biggest demonstration since the protests against food shortages in 1953.

7 October – *East Germany* Mikhail Gorbachev visits and urges Erich Honecker and the Politburo to adopt reforms.

9 October – *East Germany* 70,000 demonstrate in Leipzig.

16 October – *Bulgaria* Under the world spotlight of an environment conference in Sofia there is organised political opposition for the first time in 40 years.

18 October – *East Germany* Erich Honecker quits and Egon Krenz is appointed leader.

23 October – *Hungary* New Hungarian Republic declared along multi-party democratic lines.

26 October – *Bulgaria* Forty environmental activists arrested and beaten.

3 November – *Bulgaria* Thousands of environmentalists demonstrate without intervention from the police.

7 November – *East Germany* Government resigns followed by the Politburo. Hans Modrow made prime minister.

8–9 November – *East Germany* The Berlin Wall is reopened and thousands cross freely to the other side in a weekend of celebration.

10 November – *Bulgaria* Todor Zhivkov, in power for 35 years, is ousted by Petar Mladenov with the help of the Central Committee.

17 November – *Czechoslovakia* Police violently break up a demonstration by 50,000 people in Prague. One student killed.

18 November – *Czechoslovakia* Public protest in Prague against police violence.

18 November – *Bulgaria* Fifty thousand demonstrate for democracy in Sofia.

19 November – *Czechoslovakia* Civic Forum, a loose alliance to oppose the government, formed by the writer Vaclav Havel and friends.

20 November – *Czechoslovakia* 200,000 demonstrate for democracy in Prague.

23 November – *Czechoslovakia* Alexander Dubcek, officially banned after the events of 1968, makes his first public address.

24 November – *Czechoslovakia* Milos Jakes and Politburo resign.

3 December – *Czechoslovakia* New Government formed though with the Communists the dominant power.

4 December – *Czechoslovakia* 300,000 protest at the New Government.

6 December – *East Germany* Egon Krenz resigns.

7 December – *Czechoslovakia* New Government collapses.

10 December – *Czechoslovakia* 'Government of National Understanding' formed with a majority of non-Communists.

11 December – *Bulgaria* The Communist Party proposes an end to the one-party system and that multi-party elections be held.

16–17 December – *Romania* Protests in Timisoara are violently broken up by the Securitate.

21 December – *Romania* Nicolai Ceausescu shouted down at a public address in Bucharest and the Securitate fire on the crowd killing many.

22 December – *Romania* The army backs the people and takes on the Securitate. Nicolai and Elena Ceausescu flee Bucharest. Fighting continues for four days with estimates of up to 4000 killed.

23 December – *Romania* National Salvation Front headed by Ion Iliescu takes power. Free elections are promised.

25 December – *Romania* The Ceausescus are captured (or were already captured), put on trial, and summarily executed by an army firing squad.

29 December – *Poland* The Communist Party is eliminated as an important part of the Government.

30 December – *Czechoslovakia* Vaclav Havel elected President.

Where does this all leave the traveller on the Danube? Surprisingly, despite these very real cataclysmic changes, in much the same place he was prior to them. There have been articles by uninformed or misinformed travel editors breezing on about the opening up of eastern Europe and the relaxing of restrictions. In strict terms little has changed in relation to travel visas and travel arrangements that did not already exist or was in the process of changing prior to 1989. Any that have are noted in this book. The traveller will find it easier to cope with officialdom in countries like Czechoslovakia or Romania and will certainly find it easy to talk to the locals everywhere – although this was much easier to do prior to 1989 than many made out. At the very end of the Danube the traveller will find that little has changed.

After the overthrow of the Ceausescu's I received a letter from a yachtsman I know there. His letter was euphoric.....'you've heard what happened in Romania – when we are really free in a democratic country – and we can make friendship relations with everybody without being scared of terror in our souls. Many, many years I consider that what before was a dream, now becomes a reality'. But in Romania there is still little food in the shops, the Securitate have not been prosecuted for their atrocities and are commonly believed to have 'done a deal' with the Government to stop fighting, and Romanians are disillusioned with a Government that contains many of those who served under Ceausescu. In Bulgaria the elections put the Communists back in power. In Czechoslovakia there is irritation with a Government that is not coping well with sorting out the economy. For all these countries the road to democratic freedom and economic health will be a long hard one and the traveller should not expect to see instant changes.

Sitting here in London surrounded by books and newspaper cuttings, notes and scribbled references on the events of 1989, it is difficult to get a sense of the Danube back, to see in the mind's eye the river pouring down to the Black Sea. And then a letter arrived with Bulgarian stamps on the envelope. In *Rozinante*, short on fuel and making just a knot or two in light winds, Bridgit and I cheered ourselves up one dinner time with a bottle of wine. Afterwards I wrote a note and put it in the bottle, corked it, and threw it into the sea about fifty miles off the Bulgarian coast. The note had been found and this was the reply with apologies to the effect that it had been difficult to find someone to translate it into English. The letter hoped I had arrived in Istanbul safely and described life in the small Bulgarian village. 'If you come to Bulgaria you will please come to see us. We are poor people but we will make you welcomed. Greetings from Stara Zagora.'

NOTE

This book is designed to be used by anyone going down the Danube by whatever mode of transport, to provide useful, practical information and some background to the river as well. It is a 'working' book rather than a travelogue or an essay on the Danube, though any armchair travellers interested in the river will find it useful as well. Most of the information was gathered on two trips I made, the first in 1985 starting at Donaueschingen using a variety of modes of transport, local trains and buses, walking, local ferries, a cruise boat, and several organised excursions; and the second in 1987 in *Rozinante*, a nineteen foot motor-sailer which began at Regensburg and ended up in Constanţa on the Black Sea. Any feed-back on the information in the book is welcomed and can be sent to me care of the publishers.

ACKNOWLEDGEMENTS

Various people helped me on these two trips. My thanks to Bridgit Marsh who crewed *Rozinante* and without whom the trip would have been infinitely more difficult. To Graham Sewell who helped me get *Rozinante* to the Danube and drove the ailing Rover back to England. To Richard Wilson who helped get things together. To Odile who came along for three weeks. To Ursula Deutsch of the Commission for Tourism of the Danube Countries who went out of her way to help and organised the trip on the *Oltenita*. To Joe and the other members of the Regensburg Motorboot Club. To Yener in Bodrum for organising *Rozinante's* sale and to Alvis who I hope gets much pleasure from her in the Aegean. To the Zavody Tazkeho Strojárstva Shipyard in Komárno and to Charlie for the repairs in Czechoslovakia. To several yachtsmen who will remain unnamed in Romania, I hope there wishes come true. And lastly to Willie Wilson of Imray, Laurie, Norie & Wilson without whom the second trip in *Rozinante* could not have been made. Thank you all.

Rod Heikell
London 1991

ABOUT THE CHARTS

The charts that accompany the text are designed to give a visual guide to things because it is so much easier whether on a cruise boat, ferry, or in a small yacht, to work out what is going on with a map in front of you. We all like to know where we are going. Included on the charts is information for pleasure craft users, principally information on where the channel is and where to stop for lunch or for the night, and while some may think that there is not enough here, once on the river they will see that it is. It should be remembered that the Danube is some 2380 kilometres long from Regensburg to the Black Sea and without going to the sort of complexity and size of the charts produced by the Danube Commission, and the cost, there are real difficulties in compressing information for navigation into a book of this size. Any information that will make the book more user-friendly is welcome and can be sent to me care of the publishers.

SYMBOLS

Navigable channel. For most of the Danube in Germany and Austria the navigable channel is not shown as buoyage is well established and it is possible to navigate from buoy to buoy where the channel is in doubt.

    lock and barrage

≍   bridge

⚲   kilometre mark

○   town or village

⚓   pleasure boat harbour or pontoon

F   ferry or hydrofoil berth or stop

⊓   castle or large fort

⊏⊐   ruined castle or fort

⛪   church or cathedral

The scale of the charts is 6cm to 10km or 1:1,6000 approx.

I. The Danube

Facts and figures

If you measure rivers in geographical terms, of length, drainage area, the volume of water discharged at the mouth, then the Danube is not high up in the world league of rivers. From its source in the Black Forest it is 2850 or 2880km long, around 1776 miles taking the lower figure, to the mouth at the Black Sea. The longest river in the world is the Nile at 4132 miles closely followed by the Amazon at 4000 miles. The Danube enters the table of river length in 25th place. It is not even the longest river in Europe with the Volga which starts in the Valday Range in the USSR and runs for 2293 miles to the Caspian Sea holding the title. Nor is its drainage area particularly large at 816 square miles compared to the Volga's 1360 square miles. The one record it does hold in Europe is for the amount of water discharged at the mouth. The Volga has an average discharge of around 2160 cubic metres (80,000 cubic feet) a second, while the Danube has an average discharge of 5886 cubic metres (218,000 cubic feet) a second, though some sources put the figure at 6300 cubic metres a second. This last statistic is the one that gives us a clue to the nature of the Danube because if all that water, nearly three times as much as the Volga, is escaping down to the Black Sea, then it must do so at considerable speed and inevitably with some violence.

At its source in Donaueschingen the Danube is 678m above sea level which gives a modest average fall of 24cm for every kilometre, around 15 inches fall for every mile. Geographers take the source of the Danube to be the Brege, an alpine brook which feeds into the Danube at Donaueschingen, with the source of the Brege being 1078m above sea level. From here it is a short hop across to the watershed feeding the Rhine. From Donaueschingen it would be impossible to gauge a descent of 24cm for every kilometre by eye and it can hardly account for the speed and violence of the river. It is the volume of water in the Danube that makes it the turbulent and often destructive river it is. When the snows on the Alps melt a large number of tributaries pour the water unlocked by the thaw into the upper Danube. With a continental climate heavy spring rain swells the water from the thaw and by the time the Danube has got to Passau an average 730 cubic metres of water per second is racing past Bavaria. At Passau the Inn swells the Danube to double its original size and along its passage through Austria other rivers add to it, so that by Vienna some 1600m of water per second wash by the backyard of the old Habsburg capital. In Yugoslavia the Tisza River, the second largest tributary of the Danube, drains the great Hungarian plain, and by the time the Danube is squeezed between the Carpathians and the Balkans there is so much water passing through the narrow gorge at the Iron Gates that the depth of the river here is 80m and the bottom of the river is at the same level as the Black Sea. Just before the delta the river is swollen by its largest tributary, the Sirit, which drains most of the Carpathians, increasing its flow to the 6000 or so cubic metres per second recorded at the mouth.

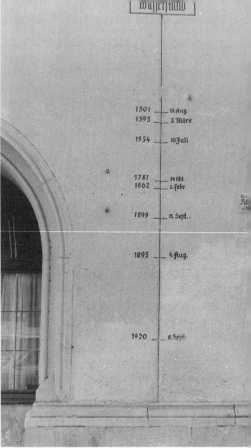

At the locks and harbours along the Danube the flow of the river in cubic metres per second is displayed so that skippers have an idea of the difficulties ahead.

The tumultuous Danube at Passau. On the Rathaus wall a scale marks the levels of flooding over the centuries.

This amount of water hurtling down a river is difficult to imagine. Small boat users will get some idea if I talk about the sort of currents encountered. When I went down the Danube in the tiny *Rozinante*, a nineteen foot sailing boat, the river carried us at some 16km an hour, around 10mph in the German and Austrian sections of the river. The speed is easily worked out by timing how long it takes to cover a kilometre from the kilometre posts on the bank. While this may not seem very much to those who travel on the land, to those of us who travel on the water in small craft it is flying. And most of the speed comes from the river itself, from the current swooshing you along. In *Rozinante* I only needed to keep the engine on tick-over to give steerage way, the rest of the speed came from all those cubic metres of water speeding towards the Black Sea. Claims have been made that in some sections of the Danube the current can be as much as 20 or 25mph, but I doubt the authenticity of these claims and so do boat owners in Germany who have spent most of their life on the river.

The Danube today is a tamer river than it ever was in the past. Massive dams hold back sections of the river, stopping the current and keeping water levels steady. In Germany there are five dams between Kelheim, where the Rhine-Main-Danube Canal will join the Danube, and Passau on the border with Austria. In Austria there are nine dams with the last dam on the Danube just before Vienna until you get to the giant Yugoslav–Romanian dam at the Iron Gates. These dams and the canalisation of parts of the the river have gone a long way towards making it usable for commercial navigation for most of the year, yet it remains one of the swiftest and most difficult rivers in

Europe to navigate and for this reason is still under-used compared with the Rhine or the Rhône.

Geographically the Danube is unique: it is the only major river in Europe that flows from the west to the east. This attribute has meant that the Danube has been used as a link between east and west for transport since very early times, an age-old water-road between Asia Minor and northern Europe. The recent discoveries at Lepenski-Vir on the banks of the Danube in Yugoslavia have overturned the prevailing archaeological theories which state that civilized man grew up around the Mesopotamian basin, spreading outwards from there to Europe. At Lepenski-Vir a large settlement of nearly sixty dwellings laid out along planned lines, evidence of farming, domesticated animals, pottery, megalithic sculptures and other artifacts have been unearthed dating back to 8000 years ago, a figure which pre-dates much of the equivalent Mesopotamian culture. Did the neolithic revolution take place by the Danube at the same time or even before the Mesopotamian culture? If it did then the Danube might well have been the first river in the world to have been navigated by man in some sort of clumsy hollowed out log or a raft tied together with hide thongs. Whether or not this is so, the Danube would have been used for thousands of years before the Greeks and the Romans arrived. Greek records show that the Celts used the Danube as a water-road to move commodities such as salt, hides, iron and, importantly, amber. In 1984 excavation began on a sunken trading ship off the Turkish coast which was found to date from 1400 BC. Amongst the cargo was found amber, a not unusual find except that the type of amber found came from the Baltic area. It is likely that the Danube was used by the Celts to transport the much prized Baltic amber to Greek colonies on the Black Sea from where it found its way into the Mediterranean.

If we take the early heroic tales of the Greeks to be a catalogue of places in the known world, then the lower Danube was well known to them. When Jason and the Argonauts sailed to Colchis at the eastern end of the Black Sea in search of the Golden Fleece, their return voyage was around the north following advice to sail counter-

Model showing navigation before the age of steam in the *Ruthoff* museum ship in Regensburg

sunwise. The Argonauts anchored off the mouth of the Danube behind an island and it is here that Jason is said to have murdered Apsyrtus, the cause of his later troubles, before continuing on down the coast to the Bosphorus. One variation on the story of the Argonauts relates that Jason sailed up the Danube into what is now Yugoslavia and then hauled the *Argo* overland to the Adriatic. Herodotus, the 'Father of History' (484–420 BC), considered the Danube, in Greek the Ister, to be the mightiest river in the known world. He names all the tributaries of the lower Danube in what is now Romania and concludes that with all these rivers discharging into the Danube it is no wonder that 'the Danube is the mightiest of rivers'. Later in the *Historia* he describes how Darius, King of the Persians, commanded his Ionian fleet to sail into the Black Sea and to the Danube.

'...he gave orders to the Ionians... to sail into the Black Sea as far as the Danube, where they were to bridge the river and await his arrival. The orders were obeyed: the naval contingent, passing through the Cyanean Islands, carried right on to the Danube, sailed up the river for two days as far as the point where the main stream divides, and here built the bridge.'

Darius' campaign against the tribes on the north side of the Danube, predominantly the Scythians, did not go well and eventually he was forced to retreat back to Constantinople.

A river which divides Europe into north and south also serves as a useful border and over the centuries the Danube has formed the borders between empires and nation states. It still does. For much of its length the Danube is the frontier between different countries on opposite banks. It is a strange feeling to sail down the line separating sometimes hostile countries and when the channel dictates, to follow the shore of first one country and then the other. For the Romans the Danube, the Danuvius, marked

Navigation on the Danube near Grein in 1840. From an engraving.

Painting showing early navigation on the Danube on a house in Passau.

The Danube in flood on the German section of the river.

the northern limits of the Empire. At times the Romans crossed the Danube in an attempt to enlarge the Empire, most notably the campaigns against the Dacians in Romania, but like Darius before them they had great difficulty with these barbarians, the unintelligible babblers, and often had to retreat to the south side of the river frontier. All along the Danube the remains of the Roman *limes* can be seen. The Romans used the river as a supply line for the garrisons and to move men along its length, building harbours and shipyards for the Danube fleets. The principal Roman fleets, of around forty to sixty galleys in a fleet, were stationed at the mouth of the Danube, Sexanta Prista at Rousse, Ratiara at Acar in the Sava, at Belgrade, Carnuntum at Petronell, Comagenis at Tulln and Arelape at Pöchlarn.

With the collapse of the Roman Empire it might be expected that the Danube river-road would fall into disuse. In fact the opposite seems to have happened, with increased trade going up and down the river. The reason for this is probably that while getting about on the Danube was a dangerous business, it was even more dangerous to travel by land. Without Roman engineers around to repair the great Roman roads they were swallowed up by the forests while the river, though tumultuous and uncertain, remained in place as it always had been. When Charlemagne advanced eastwards in the 8th century he copied the Roman model and used the Danube both as a means of transporting troops and supplies and as a defensive line. In the Middle Ages settlements and duchies spread along the river rather than into the forests. The Bishops of Passau, one of the most powerful duchies along the upper Danube in the Middle Ages, stretched from Passau down river to just above Vienna, a long meandering line of possessions which rarely deviated far from the river. Towns were awarded the right to levy tolls and trade was well established. At the lower end of the Danube Byzantium controlled trade and commerce along the river, ensuring that the route between east and west stayed open.

Part of the river trade in the Middle Ages was carrying the men and supplies taking part in the Crusades to Asia Minor. The different crusades followed different routes,

Postcard showing the Regensburg docks in 1935.

Gravel barge in Bulgaria.

but many of the early crusades proceeded along the Danube into Yugoslavia where they cut across to Constantinople from Belgrade. Peter the Hermit and Godfrey of Bouillon followed this route on the First Crusade as did Frederic Barbarossa in the 12th century. Most likely the crusaders followed the remains of the old Roman road, the Via Militaris, while supplies and equipment were sent downstream by boat. Frederic Barbarossa for one used the Danube as at Mauthausen he razed the luckless village when they had the timidity to demand a toll for the passage of his crusaders. The failure of the crusades and the growing power of the Ottoman Turks is often said to have led to a decline in commerce on the Danube. What is meant is that commerce moved away from the west to the Turks who by 1521 had taken Belgrade and by 1529 threatened to take Vienna. The Turks used the Danube to supply their army and allowed trade on the river to continue. There were numerous 'naval' battles along the river as well. When Prince Eugene of Savoy set out to take Belgrade it is recorded he did so with ten men-o-war under his command, though how they were to be used and how he was to get them safely down river is difficult to imagine.

In the 17th century with a firm Habsburg hold over most of the river, trade increased and it was possible for passengers to travel down the Danube on crude box-like boats. The town of Ulm in Germany was well known for these craft, so much so that the craft came to be known as Ulm Boxes. In 1636 William Crowne, a servant to the Earl of Arundel who was travelling to Linz, recorded in his diary that '...we took four boats to travel down the Danube, through Bavaria, on our way to Lintz'. In the 18th century Doctor Charles Burney travelled down the Danube to Vienna gathering material for his book, the *History of Music*, suffering biting cold, stale and unpalatable food when he could get it, and the dangers of the river where '...The descent is often so considerable, that the water cannot be seen at the distance of a quarter of a mile, and sometimes the noise against the rocks is as violent, and as loud as a cataract'. Trade on the river was evidently prosperous at this time as the good doctor had occasion to bemoan the cost of transporting salt upriver which he said increased 'the price of that commodity above four hundred per cent.' Only cargoes which warranted the expense of being hauled upriver in this fashion could be carried, most of the river trade being an exclusively down river business. The crude rafts would be loaded with cargo and passengers and then hurtle down river to their destination where the cargo was unloaded and the raft broken up for timber.

In the 19th century steam revolutionised transport and in 1829 the First Danube Steamship Company was founded in Vienna on the initiative of two Englishmen, J. Andrews and J. Pritchard, who undertook to build the first steam powered craft on the Danube. It was constructed in England and transported to Vienna where it was assembled. The *Franz I* puffed its way down to Budapest in 1830 and the company which was formed, the Erste Donau-Dampfschiff-fahrts-Gesellschaft, the DDSG, is still in operation today. Towards the end of the 19th century the DDSG controlled the bulk of shipping on the Danube and was the largest inland carrier in the world with some 180 steam powered craft in operation. The First World War severely interrupted navigation on the Danube, but in 1922 the Statute of the Danube restored some order, at least until 1936 when Germany pulled out of the agreement ahead of the Second World War.

After the Second World War the Danube was effectively divided between the West and the Eastern Bloc countries. Agreements were reached on river transport, but compared to other rivers canalisation was slow. There was now the upper Danube in the west and the Red Danube flowing through the Eastern Bloc countries. As ever it forms the frontier between most of the countries in Middle Europe: between Austria and Czechoslovakia for 8km; between Czechoslovakia and Hungary for 140km; between Yugoslavia and Romania for 230km; between Bulgaria and Romania for 470km; and in the delta between Romania and the USSR for 120km.

Travelling on the Danube

For the most part western Europeans, with the exception of the Germans and Austrians, seldom travel on this river. Partly it is to do with crossing the old *Iron Curtain*, going into middle and eastern Europe, and partly with the lack of information on the Danube itself. I suppose it is difficult for tour operators on the Danube to compete with pictures of sandy beaches and turquoise water in the Mediterranean or the Caribbean – do you show misty August showers in Bavaria or perhaps a riverside factory belching smoke in Romania – and consequently it is not surprising that information is hard to come by. Travel literature on the Danube is not helpful either, with many authors exaggerating the problems with eastern European bureaucrats and so, they believe, enhancing their own adventures in print. There are problems in travelling in eastern Europe, but no more than many other countries in the world. Bureaucrats in India, for example, are more obstructive than any in the Eastern Bloc with the possible exception of Romania. In fact on my first trip down the Danube I had more problems with the Austrian officials at Passau than I subsequently had in any other country. The customs officer intimated that my shabby passport might be a fake, eventually cautioning me after everyone else had gone aboard the ferry to get a new passport soon or I would not be allowed into Austria again. No other officials in any of the other Danube countries raised any problems with the same passport.

Hydrofoil connecting Vienna and Budapest.

DDSG barge and lighter in Germany

The cruise ship *Donauprinzessin*.

CRUISE BOATS

Several different companies run cruise boats on the Danube and this has to be the easiest way of seeing the river. Everything is arranged for you: formalities for passing from one country to another, your accommodation, your meals, entertainment aboard and excursions to places of interest close to the Danube. For those who want to see as much as possible in a short time a cruise on the Danube is the answer. However, if you want to vary the itinerary and do some exploring on your own, a cruise on the Danube can be too restricting. One possibility is to take a cruise for the middle section of the Danube and do some exploring on your own at the beginning and the end. A few of the cruises start at Passau, but most start from Vienna, so it is possible to have a look around the upper Danube before cruising down river. Different cruise lines have different destinations so you can choose a cruise ending up in Budapest in Hungary, Rousse in Bulgaria, Cernavoda in Romania, or do a round trip down the Danube into the Black Sea and back again.

Below I have listed the cruise boats and their operators on the Danube. Some cruise boats such as the *Donauprinzessin* can offer ultra-luxurious accommodation while some of the older boats are a little more down-market, but make up for that in character.

Donauprinzessin Operates from Passau on a round trip down to Budapest and back to Passau. The normal itinerary includes Dürnstein, Budapest, Esztergóm, Bratislava, Vienna and Melk before arriving back in Passau. Built in 1983, the *Donauprinzessin* is one of the newest and most luxurious cruise boats on the Danube. Operated by Peter Deilmann-Reederei.

Dnepr Operates from Passau down to Ismail and to Istanbul and Yalta in the Black Sea before returning to Passau. It should be possible to book part of the cruise. The normal itinerary includes Durnstein, Vienna, Budapest, Belgrade, Rousse, Giurgiu, Ismail, Istanbul, Yalta, Ismail, Rousse, Nikopol, Tekija, Belgrade, Novisad,

Budapest, Bratislava, Vienna and Linz before arriving back in Passau. This cruise is the longest on the Danube with the return trip taking three weeks including the Black Sea excursion. Operated by the Soviet Danube Steamship Company.

Theodor Körner Operates from Vienna to Ismail or Sulina on the Black Sea. Usually makes only one trip a year in late June. Operated by the DDSG in Vienna.

Oltenita and *Carpati* Operate back to back from Vienna down to Cernavoda. The normal itinerary includes Budapest, Belgrade, Turnu Severin, Giurgiu and Cernavoda or the same trip from Cernavoda ending up in Vienna. Organised tours to the delta can be arranged from Cernavoda. The ships are quite old, built in 1960, but are comfortable enough and everything works reasonably well. Operated by NAV-ROM, the Romanian State Shipping Company.

Rousse Operates back to back from Vienna to Rousse. Although the cruise starts or finishes at Vienna, it goes upriver to Durnstein as well. The normal itinerary from Vienna includes Dürnstein, Budapest, Belgrade and Rousse or the same trip from Rousse ending up in Vienna. Operated by the Bulgarian State Shipping Company.

Booking a cruise on any of these boats should be possible at any major travel agent such as Thomas Cook. If there is some difficulty two Austrian companies should be able to help. The DDSG, A-1020 Wien, Handelskai 265, ☎ 26 65 36, telex 13 47 89, handles bookings for most of the companies including the Soviet Danube Steamship Company. Luftner-Reisen, Reisebüro Dr W Luftner GmbH KG, A-6020 Innsbruck, Südtiroler Platz 4, Postfach 509, ☎ 22 423, telex 05 35 13 also handles bookings for most of the companies including NAVROM and the Bulgarian State Shipping Company.

Hydrofoil connection at Budapest

To get an idea of what to expect on a cruise I've reproduced the itinerary for the downstream cruise run by NAVROM on the *Oltenita/Carpati*.

Sunday
1200 Departure from Vienna. During the afternoon the ship passes Hainburg, the Austrian/Czechoslovakian/Hungarian borders.

Monday
0200 Arrival in Budapest.
0800 Passport control on board.
0900 Departure of the buses from the harbour for a sightseeing tour of Budapest. Lunch on board. Afternoon free.
1530 Passport control on board for departure.
During the night passport control for Yugoslavia at Bezdan – around 0200!

Tuesday
1000 Ship passes Petrovaradin and Novisad.
1500 Arrival in Belgrade.
1600 Departure of buses for sightseeing tour of Belgrade.
2300 Departure from Belgrade.

Wednesday
Passport control early in the morning for leaving Yugoslavia at Veliko Gradiste. The ship enters the Iron Gates. Passport control on board for entrance into Romania. Passage through the Iron Gates lock.
1500 Arrival in Turnu Severin. Evening programme.

Thursday
0200 Departure from Turnu Severin.
2000 Arrival in Giurgiu.

Friday
0800 Departure of buses for sightseeing tour of Bucharest. Afternoon free.
1700 Departure of buses from Bucharest for Giurgiu.
1900 Departure of ship from Giurgiu.

Saturday
0700 Arrival in Cernavoda. End of the cruise. Transfer to buses for those who have booked tours of the delta or Transylvania.

LOCAL FERRIES

It is possible to cruise most of the Danube using the local ferries in the countries along the way. There are a few gaps where you will have to travel overland to pick up the next ferry or excursion, notably between Budapest and Belgrade and again between Belgrade and Romania, if you cannot get a one way ticket on the excursion from Belgrade to the Iron Gates. For the independent traveller this method of getting down the Danube allows you a lot of flexibility and you will end up seeing more than an organised cruise on the Danube allows. The drawback is that you must make your own arrangements for accommodation on an *ad hoc* basis along the way and this can mean a lot of footwork in the popular places and gritting your teeth in Bulgaria and Romania where independent travel can be difficult.

Below I have listed the services available going down river from Regensburg, though there is no reason why you can't do the trip in reverse starting in Romania.

Regensburg to Passau The *Agnes Bernauer* runs on Sundays between April and September from Regensburg to Passau stopping at Straubing, Deggendorf, Niederalteich, Vilshofen, and Windorf. On the Saturday it does the upriver trip from Passau to Regensburg. In Regensburg there are daily trips around the river in the summer and cruises from Kelheim just upriver to Weltenburg Abbey. Tickets can be obtained in Regensburg or on board.

Passau to Linz and Vienna The DDSG run the *Stadt Wien* and *Stadt Passau*, two diesel driven paddle-wheel ferries from Passau to Linz and Vienna, on a regular back to back service through the week from May to September. The ferry stops at Obernzell, Engelhartszell, Niederranna, Wesennufer, Obermühl, Neuh-Unterm, Aschach, Wilhering, and Linz on the first day. In the morning it continues to Mauthausen, Grein, Ybbs, Marbach, Pöchlarn, Melk, Aggsbach, Spitz, Weisenkirchen, Dürnstein, Krems, Tulln, Greifenstein, Nusdorf and Vienna. The paddle-wheelers are a delight and there is no better way to see this stretch of the Danube. Cabins can be booked on board for the overnight stay at Linz and there is a restaurant on board. Tickets can be booked at the DDSG offices in Passau, Linz or Vienna.

Melk to Krems The DDSG run the *Wachau* on a daily round trip from Melk down river to Krems and back again from May to September. There are rail connections from Linz or Vienna if you want to do this trip along the Wachau Valley. Tickets at Melk or Krems or any DDSG office.

Vienna The DDSG run round trips up the Donau Canal and down river to the other end of the canal. The excursion is fairly dull and most people are asleep by the end of it. The DDSG also has the only steam-powered paddle-wheeler, the *Schönbrunn*, launched in 1913, which does charters along the river. Tickets from the office on the Donau Canal for the excursion boats. Enquire at the DDSG office for the *Schönbrunn*. The Hungarian State Shipping Company, MAHART, run the *Rakoczi* on an excursion down to Bratislava and back to Vienna, though they do not stop anywhere. Tickets at the IBUSZ office in Vienna.

Vienna to Bratislava The Czechoslovakian State Shipping Company CSPD run two hydrofoils, the *Voschod* and *Meteor*, on a daily service from Vienna to Bratislava from May to October. It is possible to do a day round trip. Tickets in Vienna or Bratislava.

Vienna to Budapest The Hungarian State Shipping Company, MAHART, run a hydrofoil service between Vienna and Budapest from April to October. The trip takes only five hours and you don't see much of the Hungarian Danube Bend at 25 knots. Tickets at IBUSZ offices in Vienna or Budapest.

Budapest A daily ferry service operates between Budapest and Esztergóm stopping off on the way. There are also organised excursions along the Danube bend by boat or by bus from May to October so that you can see at leisure what you missed at speed on the hydrofoil. Tickets for excursions from the IBUSZ office in Budapest and from the Vigado tér boat station for the ferry.

From Budapest there are no ferry services down to Belgrade. It may be possible to take a berth on a cruise ship for this leg or even onwards to Turnu Severin in Romania, but most likely you will have to go overland by train.

Belgrade A hydrofoil makes a round trip from Belgrade to Kladovo at the Iron Gates dam in the summer. It may be possible to take a one-way fare and cross over to the Romanian side from Kladovo. Tickets from the Beogradbrod Travel Agency in Belgrade.

Upper Romania A ferry is supposed to run from Turnu Severin to Călărasi, stopping off at towns along the way, but the authorities and the agents of NAVROM give only sketchy information about the services and the frequency. The usual reply to enquiries will be advice to book on a Danube cruise on the *Oltenita* or *Carpati*, or take an organised bus tour. If you want to track down this service you will have to have almost unlimited patience and a bullish determination.

Bulgaria A daily hydrofoil service runs between Vidin and Rousse stopping off at Lom, Kozlodj, Oraichovo, Nikopol and Svištov, reaching Rousse after nearly six hours. Tickets are sold at the dock office only an hour before departure, though as a tourist you may be able to get one in advance. From Vidin a ferry shuttles back and

Casting off for the DDSG *Stadt Passau*

forth to Calafat in Romania on the opposite side of the Danube. Getting accommodation in Bulgaria can be an expensive business as the Bulgarians like you to stay in purpose-built 'western style' hotels for which you pay in hard currency. Getting cheaper accommodation is a matter of persisting with the tourist office until you wear them down and a cheaper hotel or a room is found.

Danube Delta Hydrofoils and ferries run daily from Tulcea upriver to Galati and down river to Sulina. Tickets can be obtained from the NAVROM office in Tulcea, but only half an hour or an hour before the hydrofoil or ferry leaves. As elsewhere in Romania, the tourist agency would prefer you to go on an organised excursion and in many ways this is the best thing to do. Accommodation in the delta is best booked in advance at TAROM, the tourist agency, otherwise it may be difficult to find. Camping out is a battle with the mosquitoes and midges which infest all parts of this waterland, a purpose-made breeding ground for them. In the delta itself it is possible to hire rowing boats, though the strong currents make getting around difficult and you will not see very much in this way.

Danube–Black Sea Canal A cruise boat plies the canal from the Agigea end, though it is unlikely that you can just turn up for this trip without booking an excursion from Constanţa and the excursion must rank as one of the least interesting on the Danube.

The navigable channel is well buoyed for the most part: green torpedo buoys with a conical topmark and red torpedo buoys with a square topmark. Remember the Danube is buoyed from seawards as is normal practice.

Kilometre markers along the bank mean you always know where you are although they can be overgrown by vegetation in places. You can also work out your speed by timing between the kilometre posts.

NAVIGATION

Contrary to some statements I have read, there are charts of the Danube published by the Danube Commission based in Budapest. These pilotage charts are in book form, folding out like a complex origami construction or are very large format (1450 x 280mm/14 x 11 inches), and cover the Danube from Regensburg to the Black Sea in twelve volumes. The scale of between 1:10000 and 1:25000 makes them much too bulky to use as you are flipping from one chart to the next every five minutes on the swifter sections and the complete set weighs in at around 9kg. When the Danube Commission was set up the Soviet Union had a heavy hand in its formation and so the language of the Commission and hence of the charts is Russian and for some obscure reason, French. However, charts are charts and they are easy enough to follow. You don't really need them as the Danube is well buoyed in the upper stretches, reasonably so in the middle stretch, and just adequately in the lower stretch through Bulgaria and Romania. If you do want them they can be ordered from Freytag, Berndt und Artaria or Christian Bernwieser in Vienna (see Appendix III) though be warned that the entire set costs well in excess of £250.

The Danube is buoyed from the seawards direction as is normal practice, with green and red torpedo buoys. In Germany and Austria the buoyage is excellent and though I had the Commission charts on board, I rarely referred to them. In Hungary and Yugoslavia the river is buoyed at dangerous spots or where the river divides into channels, though occasionally you may strain your eyes to pick up a buoy or arrow signposts on the bank or an island showing you the channel. In Bulgaria and Romania you will have cause for confusion as the channel often changes as sandbanks form and obstruct what was formerly the main channel; even the latest Commission charts were in error, and buoyage or arrows showing the channel are few and far between in places though any really dangerous sections are adequately buoyed. There are also markers on the river bank or islands in the lower stretches showing which side the channel is. When there are no buoys showing the channel keep to the side where the river bank markers show the channel to be. Where there is a single buoy or a single channel marker on the bank keep to this side but inside the channel – with a marker on the bank this takes a little judgement as to how close the channel is to the bank. As in all rivers the channel nearly always follows the outside of the curve of the river bank – the water rushing along is deflected by the bank and as the force of the current is greatest here the channel is scoured out around the outer curve of the bank. Only when the current is less do other factors enter the equation determining where the deepest channel is as well as man-made factors like weirs and training walls. Dangers are also marked and a few sections have leading marks for the channel. Bridges are marked in the normal way with a yellow diamond showing the navigable arch and other waterways signs are straightforward, such as areas where you can't anchor or corners where you should sound your horn. All in all navigation is not a problem at all and after a day or two you will be quite relaxed about it. In Appendix II there is a glossary of the common signs used on the Danube.

Depths in the Danube change, naturally enough, according to the level of the river and these changes can be surprisingly quick. All along the river there are the *pegel*, depth gauges to show the water level, which is announced on VHF as well, but the figures given are not for the depths in the river, but for a theoretical height above sea level which unless you are familiar with the system is best ignored. In the upper Danube in Germany and part of Austria the Commission attempts to maintain a minimum depth of 2·5m with the present canalisation programme increasing the minimum depth to 3m in the near future. Throughout the rest of the Danube the Commission attempts to maintain a minimum depth of 3–3·5m. On my trip down the Danube I rarely encountered depths of less than 5m except when I left the channel and often a quick perusal of the depth-sounder showed depths of 15 or 20m for considerable stretches of the river. In the Gorge of Kazan I recorded the greatest depth at 79m. The river level fluctuates dramatically at times and can rise or fall two or more metres in as many days. At Regensburg the members of the Motorboat Club suggested I wait a couple of days as the river level was 3m above the normal level. In two days I measured a drop in the water level of two metres! – before I set out. High and low water on the Danube varies for the upper and lower Danube. On the upper Danube low water is in January and February and high water in July and August. On the lower Danube low water is in September and October and high water in April and May.

Locks on the Danube are all huge and all automatic. In Germany and Austria berth before the dock and call the lock keeper from the phone provided. Unless your German is very good the distorted voice that talks to you over the loudspeaker system will be unintelligible. What he is usually saying is to wait, in case commercial traffic is imminent, before proceeding through. Luckily there are traffic lights to tell you what is going on. In *Rozinante* we never waited more than an hour and often we were locked through by ourselves, a nineteen foot speck in locks to International Waterways Standards. Most of the locks have sliding bollards and there is no turbulence at all. The only danger is the wash from the propellers of the large tugs when they move out. If you are locking in with commercial craft you will usually be squeezed in last. At the twin locks at the Iron Gates and the lock at Prahovo it is a matter of hanging around until there is enough commercial traffic to fill the lock. Again you will be squeezed in at the end. There is no turbulence and there are sliding bollards.

PRIVATE PLEASURE BOATS

Taking your own boat down the Danube is the ultimate way of seeing and experiencing the river. You can stop in places that cannot be visited in any other way, you carry just about everything you need with you, and you get a feel for the force and drama of the river that can only be experienced by being upon it. It is not without difficulties, especially in Bulgaria and Romania, but these are not in any way insurmountable and the trip, though it will undoubtedly be eventful, will provide a fund of tales to relate on long alcohol warmed evenings in your local. Most of the information that follows is derived from my second trip down the Danube in 1987 in the diminutive nineteen foot *Rozinante* and though I have added material from other sources to round it out, it makes no pretence to be comprehensive – if it did it would take half the adventure out of the trip.

TYPES OF CRAFT

All types of craft from large motor-sailers, trimarans and catamarans, large yachts and motorboats to small motor-sailers like *Rozinante*, small motorboats, inflatables, canoes, kayaks and even two toy-like inflatables sold for children on the beach and tied together with three large Germans aboard, have descended the Danube. The problem is not so much what to go in, but how to get it to the Danube. Until the Rhine-Main-Danube Canal is finished, possibly in 1993 though the odds are it will be later than this, a boat must be taken overland to the Danube, either from its normal berth or from Nürnberg if you have come up the Rhine and the Main and the completed part of the canal. There is also the problem of what to do at the bottom of the Danube. If your craft is not seaworthy enough to tackle the Black Sea and go on into the Mediterranean it is a difficult slog back up against the current, a trip only really practicable if you have very powerful engines, a boat that will plane, or if you can get a tow with a barge. The types of craft that make the trip down the Danube can be put into four categories.

i. *Sea-going craft* A number of craft proceed up the Rhine, often with the help of a tow from a barge, and then proceed along the Main and the completed section of the Rhine-Main-Danube Canal to Nürnberg. Here masts can be taken down and transport arranged to Kelheim or Regensburg, the two logical places to aim for on the upper Danube. The transportation costs to the Danube from Nürnberg are not cheap as loads over a certain width must obtain special permission and be accompanied by a police escort. The transportation company may arrange a crane and suitable strops at the Danube end or you may be able to use the crane at the Regensburg Motorboat Club for smaller craft. An alternative to sailing on your own bottom to Nürnberg and getting transported from there would be to transport the boat overland all the way to the Danube as I did with *Rozinante*. I encountered no problems with customs, in fact they hardly glanced at the boat, trailing from England through Belgium and Germany, a trip which took two days from London to Regensburg. At the bottom of the Danube it is a reasonably straightforward trip to Istanbul in Turkey and then down through the Dardanelles to the Mediterranean.

ii. *Small inland craft* Small motorboats, yachts, even large dinghies and semi-rigid inflatables, can be trailed down to the Danube and put in the water in Germany or Austria. It would then be possible to explore part of the river, haul the boat out, and then proceed further downstream to explore a different part of the river. Alternatively the car and trailer could be left while you go off downstream, then the car and trailer collected and driven down to pick the boat up. While it would be feasible to do all of the Danube in this way, it would be a long haul down to Yugoslavia or Romania from a starting point in Germany to collect the boat and it is really only practical between Germany and Hungary.

iii.*Inflatables* An inflatable has to be one of the best ways of getting around the river. On the second trip I met two Belgians in Esztergóm who seemed to have it all worked out. They had a large inflatable with a lockable wooden chest beside the steering position, a raised plywood platform forward with a permanent sun awning over it that they could sleep on, and a 10 hp outboard to power the craft. When they reached Romania the platform and the awning and any other extraneous bits were to be thrown away and the rest, the inflatable, the steering mechanism, the outboard and their kit went into the wooden chest to accompany them on the return rail journey back to Belgium. An inflatable, floating as it does right on the surface of the water, has the advantage of being able to nose into interesting places out of the main channel and into berths sheltered from the wash of passing craft. I would probably add another outboard engine to the ensemble as getting spares is next to impossible in Bulgaria and Romania, but otherwise it seemed the ideal answer for exploring a river.

iv.*Canoes and kayaks* In most of the countries along the Danube you will come across canoes and kayaks out and about on the water. It is an ideal low-cost way of getting about on the Danube and there is no reason why you shouldn't do the whole length of the river from somewhere like Ulm to the delta in Romania – assuming you are hardy and fit that is. Every year the German Canoe Federation organises an international trip down the Danube starting at Ingolstadt and finishing in Silistra. It is billed as the longest sporting-canoeing-and-rowing event in the world and it probably is. It is co-organised by all the sporting clubs of the countries along the way and you can do the whole trip or as many stages as you want. Though it has an element of competition to it, it is more of an excursion than a race. The trip is self-sufficient in that those taking part carry everything they need with them and stay overnight in

Rowing four taking on the Danube at Ulm.

campsites so the trip is only for those who are fit and have some experience. Though some kayaks take part, the favoured craft seem to be two or three man canoes, presumably because of their load-carrying ability. The German Canoe Federation insists on certain safety equipment and makes other recommendations which I reproduce in part below, advice which should be followed by anyone venturing onto the Danube in a canoe or kayak.

- Trips in the dark or at night are strictly forbidden.
- Camping outside campsites provided by the TID (Tour International Danubien) is prohibited as protection through local police cannot be guaranteed.
- Never go out alone in a boat. Mutual help can turn out to be necessary. Always keep within earshot under bad weather conditions.
- In every boat there has to be a life-jacket, a whistle, buoyance, a protective cover and a handhold or rope.
- Recommendation for rowers: bring a cover for bow and stern, and a bilge pump.
- In strong winds or a heavy swell the wearing of a life-jacket is obligatory.

In addition the TID recommends the following equipment for the trip:
The boat should be made unsinkable. The usual equipment for boat trips comprises a tent, a cooker and cooking utensils. If you use a camping stove you need to bring along enough cartridges or bottles of gas. From Vienna on there won't be any possibilities to buy cartridges or to fill up bottles of gas. Don't forget a canvas bucket. Drinking water is not always available. Make sure you have only light luggage, the less luggage the better – you may be surprised how little you need.

For further information on the TID contact the German Canoe Club Federation, Friedrich-Beuer-Strasse 42, D-5300, Bonn 3, Germany.

EQUIPMENT AND PREPARATION

For most craft the passage down the Danube will be carried out under power and special attention needs to be paid to the installation and maintenance of the main engine. Sufficient spares for all the likely problems that might be encountered should be carried as after Austria spares for most major marine engines and most outboards are non-existent despite agents for some of the better known makes in Hungary and Yugoslavia. In Bulgaria and Romania you are entirely on your own. A comprehensive set of spares including a spare injector and a complete water pump should be carried and a comprehensive tool kit. If at all possible a back-up engine, a small outboard will do for most craft, should be carried. In Czechoslovakia the stern tube on *Rozinante* ripped out and although a repair was cobbled together in Czechoslovakia, I relied heavily on a small outboard for getting in and out of places – though we sailed whenever possible and ended up sailing most of the length of the Danube!

Where most preparation is needed is in ensuring you have a sufficient capacity for fuel and provisions. In many of the Eastern Bloc countries, including Czechoslovakia, Hungary, Bulgaria and Romania, it is prohibited to store fuel, diesel or petrol, in plastic containers, though you may get the filling station attendant to turn a blind eye. Most of your fuel after Austria will have to be obtained at filling stations and carried in jerry cans, often a considerable distance from the river. Consequently sufficient reserve supplies must be carried and you should fill up wherever possible. On *Rozinante* there was a 10 gallon main tank for the 8hp diesel and I carried a 5 gallon jerry can of diesel.

For the 4hp outboard there was a 2½ gallon petrol tank and I carried two 4 gallon jerry cans of petrol in reserve. In Romania it can be difficult to find fuel at all and so sufficient reserves should be taken to get you through Romania and down the Black Sea to Bulgaria or to Istanbul. In *Rozinante* I failed to find fuel and for the Black Sea trip we had to sail most of the way to Istanbul – it took four days to cover 200 miles with no fuel to motor with when there was little or no wind.

In most of the countries provisioning is no problem. Germany, Austria and Hungary are the best places to stock up. In Czechoslovakia it can be a problem finding many things, but Hungary comes soon afterwards to provision up for eastern Europe proper. In Yugoslavia most items can be found in the larger towns and cities. In Bulgaria it can be difficult to find many items, especially in the smaller places, but compared to Romania it is bountiful. In Romania you will have to queue for anything and even at the head of a queue you will not find a lot to buy however many Romanian *lei* you have. In *Rozinante* I stored sufficient provisions to get us through Romania and I suggest anyone else do likewise. Don't even bargain on getting basics like bread, eggs and fresh vegetables. Most Romanian shops seem to be exclusively stocked with tomato paste and pickled vegetables and if you can live on these then you might survive – otherwise be prepared.

FORMALITIES

All the normal visa requirements outlined in the next section on the countries along the Danube are required and should be obtained before leaving. Most people do not require a visa for Germany, Austria and Yugoslavia, but for Czechoslovakia, Hungary, Bulgaria and Romania many nationals will need a visa. Apart from this you will need registration papers for the boat: for the United Kingdom either full Part I Registration (the *Blue Book*) or the Small Ships Register papers administered by the RYA are satisfactory. In addition you should have a certificate of competency or for craft over 20 tons, a Master's ticket and insurance papers, although when I enquired of a number of insurance companies about insurance for the Danube they laughed me out of the room though they were quite happy to take my money for insurance in home waters – but then nobody expects insurance employees to exercise a little imagination and ask where the Danube is or goes to. As it turned out I was never asked for insurance documents in any of the Danube countries. For medical and general insurance I used *Europ Assistance*, as I have on past trips, and I can recommend their service.

In the different countries along the Danube the formalities are as follows:
i. *Germany* You are not required by law to have a certificate of competency or insurance as it is not needed if it is not required in the country of origin. At no time did customs inspect *Rozinante* either on entry by land, craning her into the water at Regensburg, or on leaving Germany on the river. However if you enter by sea it would be wise to clear out of Germany at Passau.
ii. *Austria* Clear into Austria at Passau. On *Rozinante* I could not find anywhere safe or legal to tie up – a policeman threatened to give me a ticket for berthing on the town quay! – so I did not clear out of Germany or into Austria. There is a customs station at Engelhartzell but it was not manned when I passed and German pleasure craft seemed to ignore it, so I did too and no-one seemed to mind. You clear out of Austria at Hainburg where the customs were very relaxed and friendly, though concerned at the size of *Rozinante* and the length of the trip ahead.
iii.*Czechoslovakia* Before Bratislava you were once met by a patrol boat and escorted into a pontoon on the right bank. Care needs to be taken as it is shallow alongside and the current is strong. The relevant officials, customs and immigration will come from Bratislava to carry out the relevant paperwork. When you leave Bratislava you must clear out and clear in again at Komárno on the border with Hungary. Before leaving to cross the river to Komárom in Hungary you must go onto the pontoon in

the river and be processed by the relevant officials in the office above. This procedure may change in the future.

iv. *Hungary* Clear in at Komárnu where the relevant paperwork will be carried out, a lengthy though friendly process. In Hungary tourists must normally register with the police every night, a process which is automatically carried out by the hotel staff of any hotel you stay in. On a boat there are no such checks and normally there will not be a problem, but should you venture ashore to stay in a hotel, as we did, the system hiccups and our passports were taken by the police. I had to report to the police station in the next major town to retrieve them where I was interviewed by the police. This is unlikely to happen now. You clear out of Hungary at Mohács.

v. *Yugoslavia* Clear in at Mohács in an office right alongside the Hungarian office. Here the relevant paperwork will be carried out, like Hungary a lengthy though friendly process. You are then free to cruise the length of the Danube in Yugoslavia stopping wherever you want to. In some of the river ports your papers may be checked by the authorities. To clear into Romania clear out of Yugoslavia at Veliko Gradiste and clear into Romania at Moldova. To clear into Bulgaria clear out of Yugoslavia at Kladovo and clear into Bulgaria at Vidin. It is worthwhile stocking up with cigarettes, *Kent* or *Marlboro*, at the duty free shops even if you don't smoke as these two brands can be used as a medium of exchange – a polite way of putting it – in Bulgaria and more especially in Romania.

vi. *Bulgaria* Just over the border marked by the Timok River there will be a patrol boat moored by the bank that will want to inspect your papers. They will then tell you to clear in at Vidin. The relevant offices are actually two miles upstream of Vidin at the ferry and commercial port and you should stop here or you will have to

From Donaueschingen the local train follows the course of the Danube to Regensburg.

bash back against what is still a strong current on the lower Danube. You will be issued with the relevant papers detailing the ports you are going to visit though I visited several places that I hadn't listed. Your papers may be checked by a patrol boat, but otherwise you are free to potter along the river until the last port of call, usually Rousse. Clear out of Rousse for Giurgiu across the river.

vii. *Romania* Clear in at Moldova or Giurgiu. The paperwork is extensive in Romania and you should allot the best part of a day for it. In the past when you arrived you were allotted an armed guard, usually a young lad doing his national service, to keep an eye on you. An armed guard was posted day and night in Romania in all ports, but in my experience these lads were all polite and helpful, usually wanting any backhanders that were going like cigarettes, coffee and western magazines. At all subsequent ports a guard was posted and the authorities would check the papers. I anchored in the river on several occasions and nobody seemed to question what had happened to the 'missing' day at the next port. The procedure may change in the future.

If you are transitting the Danube–Black Sea Canal then the relevant paperwork and a pilot, the latter mandatory on all craft even on all nineteen feet of *Rozinante*, are dealt with at Cernavoda. The pilot accompanies you to Agigea and luckily we managed to get a tow from a tug going through, otherwise the pilot would have been on board for a couple of days! At Agigea more paperwork is carried out and the canal fee paid. The canal fee is calculated on engine size: in 1987 0–20hp was $20, 20–40hp was $30, 40–60 hp was $40 and so on. There have been reports of extortionate amounts of money being demanded for the transit, but if the transit is in company with a commercial craft then the above amounts are charged. The fee can be paid only in US dollars or deutschmarks (or yen if you happen to have them). It cost $20 for *Rozinante* and several packets of *Marlboro*. From Agigea you lock out into the vast commercial port of Constanţa. You must motor through this maze of breakwaters and jetties to the old port of Constanţa just up the coast to the north. If you are proceeding to the Danube delta, clear out from Tulcea or Sulina. It should be noted that private pleasure craft cannot explore the delta but must stick to the main channel.

DANGERS TO NAVIGATION

i. *Debris in the river* Bits of debris, mostly logs and large branches, are rated as the greatest danger in the river by users in Germany and Austria. If a log or large branch becomes waterlogged it will float just under the surface and if you run over it the propeller can be severely damaged. There may also be damage to the stern gear, couplings, gearbox and to the engine mounts. I saw one motorboat that had both propellers crumpled into a metallic pulp after hitting a log. Another boat I looked at was getting a new gearbox after hitting a log with its propeller. It is also possible to damage the hull of a craft on a large submerged log. I saw several fully grown trees some 10m long and around a metre thick floating in the Danube. The only guard against this danger is constant vigilance – you become very attuned to spotting lumps of wood in the water after a few days.

ii *The current* In places the Danube is roaring along at close to 12mph, around 20kph, and care is needed to line a boat up to go through a bridge arch or to avoid other traffic on the river. You have to learn to start cutting across the river well before the time you would need to in still water. This applies especially when coming into pontoons or basins as in places it will be impossible for a just adequately powered boat to make any headway against the current. If you have a shallow draught craft drawing less than a metre you may be able to pick up a counter-current close to the bank – but don't count on it. Always remember that the current can be your friend as well as your enemy. If you turn around into the current you will be able to hold the boat virtually in the same spot except in the very swift sections of the Danube. This technique should be used when approaching harbours or pontoons which can be done very slowly motoring into the current. With a little experience you can get a boat to literally slide sideways across the river. If in doubt over the channel or when there is a danger ahead the same technique can be used to give yourself breathing space while you figure out where the channel is or to avoid a threatening barge train.

iii.*Commercial traffic* Commercial traffic on the Danube is a frightening experience for the first one or two encounters, after that you will be more relaxed about it. Traffic normally keeps to the starboard side of the river as is normal practice. However barge convoys, both pusher-tugs but more particularly barge tows, often need to line themselves up for corners or difficult sections of the channel from the wrong side of the river. The tugs, both pusher-tugs and towing tugs, and powered barges, have a board signal showing you the side to pass on, but you will normally see the flashing strobe lights they are required to use showing the side to pass on before you ever see the board signal. The lights show up well even in bright sunlight and it is a rare occasion when you will be confused about what is going on. Commercial traffic has right of way on the river and any pleasure boat skipper who obstructs one of these river leviathans needs his head examined – you wouldn't step out in front of a double-decker bus so don't put a small pleasure craft in front of several thousand tons of a barge train and the thousands of horsepower pushing or pulling it.

iv.*The weather* Though you are on a river, the weather can still affect your movements and at times the safety of a craft. Heavy rain can reduce visibility to less than a 100m and at such times it is wise to stop if at all possible. There can also be a river

Leviathans of the river: small craft should keep well clear.

mist in the morning which reduces visibility, though rarely to levels which make navigation dangerous. On the wider section of the Danube there can be severe gales at times, and I do mean gales where the wind gets up to 30–40 knots and can whip up a surprising swell – I encountered swells of up to two metres on several occasions with the wind gusting to 40 knots. At times these storms, the worst are the autumn storms on the lower Danube, bring all navigation on the Danube to a halt and even the huge push-tows are held up by the weather. In *Rozinante* I was caught out on two occasions by these storms, once anchored out in an open stretch of the river which necessitated hauling up the anchor and going downstream in the dusk until we found a sheltered spot to anchor, and again at the Iron Gates dam where the force of the wind made it dangerous to operate the lock gates and we had to anchor in a small bight and keep an anchor watch.

HARBOURS, PONTOONS, AND ANCHORING

Where to stop for the night along the river varies from country to country. In Germany and Austria there are numerous pleasure craft marinas or clusters of pontoons with all facilities available – water, electricity, fuel, a restaurant and bar. Often you can use the ferry pontoon if a ferry is not due in until the next day. In Hungary there are sufficient pleasure craft facilities to get by, though they are not up to the standard of those in Austria. In Yugoslavia there are pleasure craft harbours or pontoons, though you will have to use commercial pontoons or harbours some of the time. Once out of Yugoslavia pleasure craft facilities dry up and you will have to berth wherever you can at pontoons or commercial harbours.

In Germany and Austria it is unwise to attempt to anchor as the river bed is mostly composed of gravel or, worse, smooth rock, and though the locals may sometimes anchor for lunch, they rarely do so for the night. The swift current can quickly whip you downstream onto a gravel bank or rocks should the anchor drag and getting off against the current may be impossible without assistance. Below Budapest where the Danube slows and spreads out the bottom is often mud or sand, especially behind islands or 'headlands', and there are numerous wonderful places to anchor for the night. You could be in the Mediterranean or the Caribbean. However care needs to be taken to check the composition of the river bed as there is still gravel in places all along the Danube. In Hungary and Yugoslavia there appeared to be no restrictions on where you could anchor. In Bulgaria you must list your itinerary and obviously you won't know where you are going to anchor – however the authorities seemed not to be worried about it and I anchored in several places in between the listed ports on the itinerary. In Romania caution was needed, but nonetheless I anchored off in a deserted stretch of the river and no-one objected.

In a small boat you can run in to sloping muddy banks and just nose in until you can get a line ashore. This technique should only be used where there is no commercial traffic passing or the wash may damage the boat by bashing it up and down on the bottom and the bank. The technique is useful because close to the bank you are usually out of the current and also you can simply jump ashore. One other technique which is useful when hanging off a pontoon is to put a strong bucket out the back on a length of rope. This will keep you from sheering around in the current and from being bashed against the pontoon should there be a lot of wash from commercial craft.

In Appendix I there is a list and brief details of harbours, pontoons and anchorages along the Danube.

The Danube in Upper Austria
Austrian National Tourist Office

CYCLING AND WALKING

In 1934 Patrick Leigh Fermor walked down the Danube and in the same year Bernard Newman cycled down it on his trusty bicycle *George*. Bernard Newman completed his trip in a matter of months, but Patrick Leigh Fermor was still on his way to Constantinople well into the second year, so there is a moral here for anyone who is contemplating cycling or walking the whole length of the Danube: if you have the summer then it is a cycling trip, if you have two years then it can be walked. Not that many will seek to emulate the Patrick Leigh-Fermors or Bernard Newmans of this world who belong to an older tougher age of travelling.

A cycling or walking trip of the Danube will most likely be confined to a part of the river and is perfectly feasible in Germany and Austria where the Germans and Austrians are out in their hundreds every weekend hiking or cycling along the river bank. The *Treppelweg*, the path built along the side of the river for horses to haul barges upstream before the age of steam, is largely intact in these two countries and it is feasible to walk or cycle the length of the Danube from around Ingolstadt all the way down to Vienna, though cyclists will have to cut inland in places. There are plenty of *Gasthäuser* to stay at in towns and villages along the way and to my mind it would make an ideal walking or cycling tour.

In the countries below Austria things become more difficult. It would be wise to leave Czechoslovakia out altogether as the tracks and roads do not follow the river where it spreads out into a marshy waterland. From Austria you can cut across into Hungary and rejoin the Danube before the Danube bend. From the river it looks possible to continue all the way to the border with Yugoslavia where the Danube again spreads out into marshland and you would have to skirt around this section until the Fruska Gora. From here it is possible to get to the Iron Gates and either continue on to Bulgaria or cut across to Romania. The Romanian side would be difficult after Turnu Severin because of the extensive lakes and marshland bordering the river. From Giurgiu you could, the authorities permitting, go on to the Danube delta.

The countries along the Danube

The following section deals briefly with practical details about the countries along the Danube, though I have omitted the USSR as few people go there on a trip down the Danube, except for those on the Russian cruise ship *Dnepr* who see Ismail briefly. I do not deal with the history of the countries here, that would need an extra couple of volumes just to scratch the surface of, for example, the rise to power of an Austrian vegetarian who threatened to rule Europe, the Habsburgs who did rule central Europe, the Hungarians invaded and conquered by everyone who came through central Europe over the centuries but still fighting for their freedom, the Southern State of the Slavs brought together by the charisma of Tito, the tinderbox of the Balkans and the troubled history of Romania.

GERMANY

(Figures are for post-unification Germany and combine what was formerly West and East Germany.)

Area 356,963 sq kilometres (137,822 sq miles)

Population 78,666 (Note: population is difficult to ascertain due to migration from other eastern European countries.)

Government Federal republic, multi-party, decentralised.

Capital Bonn (285,000). Soon to be Berlin.

Language German. Some English spoken in larger towns.

Religion Protestant (49%) and Catholic (44%)

Time zone UT+1 DST April to September

Currency Deutschmark (Dm) = 100 Pfennig

Banks Open 0800–1230 and 1330–1600 though there are local variations in different towns. Eurocheques, major credit and charge cards and travellers cheques are accepted.

Mail Reliable. *Poste Restante* service is good.

Telephones Entirely automatic and international calls can be made from phone booths.

Medical Probably the best medical facilities in Europe with more doctors and hospital beds per head of population than any other country in the EC. Reciprocal agreement for medical treatment with other EC countries. If you have to pay for medical treatment it is expensive.

Internal travel Reliable trains and buses to most destinations. Internal flights to major cities. Car hire in all the larger towns and cities. Taxis commonly available.

International travel International flights to Frankfurt, Hamburg, Munich and Cologne. Rail travel from most European countries.

Public holidays

Jan 1	New Year's Day	*Movable:*
Jan 6	Epiphany	Good Friday
May 1	Labour Day	Easter Monday
Jun 17	National Unity Day	Ascension
Aug 15	Assumption	Whit Monday
Nov 1	All Saints Day	Corpus Christi
Dec 25	Christmas Day	Day of Penitence
Dec 26	St Stephen's Day	

Entry requirements No visas are required by EC nationals nor by holders of most western passports. Usually there is only a cursory check on passports when you enter Germany.

Marbach with the church of Maria Taferl behind. *Austrian National Tourist Office*

At Passau the Inn, seen here, doubles the volume of the Danube

Downstream from Linz – the Danube is not all sleepy villages and farmland

Food and drink German regional cuisine is largely composed of thick soups, stews, sausages and grilled or roasted meats. It is solid stuff often accompanied by potato salad and the ubiquitous *Sauerkraut*. Fish, often herrings, is widely available. If you are watching your figure Germany is a disastrous place to eat, but otherwise the solid fare is good value and I for one became addicted to *Gulaschsuppe*, a spicy meat-laden soup which is a meal in itself.

German beer is excellent, certainly amongst the best in the world, and you can choose almost any and be satisfied. German wines are also good and local *schnapps* are well worth trying, though be prepared for the lethal consequences of a *Jaegermeister* or *Barwürtz*.

AUSTRIA

Area 83,849 sq kilometres (32,374 sq miles)

Population 7·6 million

Government Federal republic, multi-party, centralised in Vienna.

Capital Vienna (1·7 million)

Language German, some English and French spoken.

Religion Catholic with a Protestant minority.

Time zone UT+1 DST April to September.

Currency Schilling (S) = 100 Groschen.

Banks Open 0800–1230 and 1330–1530 though there are some local variations. Eurocheques, major credit and charge cards and travellers cheques accepted.

The Schlögen Schlinge, (the sling of Schlögen), in Austria where the Danube swings in a huge U-bend back on itself. The ruins of Haichenbach castle sit atop the Schlinge. *Austrian National Tourist Office*

Mail Reliable. *Poste Restante* service is good.

Telephones Largely automatic and international calls can be made from phone booths.

Medical A high standard of medical treatment. Check for reciprocal agreements as the cost of medical treatment is high.

Internal travel Reliable and efficient rail and bus transport to most destinations. No internal flights to speak of. Car hire in the larger towns and cities. Taxis commonly available.

International travel Flights from most places to the international airport at Vienna. Rail connections from most European countries intersect at Vienna.

Public holidays

Jan 1	New Year's Day	*Movable*
Jan 6	Epiphany	Easter Monday
May 1	Labour Day	Ascension
Aug 15	Assumption	Whit Monday
Oct 26	National Day	Corpus Christi
Nov 1	All Saints Day	
Dec 8	Immaculate Conception	
Dec 25	Christmas Day	
Dec 26	St Stephen's Day	

Entry requirements None except for South African nationals who must obtain a visa in advance.

Food and drink Breaded veal, *Wiener Schnitzel* and chicken, *Wiener Backhändl*, are the two well known Austrian specialities. I found their various salads excellent and also the soups. Dishes from Czechoslovakia and Hungary are also common. Viennese desserts are justly famous, try *Sachertorte*, chocolate cake with jam, *Apfelstrudel*, apple pastry and *Topfenstrudel*, cheese cake, before moving on to the less well known desserts.

Austrian beer is always good. Austrian white wines are good, the reds less so. Coffee is an institution in Austria and comes in a bewildering array of types. Keep trying until you get what you want – in one Viennese café it was said they kept a chart with the different shades of brown on it so you could choose the shade of coffee you wanted.

CZECHOSLOVAKIA

Area 127,869 sq kilometres (49,373 sq miles)

Population 15 million

Government Newly formed federal republic, multi-party. Until 1989 the government was single party Communist.

Capital Prague (1·2 million)

Language Czech and Slovak. German quite common.

Religion Catholic with a Protestant minority.

Time zone UT+1 DST April to September.

Currency Czechoslovak crown, the koruna = 100 halers

Banks Open 0800–1600. Foreign currency, Eurocheques and travellers cheques can be changed at *Cedok*, the state tourist office. Major credit and charge cards accepted in some places in the popular tourist spots. Limited black market in currency exchange.

Mail Generally reliable but slow.

Telephones International calls are best made from a hotel. Direct dialling in some places.

Medical A good standard of medical care in the larger towns and cities. Minor treatment is free, major treatment must be paid for where no reciprocal agreement exists. Charges are moderate, but must be made in foreign currency.

Internal travel Trains and buses run to most destinations, but they are often overcrowded. On local public transport you must buy a ticket in advance and punch it on the automatic puncher on the bus or tram. Internal flights to major cities. Car hire in the major towns and cities. Taxis are scarce and it is best to have one called.

International travel Flights to Prague and some to Brno and Bratislava. Trains from Europe go to Prague and Bratislava.

Public holidays

Jan 1	New Year's Day	*Movable*
May 1	Labour Day	Easter Monday
May 5	Uprising Day	
May 9	Liberation Day	
Dec 25	Christmas Day	
Dec 26	St Stephen's Day	

Entry requirements Visas are no longer required by most EC nationals and Swiss, Austrian, USA and Canadian nationals. Most other nationals can obtain a visa at the border or from a Czechoslovakian Embassy.

Food and drink Traditionally roast or grilled meat, especially pork, often served with *knedliky*, dumplings and *sauerkraut*. Hungarian *gulǎs*, goulash, is also common. In Bratislava I had excellent pancakes stuffed with diced pork and a mushroom and cream sauce.

Czechoslovakian beer is renowned, but it is difficult, often impossible, to find the famous brand-names. The red and white wines are good and there are imported wines from Hungary and Bulgaria.

HUNGARY

Area 93,030 sq kilometres (35,519 sq miles)

Population 10·6 million

Government Newly formed federal republic, multi-party. Until 1989 the government was single party Communist.

Capital Budapest (2 million)

Language Hungarian, some German and a little English.

Religion Catholic (65%), Protestant (25%) and an Eastern Orthodox minority.

Time zone UT+1 DST April to September.

Currency Forint = 100 fillers.

Banks Open 0900–1300. Exchange also possible at *Ibusz* offices. Eurocheques, travellers cheques and major credit and charge cards widely accepted. There is a black market in currency, but as the rate is only 10% or so above the official rate it's hardly worth bothering with.

Mail Generally reliable.

Telephones International calls are best made from a hotel. It may take a little time to get through, though usually less than an hour.

Medical Medical care is of a high standard. In an emergency care is free, otherwise fees are relatively low.

Internal travel Buses and trains serve most destinations. There are no internal flights. Hire cars at major towns and cities. Taxis are common and relatively cheap.

International travel International flights to Budapest. Rail service to most destinations in Europe.

Church on the *Puszta* in Hungary

Public holidays

Jan 1	New Year's Day	*Movable*
Apr 4	Liberation Day	Easter Monday
May 1	Labour Day	
Aug 20	Constitution Day	
Nov 7	Anniversary of October Revolution	
Dec 25	Christmas Day	
Dec 26	St Stephen's Day	

Entry requirements Visas are no longer required by EC nationals and most other European and Scandinavian nationals. Most other nationals can obtain a visa at the border or from a Hungarian Embassy.

Food and drink Gulăs, goulash, is, of course, the national dish, though there are a range of different goulashes, some regional. Other dishes are *paprikas csirke*, (paprika chicken), stuffed cabbage and other goulash-like stews. Also good near the Danube are the fish dishes, especially *halaszle*, fish soup. Pepper salads are common, in fact the pepper is essential to Hungarian cuisine. Desserts are the equal of Austrian desserts with cakes common and my favourite, a *palacsinta*, pancake, filled with cottage cheese and chopped nuts with icing sugar on top. The cuisine is invariably excellent and also cheap.

Beers are good. The wines are invariably good and often excellent. The reds, such as the well known *Egri bikaver*, Bull's Blood, are robust and full-bodied although there are lighter reds as well. Hungary is the home of the inimitable *Tokay*, usually drunk in the west as *Aszi*, a sweet dessert wine, but also available as medium sweet or dry. Various liqueurs are made, my favourite being *barack*, made from apricots.

YUGOSLAVIA

Area 255,804 sq kilometres (98,766 sq miles)

Population 22·8 million

Government Federal peoples' republic, single party Socialist, though it is currently in the throes of becoming a multi-party system.

Capital Belgrade (Beograd) (1·3 million)

Language Serbo-Croat, using both the Roman and the Cyrillic alphabet. German spoken along the Danube. Italian along the coast.

Religion Eastern Orthodox (42%), Catholic (25%) and Muslim (10%).

Time zone UT+1 DST April to September

Currency Dinar (din)

Banks 0700–1900 though there are many regional and local variations. Eurocheques, travellers cheques, major credit and charge cards widely accepted.

Mail Generally reliable. *Poste Restante* can be used in major towns and cities.

Telephones Mostly automatic in the larger towns and cities. Direct dialling to most places. Telephone calls are best made from a hotel.

Medical Medical treatment is average to good. There are reciprocal agreements with many western countries, otherwise costs are moderate. Emergency treatment is usually free.

Internal travel Buses and trains serve most destinations. In the cities trams and buses are often crowded. Internal flights to many parts of the country. Hire cars in the tourist centres and cities. Taxis common.

International travel International flights to Belgrade and to some other destinations in the summer. Rail connections to most European destinations.

Public holidays

Jan 1, 2   New Year
May 1, 2   Labour Days
July 4   Veterans' Day
Nov 29, 30   Republic Days

There are also various regional holidays.

Entry requirements Most western nationals do not require a visa except for Australians, New Zealanders, South Africans and Greeks, who should obtain a visa in advance though it can be obtained, with some hassle, on the border.

Food and drink Yugoslav cuisine is not the greatest, usually consisting of pork or veal grilled or fried with a squidgy mess of vegetables. On the river try the spicy fish soup which is often good.

Beers are good, of the lager type. Wines, both red and whites, are invariably good and often excellent. The national liqueur is *sljivovica*, plum brandy, fiery but addictive.

BULGARIA

Area 110,911 sq kilometres (42,823 sq miles)

Population 9 million

Government Quasi-multi-party with the old Communist party still in power. Once known as the model Soviet satellite state.

Capital Sofia (1 million)

Language Bulgarian, some German and French spoken. Cyrillic alphabet.

Religion Bulgarian Orthodox with a Muslim minority.

Time zone UT+2 DST April to September

Currency Lev (plural leva) = 100 stotinki

Banks Open 0800–1200. Exchange offices at *Balkantourist* hotels and tourist offices. There is a black market operating but be warned it is illegal with stiff penalties.

Mail Mail may be opened and packages have been known not to arrive. You can have mail sent to *Poste Restante* in the larger towns and cities.

Telephones International calls are best made from a hotel, but expect to wait for at least an hour for your call to get through.

Medical Medical care is average. Emergency treatment is free and fees for any other treatment is moderate.

Internal travel Rail and bus services to most destinations. The trains and buses are often overcrowded but generally reliable. Internal flights to a number of places. Car hire in the major tourist centres. Taxis are rare.

International travel Flights to Sofia. Rail connections to Europe and Turkey.

Public holidays

Jan 1	New Year's Day
May 1, 2	Labour Days
May 24	Saints Cyril and Methodius; Alphabet, Education and Culture Day
Sep 9, 10	Socialist Revolution Days
Nov 7	Anniversary of October Revolution in Russia

Entry requirements Most western nationals must obtain a visa **in advance** before entering Bulgaria. This normally takes ten to fourteen days so don't leave it too late. Visas cannot be obtained at the border. The nationals of Austria, Denmark, Finland, Iceland, Norway, Portugal and Sweden do not need a visa. South Africans will not be allowed into Bulgaria. Independent travellers are subject to currency exchange regulations, at the moment you must change $15 a day for every day you are in Bulgaria, though those on a package holiday are exempt from this requirement. I was not subject to the currency exchange regulations on my trip in *Rozinante* though whether this was an oversight or policy I'm not sure.

Food and drink Grilled or roasted meats are common, and spicy sausages will often be found. Most of the items on a menu will not be available, but there is usually a choice of two or three things except in out of the way places.

The beer in Bulgaria, in my experience, was watery and sour. Wines on the other hand, especially reds, were always good and often excellent.

ROMANIA

Area 237,500 sq kilometres (91,699 sq miles)

Population 21·2 million

Government A newly formed provisional government. A multi-party system is to emerge, though slowly it appears. Formerly single party Communist along what can only be called Stalinist principles under Ceausescu.

Capital Bucharest (2 million)

Language Romanian, some French, German and Italian spoken.

Religion Romanian Orthodox (75%) and Catholic, Protestant and other minorities.

Time zone UT+2 DST April to September

Currency Leu (plural lei) = 100 bani

Banks Open 0800–1330. There are currency exchange offices at *TAROM*, the state tourist offices. Eurocheques and travellers cheques accepted. Major credit and charge cards can be used only in a few places. It is no longer necessary to exchange $10 a day and the *lei* is now allowed to float freely against other hard currencies. There is a black market and you will often be pestered to 'change money, change money' – however the dealers have a well practiced slight of hand and you may find you don't have as many *lei* in your hand for your dollars or pounds as you should have.

Mail Care is needed as mail is often checked and packages are known not to arrive. You can have mail sent to *Poste Restante* and collect it for a small fee.

Telephones International calls are best made from a hotel and even then you will have a long wait before the call goes through.

Medical Medical care is average to poor. Fees are moderate.

Internal travel Bus and train service to most destinations though it is always over-crowded and sometimes unreliable. Internal flights to some destinations. Hire cars in a few places. Taxis are rare.

International travel International flights to Bucharest. Train service with most European connections.

Public holidays

Jan 1, 2   New Year
May 1, 2   Labour Days
Aug 23, 24 Romanian National Days

Entry requirements EC nationals and most European and Scandinavian nationals can obtain a visa at the border – no photographs are required. Alternatively a visa can be obtained from a Romanian Embassy before departure. It would be wise for some nationals outside Europe to check with an embassy before departure.

Food and drink If you are on a tour the food will be not too bad but if you are fending for yourself the food is abysmal. Restaurants normally have only one or two of the items on the menu and food will run out in poorer establishments. I queued at a pizza restaurant and just as I was about to be served, pizzas ran out for the evening. That was it, no more food! During two trips to Romania I have yet to come across a national cuisine, most of the food being a poor imitation of an 'international cuisine'. Despite the apocalyptic events of 1989 and 1990, the food situation has only marginally improved in the cities and hardly at all in the countryside.

The beer is OK. Romanian wines are said to be excellent, but those kept for internal consumption were mediocre and most Romanians seemed to prefer Bulgarian wines.

Rhine-Main-Danube canal

The idea of linking the Rhine and the Danube and being able to navigate right across Europe from the Black Sea to the North Sea has occupied the minds of engineers from early medieval times to the present. We have no evidence that the Romans contemplated such a canal though I am certain that Roman engineers were consulted by Roman generals on the feasibility of such a project. It would not have been beyond the technology of the time, after all the Romans constructed navigation canals in England, France and Italy, constructed flash locks to overcome difficult slopes, and had a competent knowledge of hydrodynamics as the construction of their aqueducts clearly showed. However the first attempt to link the Rhine and the Danube was under Charlemagne who started construction of the Fossa Carolina in 793. It was a short canal, only 2000 paces, roughly 2000m long by 9m wide, to link the Rivers Altmühl and Regnitz, which would enable navigation from the Danube to the Rhine. However, difficulties were encountered cutting through the marshy land between the two rivers and work proceeded slowly. At the end of autumn it was decided to abandon the canal. Parts of the Fossa Carolina can still be seen at Graben, a village near Weissenburg between Nürnberg and the Danube.

A canal to link the Rhine and the Danube was not attempted again until the 19th century under Ludwig I. Ludwig had a route surveyed in 1828 and in 1832 a route between Bamberg and Kelheim was agreed upon. In spring 1837 work began with a work force of 6000 men and an early steam shovel. The work force was to increase to 9000 men at times. The canal between Bamberg and Nürnberg opened in 1843 and the complete canal from Bamberg to Kelheim was open in 1846. It was an audacious project for the times. The canal was 172km long, with a width of 10·5m and a depth of 1·45m. From Bamberg it followed the Regnitz valley to Nürnberg around Neumarkt and along the Sultz valley to Dietfurt and the Altmühl valley to Kelheim. From Bamberg on the Main it rose 180m to the summit reach which was 457m above sea level and then dropped 80m to Kelheim where there was a basin for craft to wait until the Danube was suitable for navigation. There was a total of 101 locks as well as aqueducts and cuttings. The canal could take barges up to 32m long and 4·45m wide of around 100 tonnes capacity. By 1850 it was handling nearly 200,000 tonnes of cargo a year, a record capacity that was to go slowly downhill over the succeeding years.

In 1925 Negley Farson on *Flame* was probably one of the last people to record a passage on the Ludwig Canal. First he had to get up the River Main which although canalised, nonetheless had a swift current flowing down. To get from Aschaffenburg to the canal a *Kette-Boot* operated so that barges, and *Flame*, could get up against the current.

'The *Kette-Boot* itself is one of the most surprising contraptions imaginable. Looking like a marine architect's nightmare, it performs the remarkable feat of pulling itself, on a continuous chain, 190 miles into the Bavarian mountains to Bamberg...The captain told us that in his twenty-five years with the *Kette-Boot* he had known periods of three months to pass before it could get up to Wurtzburg. The engineer, nursing his 120 horse-power motors, explained the intricacies of machinery, but, when asked about the chance of arriving at Bamberg with the *Kette-Boot*, shrugged his shoulders. The stoker hung his cap over the pressure gauge to indicate that if a high head of steam could do it it would be done. Meanwhile, with eight barges in tow and *Flame* lashed alongside, the *Kette-Boot* clanked up the Main.'

Negley Farson and *Flame* did make it to the Ludwig canal where they cruised through a Germany shattered by the settlement terms of the First World War – 'Germany is troubled with people tramping the country for work' – along the weed-choked canal. By 1925 there was virtually no commercial traffic on the Ludwig canal. The Main and the canal itself were beset with a severe water shortage in the summer so

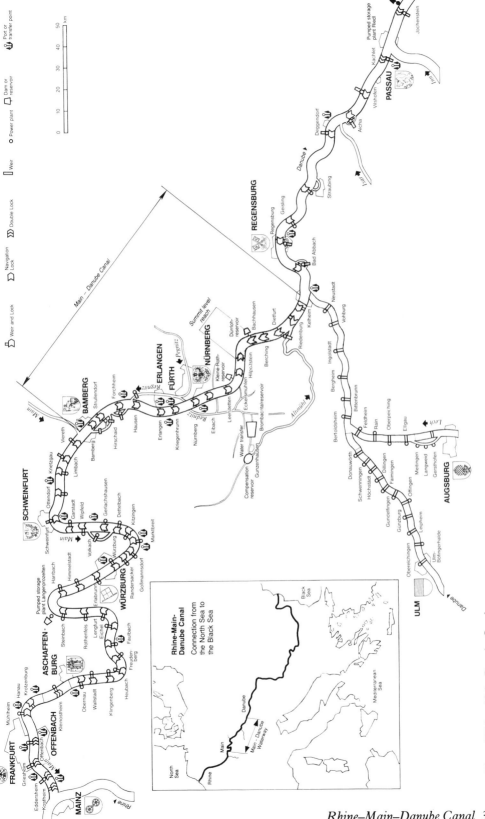

Plan of Rhine–Main–Danube Canal.

Rhine–Main–Danube Canal 35

that traffic often could not get up to Bamberg or through the canal. Added to that there was the turbulent upper Danube from Kelheim down to Passau which was often too dangerous for craft to use. It is said that Germany used the Ludwig canal during the Second World War to get E-boats to the Danube and thence down to the Black Sea and the Mediterranean, but unless the E-boats drew less than 1·45m, in fact considerably less since the canal was by then in a bad state of repair and probably severely silted up in places, then this tale is unlikely to be true.

Before Negley Farson and *Flame* passed through the Ludwig canal it had already been decided to build a new Rhine-Main-Danube canal capable of taking large barges up to 1500 tonnes. In 1921 it was agreed that a new canal should be built from Aschaffenburg, where the *Kette-Boot* started its long haul to the Ludwig canal, to Bamberg and then to Kelheim roughly following the route of the old canal. The scheme also included a canalisation programme for the upper Danube. The Rhein-Main-Donau AG (RMD) company was to build the canal which would then be handed over to the State, but the company would retain ownership of the hydroelectric plants installed in the various barrages to be built and retain the profits from these up till the year 2050. The project was to be built in stages: the canalisation of the Main for 297km between Aschaffenburg and Bamberg; the Main-Danube canal for 171km between Bamberg and Kelheim; and the canalisation of the Danube for 209km between Kelheim and Passau on the German-Austrian border. Initially the size of the waterway and the locks on it reflected the type of traffic predominant at that time and it was envisaged that motorised barges of around 1500 tonnes would be using the canal. Since that time the type and size of commercial traffic has altered substantially and now the Main-Danube canal and the Danube between Kelheim and Passau is being constructed to meet Waterway Category IV standards which can take craft up to 185m long by 11·4m wide with a cargo capacity of 3300 tonnes.

The canalisation of the Main was completed between 1926 and 1962 although some sections will have to be further modified because of the revised size of the vessels that will use the whole system. The Kelheim to Passau section is still under construction although the works already completed mean that an increased amount of commercial traffic is already using this section. There is still a considerable amount of work to be done canalising the river and three new barrages and locks have yet to be built at Deggendorf, Aicha and Vilshofen. The Main-Danube canal is still not finished despite the fact that I have read of completion dates starting in 1976 and going through to 1993. 1993 is still the official date given for completion, but most of the experts reckon that it will be closer to 1995. The Main-Danube canal is complete as far as Nürnberg, with the section to the Dürrloh-Reservoir under construction and sections at Dietfurt and Riedenburg also under construction. A long section between Bachhausen and Dietfurt and another section after Dietfurt is still in the planning stage.

The Rhine-Main-Danube canal has been plagued not only with engineering problems, but also with political tensions. Environmental lobbying and worries about the escalating cost of the canal threatened to bring the whole project to a halt in 1983, but these worries have been overcome and work is continuing on it. While I sympathise with the environmental lobby, I think its conservation policies do not stand up to a wider environmental argument bringing in the relative efficiency of water transport (one horse-power will transport 150kg by road, 500kg by rail and 4000kg by water), thus saving fuel and reducing the use of hydrocarbon fuels, and the generation of hydro-electric power which compared to hydrocarbon or nuclear generation of power is considerably better environmentally.

The problem which plagued the original Ludwig canal, lack of water in the summer months, has been overcome on the Rhine-Main-Danube canal by a number of means. One of these is to use water saving locks with side-ponds which take up to 60% of the water from the lock when it is emptying rather than letting it flow away downstream. The water then flows back into the lock by gravity when the lock is filled again. In addition water will be pumped up from the Danube basin to the Regnitz-Main area, where there is a scarcity of water, both for the canal locks and for irrigation. The water will be pumped up to the reservoirs at night when there is little demand for electricity. If water in the Danube reaches low levels there is a back-up system whereby flood-water from the River Altmühl will be stored in a reservoir and can be pumped up to the canal summit. The environmental lobby has also pressured the RMD to conserve the surrounding countryside and landscape the canal. Basically what will happen is that the canal will be made to look like a river as much as possible with the width of the canal varied, subsidiary channels built, different water levels out of the channel to pro-mote river life, gravel bank islands out of the channel, variations in bank height and trees planted along the banks. At the moment it seems difficult to visualise this riparian arcadia depicted in the literature of the RMD when all there is is mud churned by huge earth-moving equipment and stark concrete, but I have no doubt that German thoroughness in these matters will transform the building site into a garden.

The legal status of the Main-Danube canal is an interesting one as it is not covered by the agreements which govern navigation on the Danube. It is a national waterway exclusively under German regulations. However, bilateral shipping agreements have been offered to the countries along the Danube and an agreement has already been signed with Austria. It is unlikely that some Danube countries will be excluded from using the canal although fears have been voiced that subsidised eastern European ship-ping companies, especially the huge Soviet fleet already operating on the Danube, could undercut western shipping companies and take a disproportionate share of ship-ping business in Germany.

For pleasure craft users there are not likely to be any complications concerning use of the canal and the age old dream of sailing clear across Europe should be a reality sometime in the 1990s. It would then be possible to do a 'Grand Tour' starting in Hol-land and crossing Germany to the Danube where you can pass through Middle Europe to the Balkans and out into the Black Sea. From here you can enter the Mediterranean at its eastern end, cruise the length of the Mediterranean and return to northern Europe through the French canals or sail out into the Atlantic and around through Bis-cay back to the north. It's a thought for the adventurers out there amongst you.

Travellers on the Danube

When I started out doing the research for this book I little imagined that I would come across as many travellers' tales recounting voyages down the Danube as I subsequently did. It seemed that every book I found describing a trip down the Danube led to an-other and another until I had to call a halt to what was becoming an obsession on my part, this collecting of volumes and histories relating adventures on the Danube. One thing that became clear was that before the Second World War, right back into the 19th century, there had been a greater interest in the Danube and the countries along its length than when the Iron Curtain was pulled across Europe, as if the phrase as much as the border ruled out central and eastern Europe for travellers and hence ruled out the Danube as a water road for travelling along. There have been only two popular accounts of voyaging in small boats on the Danube since the Second World War and a handful of general travel books describing the river, most of them recent, as interest is rekindled in a greater Europe that includes those long lost cousins in the centre and east of the continent.

Most of the accessible tales of trips down the Danube are, naturally enough, from the 20th century, but there have been a number of travellers in the centuries preceding our own who rate a mention.

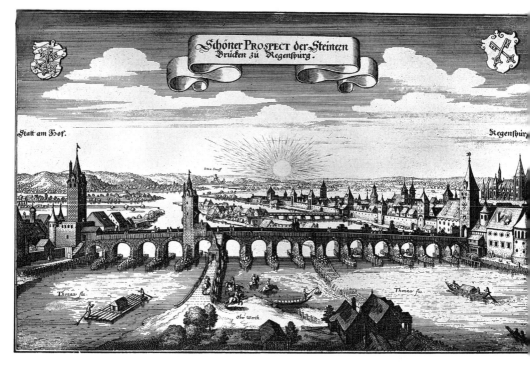

Regensburg in 1657. From a woodcut by Matthaeus
Merian.

One of the earliest accounts was by William Crowne, a servant who accompanied the
Earl of Arundel to Linz and kept a diary of his experiences. In 1636 the Earl of
Arundel was sent to Linz by Charles I who hoped to reconcile the opposing forces in
the Thirty Years War. As it turned out the Earl accomplished nothing and returned to
England without even getting the opposing forces to talk to each other, but William
Crowne's diary survived relating the trip down the Danube from Regensburg to Linz.
Most of the account deals with the havoc and ruin resulting from the war and of the
war-weary population they encountered along the way. The party 'took four boats to
travel down the Danube', staying in inns for the night along the river until they
reached Linz. The journey was accomplished in around three days travelling time, a
relatively swift journey averaging 81km a day, a speed which could never be equalled
by carriages on the roads of the time.

In the early 1770s Doctor Charles Burney travelled down the Danube from Landau,
which is actually on the River Wörth and joins the Danube just below Deggendorf, to
Vienna, while researching his book on the history of music. He kept an account of his
travels, published in 1773 as *Doctor Charles Burney's Continental Travels* in which he describes his experiences on the Danube. His *History of Music* was published later and
became the definitive work on the subject. The doctor travelled on one of the crude
rafts with a shelter on it common on the river at that time. His journey was not a comfortable one; it was cold, 'I forgot to bargain for warm weather; and now it is so cold,
that I could scarcely hold the pen, though but the 25th of August!' he wrote, and as for
food, 'My provisions grew short and stale, and there were none of any kind to be had
here!' It took a week for the trip from Landau to Vienna, an average speed of just over
55km a day to cover the 390km, a little slower than it took William Crowne to cover
his shorter journey.

By the 19th century travelling on the Danube was a lot more civilized and a good deal faster. Even by the mid-19th century there was as yet no railway line connecting one end of Europe to the other and road transport was slow and uncomfortable and in places dangerous. In 1830 the DDSG was operating the first steam-powered passenger ship between Vienna and Budapest and by the last decades of the 19th century it was possible to travel comfortably and in some style along the whole length of the Danube from Passau to the Black Sea and then on to Constantinople. In 1840–41 C. W. Vane, the Marquess of Londonderry, travelled up the Rhine and down the Danube en route to Constantinople. An account of his travels, *A Steam Voyage To Constantinople*, was published in 1842 and it is interesting to compare his style of travel with that of Doctor Burney: 'Two separate cabins, for Lady L and myself, with our own beds, made our accommodation all that could be desired. The cuisine on board was also very fair. The captain, an intelligent agreeable man, spoke many languages, and was the best specimen of the kind we met.' The passage proceeded smoothly and comfortably to Drenkova (km 1016) at the Iron Gates where the party 'were now divided into two large eight or ten oared barges, with flat-bottomed boats following, bringing luggage and carriages.' After the comforts of the steamer the Marquess found the open boats 'as rudely constructed as at the origin, probably, of this savage race', exposed to the elements, and not the sort of comfort that a man of his rank was accustomed to. They rejoined a steamer at Skela Gladova (Kladovo) though this was a cramped and ill-run ship in the Marquess' estimate.

'All this and more was crowded on an arena both filthy and black with the coals of the steam-boat, mixed with flakes of water, and nothing to wash the decks; while the oil of the engines, and the stench of garlic issuing from a four feet cupboard, by way of

Scene depicting a passage from the *Nibelungen* where
Kriemhilde is welcomed at Passau.

kitchen (from which effluvia, no part of the deck was to be free), formed an ensemble that certainly no delicate female should ever be exposed to, even by a speculative mamma or from curiosity to see foreign parts.'

The Marquess was so upset at the arrangements he considered taking his carriage (he travelled as many others did with his own personal carriage shipped on board) overland to the Black Sea to take a steamer from there, but was informed 'the roads over the mountain were impracticable' and that in a local Turkish wagon 'it would take us four or five weeks'. From Galatz a steamer was taken to Constantinople and the Marquess was comfortably accommodated once more. The whole trip from Vienna to Constantinople was accomplished in something like twelve days, a swift journey compared to going overland and also a relatively comfortable one despite the protestations of the Marquess.

Towards the end of the 19th century voyaging in small boats was becoming increasingly popular and one of the pioneers of the sport was John MacGregor. MacGregor was one of those hale and hearty Victorians that wandered around the world in utter disregard of hardship and danger with an almost messianic view in what an Englishman could do whatever the odds. In his book *A Thousand Miles in the Rob Roy Canoe on the Rivers and Lakes of Europe* he describes his adventures on a number of rivers and lakes of the Continent and a cruise down the Danube from Donaueschingen to Ulm with prose that makes it all sound easy as long as you have the right attitude and fortitude, the stuff of every right-thinking Victorian. MacGregor was this and more. He gave most of the royalties of his books to charitable organisations, profits from the first and second editions of *A Thousand Miles in the Rob Roy Canoe* went to the Royal National Lifeboat Institution and to the Shipwrecked Mariners Society. He helped to found the *Boy's Own Paper* in which he described his adventures in Europe, on the Baltic, and later a trip down the River Jordan. He was a religious man, in the manner of the times, though not overbearingly so.

But there is something else tucked into MacGregor's tales, a familiar cry of the heart, echoed in todays conversations on travelling, the oft heard derision of package holidays and the sun, sea and sand brigade. Of getting away from it all. MacGregor wanted to get away from it all, from railway and boat trips full of tourists. He was escaping from the hordes as well. 'Year after year it is enough of excitement to some tourists to be shifted from town to town, according to the routine of the excursion ticket.' He wanted the youth of England to emulate his example and get away from the fogs of London and the mills of Manchester, from the seaside resorts at Blackpool and Brighton to the healthy open-air life afloat. His book was not to be a guide-book of any sort. 'Fancy the free traveller, equipped for a delicious summer of savage life, quietly submitting to be cramped and tutored by a *Chart of the Upper Mosel*'; and he goes on to derisively quote from such a guide. MacGregor didn't have much time for *Murray's* handbooks and *Baedeker*. Nor did he have a lot of time for some of his countrymen. 'All being ready, and the weather very hot at the end of July, when the country was caught in election fever, and MPs went to scramble for seats, and the lawyers to thicken the bustle, and the last bullet at Wimbledon came 'thud' on the target, it was time for the Rob Roy to start.'

As a low cost way of getting afloat MacGregor designed the Rob Roy canoe. 'The Rob Roy Canoe was built of oak, with a deck of cedar. She was made just short enough to go into the German railway wagons...' With one small bag and the clothes on his back, MacGregor recommended a Norfolk Jacket manufactured by Meyer and Mortimer's as tough and durable with the advantage of six pockets in it, and 'a pretty blue silk Union Jack,' he set off for the Danube. 'By dusk I marched into Donaueschingen, and on crossing the little bridge saw at once I could begin the Danube from its very source, for there were at least three inches of water in the middle of the stream.' On page 65 of the book there is a pen and ink sketch, his own, of him towing

Romanian fisherman on the Delta – I was informed he had won a medal for kayaking in the Rome Olympics.

his canoe over the wet grass at the side of the Danube past a group of peasants working in a field nearby. The silk Union Jack flutters from a short staff at the front. MacGregor is looking steadfastly ahead, the two-bladed paddle over his shoulder, trousers rolled up to the knees, straw boater firmly on his head. 'Some even ran away, very often children cried outright, and when the grey stranger looked gravely on the ground as he marched and dragged the boat, and then suddenly stopped in their midst with a laugh and an English harangue, the whole proceeding must have seemed to them at least as strange as it did to me.'

MacGregor paddled himself downstream to Ulm where he decided that the wildness of the Danube was exhausted and it was time to pack up his boat and head for another European destination. When he arrived in Ulm it was still a busy river port. 'It had boats on it, and navigation, and bridges, and railways like other great waters' and so for MacGregor 'its romance was gone'. Ulm boxes were still around, or at least their descendants which MacGregor described as 'huge in size, with flat bottoms, and bows and stems cocked up, and a roofed house in the middle of their sprawling length.' He goes on to say that a steamer was tried here in 1839, but that it got stuck on a shoal and so the attempt was abandoned and the steamer was used to run downstream from Donauwörth, a village just above Regensburg. For MacGregor this was the end of his trip down the Danube and he put the Rob Roy on a train for Lake Constance.

A fellow voyager MacGregor would have got on with was Don Maxwell. In *A Cruise Across Europe* Maxwell described a trip he made in 1905 in which he sailed and punted an eighteen foot sailing boat, the *Walrus*, from England to the Black Sea. With a friend, Cottington Taylor, they sailed across the Channel, got a tow up the Rhine to the River Main, crossed the Ludwig canal and arrived at the Danube down the River Altmühl at Kelheim. They were a casual pair and the book is written in a gung-ho style which doesn't really do justice to their trip. After being arrested as spies in Holland, getting arrested in Hungary was par for the course.

'The mate was on duty, and when he crawled outside to observe the weather he was politely requested by one of the soldiers to hand over his passport and that of his companion, and to consider himself under arrest.

The captain was awakened by the unusual sound of conversation within hearing of the boat.

'What's the matter?' he enquired.

'Arrested again,' the mate answered in a bored tone.

'Tell them to wait till after breakfast,' was the reply.'

Maxwell was just as cool when it came to facing the perils of the river. At Regensburg the medieval bridge across the river was, and still is, the most difficult obstacle on the upper Danube.

'I see, said the captain, that a perfect fiend, an old stone bridge, is charted at Ratisbon (the old Roman name for Regensburg). I think we will go and have a look at it from dry land first. With a river running like this it would be suicide to go near it by water.' The mate agreed to the proposal.

Accordingly they trudged over the hills to Ratisbon. When they reached the river, below the bridge they beheld a mass of racing waters, white with foam and flying spray. The narrow arches of the old stone bridge were nearly half their normal height, so great was the rushing stream, and a foaming wave was piled up against each pier. The roar was incessant.

'It's a beast!' shouted the captain.'

Maxwell and Taylor were unsure about what they should do. They inspected the navigable arches on the right bank, the same two arches navigable today, and decided that as there was no other way to get around, they would simply have to risk it. From a point just upstream of the bridge they used a long painter to ease the *Walrus* closer and closer to the navigable arch, then at the last minute leapt on board and disappeared un-

Buskers at the Fisherman's Bastion in Budapest.

der the bridge before they knew what was happening. 'Down she went, in fine style, with increasing velocity, until she simply leapt from wave to wave.' In the Iron Gates, the evocatively named gorge and rapids where the Danube tumbles between the Carpathians and the Balkans into Romania and Bulgaria, Maxwell inadvertently took the wrong channel and was sucked down one of the most dangerous sections of the river. The studied insouciance of Maxwell would be obnoxious if it were not for the fact that what they were doing was perilous – tugs and small boats were regularly wrecked on this section.

'For a week back, and especially since they had approached so near, almost everyone who had spoken with the 'mad Englishmen', had warned them of the terrors of this rock-strewn cataract and impressed upon them the necessity of getting a pilot. . .

'They are hailing us from the signal station on the Servian shore', observed the mate; 'evidently they mean to insist on our having a pilot'.

Both men therefore looked innocently the other way. . .

The mate suggested tea, for the kettle was boiling, and the captain agreed. It was always the characteristic of the *Walrus* that, whenever anything particularly dangerous or exciting was to be encountered, tea was served on the cabin top as an outward sign of contempt for the obstacle.'

Both Maxwell and Taylor contracted malaria in Romania. Taylor recovered but Maxwell had to be shipped home an invalid. Towards the end of the journey Taylor records that Maxwell in his delirium thought he was a book, 'not properly bound', and spent sometime trying to stitch himself together. Later he got up and started to unmoor the *Walrus* in the middle of the night. He dedicated *A Cruise Across Europe* to the Hon. Henry Charles Clement Dundas, vice-consul at Galati in Romania, who no doubt saved his life by making prompt arrangements to get him back to England. What happened to the *Walrus* is not recorded, but I like to think that in some small canal in the

Danube delta she sits beside some Lipovenian fisherman's cottage earning her keep as a fishing boat.

Just before the onset of the First World War an American, Henry C. Rowland, had a thirty-five foot motorboat constructed with a 14hp paraffin engine and set out to motor across Europe. In *Across Europe in a Motorboat* published in 1915, Rowland describes his trip in the *Beaver* up the Rhine and through the Ludwig canal to the Danube. He comes across as a resourceful individual, though conceited and eager to show the American flag to the countries along the way. Most of the trip down the Danube was uneventful until fate struck in the form of the equinoctial gales in the Black Sea. The motor was flooded and the auxiliary rig was not enough to prevent a disaster.

'Oddly enough there was nothing at all terrifying about this part of it. After the hours of cold and helpless inertia in waiting for what we thought would be certain death it acted as a stimulant and seemed to bring back all of our force. It was wild, exhilarating, tremendous, like the rush of a racing automobile, or a cavalry charge, or artillery going into action. Twice the crumbling crests of the breakers came boiling over our stern, but the canvas held and kept us from filling. The uproar of the sea was deafening; we were all howling together at the top of our lungs, and when we saw that we were through the worst of it we began to laugh and shout. Almost ashore we came down with a crash upon a reef, knocking a hole the size of one's head in the starboard bilge, but so great was the drive of the following sea that we did not sink.'

The *Beaver* was left on the beach in the Black Sea, it proved impossible to get her off for repairs, and Rowland and his companion returned safely to Paris after their near brush with death.

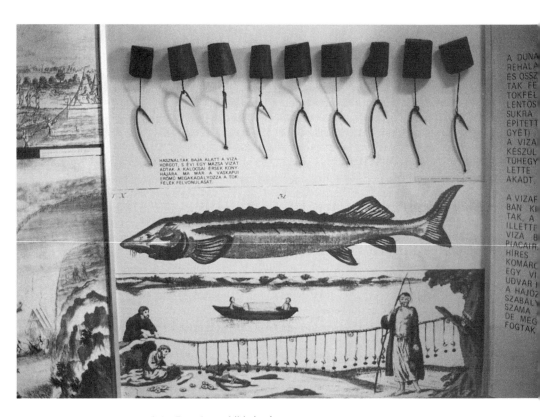

Old fishing methods of the Danube, exhibit in the Danube museum in Baja, Hungary.

Between the wars an American in the mould of Hemingway, though in his own eccentric style, sailed from England to the Black Sea with his wife. In 1925 Negley Farson took the 26 foot *Flame* on the usual route up the Rhine, through Ludwig's canal and down the Danube. Farson was an American journalist who made his home in England between his various trips through Europe and beyond. He came to England on the eve of the First World War to work in an engineering company in Manchester, moved to Russia where he sold munitions and witnessed the Revolution, served in the war with the Royal Canadian Flying Corps, went back to America after the war where he lived on a houseboat on a lake in British Columbia writing short stories and hunting and fishing to keep himself and his wife alive, went to Chicago where he sold trucks, then tiring of all this decided to sail across Europe. On the 15th June 1925 Farson and his wife, the 'crew', left Rotterdam.

Farson's tale is well-told and describes the inter-war years of unstable central Europe in some detail – it seemed half of Europe was starving. When he traversed Ludwig's old weed-choked canal he encountered numerous groups of wanderers, dispossessed by the harsh settlements after the First World War. All through Bavaria Negley Farson was treated to tales of the brutal life that Germans now led, and talk of the next war. A mechanic who repaired his engine told him of his hatred of the French and what they were doing in the Ruhr. 'All the sport carnivals, he said, had one great purpose – to fit German manhood for war.'

In Austria he was warned that he might be robbed.

'Don't leave your boat', said an onlooker; 'there are many desperate men on the riverfront. They might cut it adrift – and rob it below – on the islands.'

Below Austria was the new republic of Czechoslovakia, then Hungary under the ultra-right-wing Admiral Horthy, then the feuding Balkan states. 'The river ran between hostile nations like a line drawn between fighters...Customs posts for instance, had a nasty habit of shooting if one didn't stop.'

In the lower Danube *Flame* was shot at from the Bulgarian side.

'Moo-o! Moo-o! Bl-oo!' I heard shouts from the Bulgarian shore, saw five soldiers with their guns pointed at us, and another man waving his arms to signal us to come in.

'Well, well,' I said to the Crew; 'look at the Bulgarians.'

'Take no notice', said the Crew, who was deep in *The Smiths*; 'international waterway'.

Whack! – a bullet ploughed the water not far behind us. I saw a puff of back-powder smoke.

The Crew dropped *The Smiths*.

'They can't have!' she said.

'But – they did.'

Farson was threatened with a rifle poked in his stomach before he eventually got the soldiers to back down and let him continue on his way. The dangers of the people along the way were considerably more than the dangers of the river in these uneasy times, a situation which some writers would have you believe exists today though this is not true. The *Flame* voyaged safely through the autumn storms that beset the Danube and on to the Black Sea, arriving at the onset of winter on the 10th December 1925. What happened to *Flame* is not related, but Farson went on to become the foreign correspondent to the *Chicago Daily News* and to write further books. In 1951 the account of his journey over the Caucasus in 1929 was published as *Caucasian Journey*. In *The Transgressor* and *A Mirror For Narcissus* he described life as a foreign correspondent. He died in 1960, appropriately enough, preparing for another journey and as his son commented in the preface to *Caucasian Journey* : 'He was seventy and had done the things that most men dream about.'

Negley Farson was not the only traveller on the Danube in the years between the two world wars. In December 1933 Patrick Leigh Fermor set out from England to walk across Europe, roughly following the course of the Danube though he was to deviate

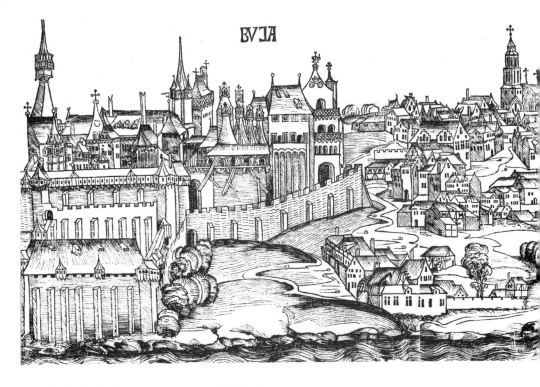

The 'Buda' of Budapest (from an engraving 1470).

often, until two years later he was riding with the Greek cavalry during a rebellion. He was 18 when he set out with five pounds a month to live on and a youthful curiosity for everything, particularly the arcane culture and languages of middle Europe. The two volumes that cover his journey from England as far as Romania, *A Time of Gifts* and *Between The Woods And The Water*, were written comparatively recently, drawing on Leigh-Fermor's prodigious memory, a little judicious reconstruction and a chance recovery of the diary he wrote on the way and accidentally left behind in a house he stayed in. His walk took him through a bitter winter to the Danube near Blenheim though he was not to see it again until 200 miles east as he zig-zagged across Germany and Austria. Germany was preparing for war, its young men caught up in the fever of National Socialism in the belief that the damage done to her in the settlement after the First World War, would be righted by the *Führer*. Along the way Leigh-Fermor stayed with old aristocratic families that he had obtained introductions to and through Germany and Austria, through the shredded Habsburg Empire in Hungary and Romania, he gives an evocative picture of the decline of these old families, some fallen on hard times, some marooned by geography in a pocket of the past, but all crumbling before the advancing doctrines of the new politics. He slept rough as well, with gypsies, in the fields and in the woods, in small *Gasthäuser* when cash allowed. In all the two books give a marvellous pastiche of a fading world with war rumbling around its edges. There are few accounts, few travel books, to rival these two dense, jumbled volumes pulling in observation and rumination on a bewildering array of topics.

I fault him on only one thing. In an appendix to *Between The Woods And The Water* he recounts a few thoughts from a recent visit where he observed the despoilation of the Iron Gorge by the construction of the Iron Gates dam, the flooding of the towns and villages, of the island of Ada Kaleh, the loss of this wild stretch of the Danube which has in effect been turned into a huge lake. It is a loss, but he goes too far.

'Others have done as much, or worse; but surely nowhere has the destruction of historic association and natural beauty and wildlife been so great. My mind goes back to my polymath Austrian friend and his thoughts on the still unhindered thousands of miles which led fishes from the Krim Tartary to the Black Forest and back again; how, in 1934, he lamented the projected power-dam at Persenbeug, in Upper Austria, 'Everything is going to vanish! They'll make the wildest river in Europe as tame as a municipal water works. All those fish from the East! They'll never come back. Never, never, never!''

I never saw the wild Danube of 1934, nor the Iron Gates before they were flooded, but I can tell Patrick Leigh-Fermor that the Danube is still the wildest river in Europe and no amount of damming will change that. I remember lying to anchor in the Iron Gates, a biting wind churning the water into a frothy white, the gates of the Iron Gates lock immobilised by the force of the wind, and though it has lost some of its savage nature, it is still recognisable as Leigh-Fermor's Danube.

In 1934, while Patrick Leigh-Fermor was striding across Europe, another adventurous soul, Bernard Newman, decided to cycle the length of the Danube.

'...I chose a bicycle – a perfectly ordinary push-bicycle – and never regretted it. I ambled along at my own pace – I was not out for speed, of course, but to see the countries and people – all my earthly requirements strapped in a pack on my carrier. . .

I guessed that the cost of living in the Balkans would be low; actually ten days in Bulgaria cost me exactly 30 shillings. So I set off with but £15 in my pocket, together with a ticket for my journey home.'

His trip had more to do with the Danube than Patrick Leigh-Fermor's, Newman's account of it was published as *The Blue Danube* in 1935, and it is less dense and in a lighter vein than Leigh-Fermor's. Newman concentrates more on the river, the people and history along the way, and on the Balkans provides a unique picture of the unsettled times – Newman was a student of Balkan history and politics and went on to write other books on the subject.

Bernard Newman cycled the whole length of the Danube, starting out at Donaueschingen in the Black Forest and finally making it along a muddy rutted track to St Gheorghiu on the southern arm of the Danube. He braved not only rough roads and inquisitorial customs officers, but gypsy vagrants who tried to rob him and an alarming ride down the rapids in the Iron Gates when the rowing boat he was being ferried in got out of control. In a sense it is *Boy's Own* stuff fifty years after MacGregor sailed his canoe on the rivers and lakes of Europe and reads something like MacGregor's prose, not badly, but out of step with the times.

After the Second World War there are few accounts of travels on the Danube until John Marriner's *Black Sea and Blue River* in which he describes his trip on the Danube in the motorboat *September Tide* in 1966. His trip is interesting because he is one of the few travellers to have ascended the Danube from the Black Sea to Vienna. The book describes what life was like in eastern Europe in the 1960s and it is interesting to find out that the Eastern Bloc countries were almost as accessible then as they are now. In fact in Romania the regime was, if anything, more tolerant then than under Ceausescu in the 70s and 80s. One of the aims of the trip was to make a documentary on the delta for the BBC, and so Marriner carried a cine photographer aboard *September Tide*, which ensured the full co-operation of the authorities in Romania who, as always, were anxious to be seen in a good light in the west. Marriner's was probably one of the last pleasure boats to transit the Iron Gates before the dam was completed and the valley flooded. His account of the difficulties he had getting through, even though assisted by a tug, shows how dramatically navigation in this section has changed since the dam tamed this part of the Danube.

'Normally the rate of current at Gura Vaii, just before embarking on the upward passage of the Iron Gates, is about eighteen kilometres an hour (say about nine knots), but on the day we passed through it had risen to twenty-three kilometres (about eleven knots). . .

...We had hardly moved. I began to wonder whether we should ever get through. Faces aboard the tug seemed to me unnaturally taut: Alexander kept looking anxiously ahead and down at his charge below. First to one side of the torrent, then to the other went *Portile de Fier* and her incubus. I could not think what her skipper was getting at...The tug, apparently despairing of getting by on the Romanian side, had swung right over to the Yugoslav. We were within six feet of the bank; I could have jumped ashore! But there was method in the madness of *Portile de Fier*, as we began to see. Slowly, very slowly, the trees ashore began to creep by us and we knew we were on the winning side.'

John Marriner and *September Tide* made it up to Vienna where he wintered over in the *Winterhafen*. It is not until 20 years later that there is another account of a trip down the Danube, made by the irascible Tristan Jones in the same year I wandered down the river for the first time. Readers either adore or hate Tristan Jone's racy prose and pugnacious adventures. In the *Improbable Voyage* he recounts his voyage and his battles against German bureaucracy, a Czechoslovakian set-up (he believed) designed to wreck his boat, Bulgarian piracy and his single-handed attempts to reform Romania and free its people. You cannot deny the allure of the ripe tales, but there is a lot of fantasy mixed into the book and worse, a jingoism, a waving of the American flag though he is Welsh, that has little to do with an understanding of eastern Europe and its peoples and promotes the sort of stereotypes that need to be dismantled rather than reinforced.

The most recent book on the Danube that goes some way to looking intelligently at the river and the peoples along it is a dense, difficult book by an Italian German scholar. In *Danube*, subtitled *A Sentimental Journey From The Source To The Black Sea*, Claudio Magris follows the trail of German scholars and other sources along its length. It is not a journey or a voyage like Tristan Jones or John Marriners following the geography of the river, rather the geography acts as a reminder for the ideas and culture that have shaped people and events along the Danube. At the end of the river Magris stands on the Black Sea and you can judge from his last paragraph whether you will want to experience the Danube with him or plump for Tristan Jones.

'Is that all then? After three thousand kilometres of film we get up and leave the cinema, looking for the popcorn vendor, and absent-mindedly wander out at a back exit. There are few people to be seen, and even they are in a hurry to leave, because it's already late and the docks are emptying. But the canal runs on, runs on, calmly and confidently flowing into the sea, and it is no longer a canal, a limitation, a Regulation, but a flowing outwards that opens and abandons itself to all the waters and oceans of the entire globe, and to the creatures living in their depths. Lord let my death – says a line of Marin's – be like the flowing of a river into the great sea.'

II. Germany

DONAUESCHINGEN TO PASSAU
The source

On the southern slopes of the Black Forest, at Donaueschingen, two alpine brooks, the Brege and the Brigach, converge to become the Danube, the *Donau* to the Germans and Austrians. In the grounds of the Fürstenberg Palace at Donaueschingen a spring bubbles up out of the ground to feed the lower part of the Brigach and the Princes of Fürstenbeg have erected a stone wall around the spring and called it the source of the Danube. It adds to the attractions for tourists visiting the palace and its grounds. Unhappy with this the owner of the spring which feeds the Brege higher up the slopes has erected a plaque stating his spring to be 'the source furthest away from the mouth of the Danube' – put this way the claim can hardly be denied. The logic of the Furstenburg source is said to be that the two brooks, the Brege and the Brigach sometimes dry up in a hot summer, while the spring in the grounds of the Prince does not.

The *Donauquelle* at Donaueschingen, claimed by the Princes of Fürstenberg to be the source of the Danube.

The confluence of the two brooks is not marked except by the reinforced concrete arches of the bridge for the by-pass around Donaueschingen. At this point it is 2850 or 2880km to the Black Sea depending on whose figures you take, around 1776 miles taking the lower figure. There are no kilometre marks here since it is not navigable. In fact the ducks swimming around could walk across it in places if they got tired of swimming. Unlike all other rivers the Danube is measured from its mouth on the Black Sea, apparently because the actual source of the river was disputed. A little further downstream it disappears underground and this was considered a complication to working out exactly where to begin measuring it. Why this should be so is a bit of a mystery since the Thames, for instance, also disappears under a boggy field downstream from its source before reappearing again.

Donaueschingen

The small town high up in the Black Forest generally accepted as the starting point of the Danube. In the Castle of the Princes of Furstenburg, a spring, the Donauquelle, is claimed to be the source of the Danube. Around the castle are fine gardens and walks. In the town a gallery in the Karlsplatz has a good collection of 15th and 16th century Swabian masters, Zeitblom, Holbein the Elder, Messkirch and Cranach the elder and the younger.

Swabian Jura

From Donaueschingen to below Sigmaringen the Danube cuts through a limestone plateau known as the Swabian Jura. During the Jurassic era (136-195 million years ago) this area was covered by the sea. The limestone laid down has been weathered and eroded into

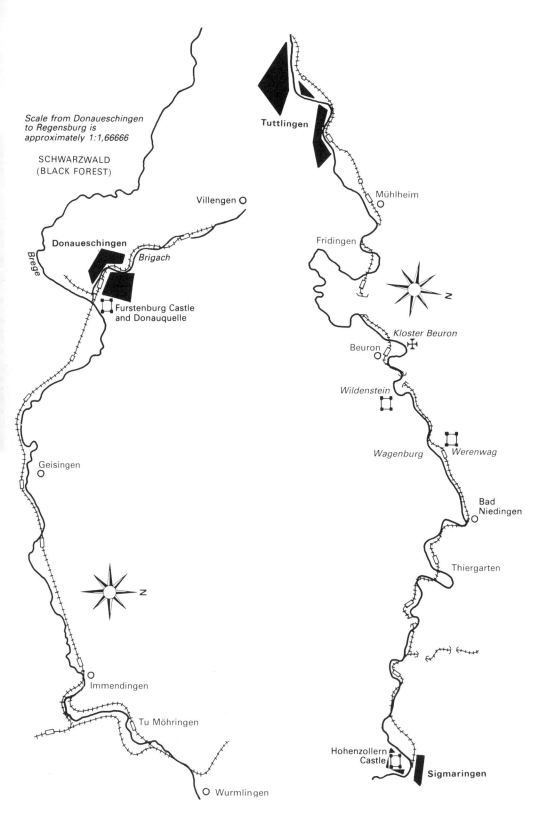

Scale from Donaueschingen
to Regensburg is
approximately 1:1,66666

SCHWARZWALD
(BLACK FOREST)

Villengen ○

Donaueschingen

Brege

Brigach

Furstenburg Castle
and Donauquelle

Geisingen ○

Immendingen ○

Tu Möhringen

○ Wurmlingen

Tuttlingen

Mühlheim ○

Fridingen

N

Kloster Beuron

Beuron
○

Wildenstein

Wagenburg   *Werenwag*

Bad
Niedingen
○

Thiergarten

Hohenzollern
Castle   **Sigmaringen**

N

50 *The Danube. A river guide*

deep gorges, pinnacles and outcrops of rock, and rocky bluffs, and the whole area is one of remarkable beauty. The railway line and a road follows the course of the Danube Valley through the Swabian Jura from Donaueschingen to Sigmaringen.

Tuttlingen
Old town with a number of attractive buildings.

Mülheim
Fortified market town overlooking the Danube with the small castle of the Enzberg Barons at one end.

Beuron
Benedictine abbey founded 1077 and renowned for its patronage of the arts, especially of choral singing. The revival of the Gregorian chant began here. The abbey buildings are not open to the public but there are wonderful views.

Wildenstein and Werenwag
Two castles built on opposite sides of the Danube.

Sigmaringen
The castle of the Catholic branch of the Hohenzollerns sits spectacularly on a rocky bluff above the river. Remodelled through the ages, it is a pastiche of different styles. Collections of furniture and furnishings and the largest private collection of arms and armour in Germany. Good collection of paintings of the Danube School in the museum nearby. The village is one of the most attractive along this stretch of the river.

The Danube School of painting Next to the castle at Sigmaringen is the museum. Before going in you exchange your shoes for great shaggy slippers something like the bottom of a string mop which make walking a little difficult, but keeps everything quite except for the shushing sound of the slippers.

The landscapes in the paintings on the walls are easily recognised as those around the Swabian valley and the Danube further downstream. Some are set in the landscape around Sigmaringen. There are stretches of the valley that can be recognised as if in a photograph. My art history is not the best, but I suspect there are few people familiar with the Danube School of painters. In the late 15th and the 16th century a school of painters developed along the Danube Valley. Cranach and

Hohenzollern castle above the Danube at Sigmaringen.

Altdorfer are names that might be recognised by some, but there are a host of minor names as well. The painters take all the traditional Biblical subjects that had been painted for centuries and that over time had seen changes in technique, lighting, materials, perspective and fashion. So the Danube School depicts Christ being scourged, judged by Pontius Pilate, crucified, stabbed in the side with a spear, the resurrection; the themes are all there just as they always had been and still are. But it isn't taking place in the parched lands of the Levant, it has been transported to the Danube. Thick pine forest, steep valleys, wooded glades, limestone pinnacles, cultivated fields, medieval towns and of course the Danube itself. Rustic peasants and town burghers from the Middle Ages are the ones doing the judging and scourging, leading Christ to the cross, jeering, whipping the bloodied figure of Christ, and just milling about. They are savage almost deformed figures, cruel faces and cruel expressions, Breughel-like figures

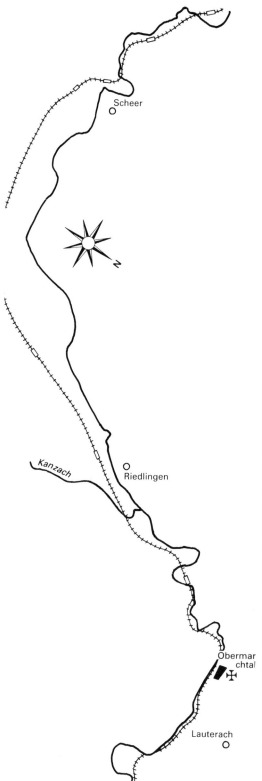

where one searches in vain for a body or a face that is not malformed. The only incongruous figures in the landscape are Christ, a few winged angels and cherubim and seraphim hovering heavily about the edges. All this is depicted in vibrant colours, as if painted in enamels, emerald green, corn yellow, deep crimson, magenta, peacock blue, sky blue, none of it dulled by time. The paintings have a powerfulness and directness about them and the more one looks at them, the more the awfulness of medieval life emerges. This is no Golden Age. In the figures there is disease and mendacity, poverty and cruelty, lack of compassion and echoes of how hard everyday life was. The figures are pocked by disease, the plague, malnutrition, congenital debilitation. There is an awful realism not found in Italian painting of the same period.

Obermarchtal

Former monastery of the Premonstratensians overlooking a gorge on the Danube. The name of the sect comes from a vision of St Augustine where a monastery site was given to him, hence *prater monstratum*, 'the meadow pointed out'.

Danube backwater in old Ulm.

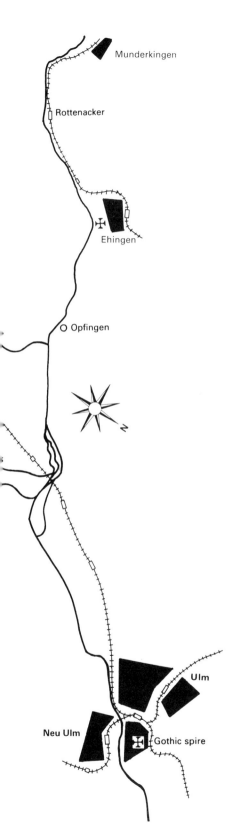

Munderkingen

Rottenacker

Ehingen

O Opfingen

N

Ulm

Neu Ulm

Gothic spire

Ulm

A large town straddling the Danube at the bottom of the Swabian Jura. Ulm was a Franconian Imperial Court in the Middle Ages occupied by alternate factions. In the 13th century it developed rapidly and was an important town on the Danube trade route between the Orient and northern Europe. Heavily damaged in the Second World War, it has mostly been rebuilt. The pride of Ulm is the Gothic cathedral started in 1377 but not completed until 1890. The spire at 161m, 528ft, is the tallest in the world. Around the Danube is the old quarter, the Fisherman's quarter with fine old buildings including a Gothic and Renaissance *Rathaus* with an astronomic clock, a fountain of 1482 and a museum with paintings by Ulm masters and 20th century works including Picasso, Klee and Kandinsky. There are pleasant walks around the old quarter and along the Danube.

Albert Einstein was born here in 1879 and no doubt it was an Ulm schoolteacher who told him he would not amount to much. Ulm's other famous son is the Tailor of Ulm who constructed a pair of silk wings so he could fly across the Danube. He failed, but every year a competition has been held for budding fliers. A few years back the deed the tailor attempted was accomplished by an eccentric German inventor.

Ulm Boxes Ulm was at one time an embarkation point for German settlers migrating to southeastern Europe. From the 18th century craft drifted downstream to Hungary, Yugoslavia, Bulgaria and Romania carrying settlers from Swabia, the Palatinate and Alsace who colonised bits and pieces of eastern Europe. Many of them are still there amongst the ethnic populations and it is still possible to recognise a distinctly German aspect to the architecture. This exodus of Germans down river made German the *lingua franca* of the river and it remains so today.

Near the old town there is a replica of the sort of craft which made the trip and which acquired the generic name of Ulm boxes. The name is accurate, as it would be difficult to call these craft boats or little ships. They were wooden flat-bottomed barges with a steering oar at each end. The barge would be loaded up with cargo and passengers arranged themselves as best they could in a wooden hut built on deck. The barges simply drifted downstream controlled by the steering oars as best they could. A large rowing boat was carried to take ropes ashore to control the descent over difficult stretches of the river and rough anchors would be thrown off the stern to slow the craft down and line it up for narrow sections and bridges. One adventurous English traveller who descended the river to Vienna on such a craft was the redoubtable Dr Charles Burney who I have mentioned earlier. In 1770 and 1772 he travelled throughout Europe and in his book *Continental Travels* he described life on one of these craft. 'I had now filled up the chinks of my cabin with splinters, and with hay; got a new button to the door, reconciled myself to my filthy blanket, and made a pair of snuffers out of a chip of deal; but alas! the essential failed: this was all external, and I wanted internal comfort! the last bit of my cold meat was fly-blown, to such a degree, that ravenous as I was, I threw it into the Danube; bread too, that staff was broken! and nothing but *Pumpernickel* was to be had here; which is so sour, as to disgust two senses at a time.' When an Ulm box reached its destination it was either hauled back upstream if the cargo warranted the high cost of this, or more commonly it was broken up for timber. Vienna was short of timber while the land around the German stretch of the Danube was heavily forested. Dr Charles Burney noted that the banks were thickly timbered and on enquiring what lay beyond was told 'huge forests'. Many of the craft going downstream were not even the roughly shaped Ulm boxes but rafts of timber with a rough shelter on top. These were designed solely to get timber downstream; any cargo or passengers were additional profit.

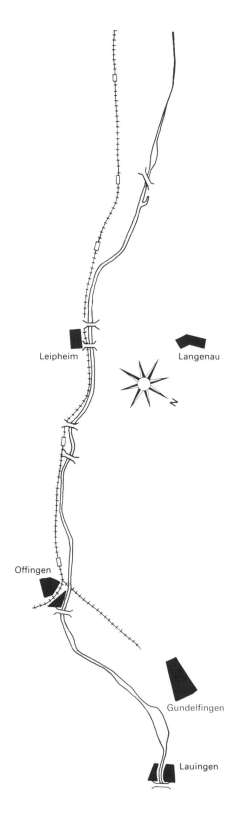

Leipheim

Langenau

Offingen

Gundelfingen

Lauingen

Wiblingen

Former Benedictine abbey near the confluence of the Danube and the Iller. Its pride is the Rococo library.

Blindheim

Known to us as Blenheim where the Duke of Marlborough defeated the superior forces of Louis XIV in 1704. Large numbers of Louis' army are said to have drowned in the Danube.

Donauwörth

A town on a steep hillside by the Danube. The Heiligkreuzkirch, (Holy Cross church), a Baroque building, dominates the town.

Neuburg

Old ducal town on the right bank. Numerous historical buildings with the central square, the *Karlsplatz*, said to be the most beautiful in Germany.

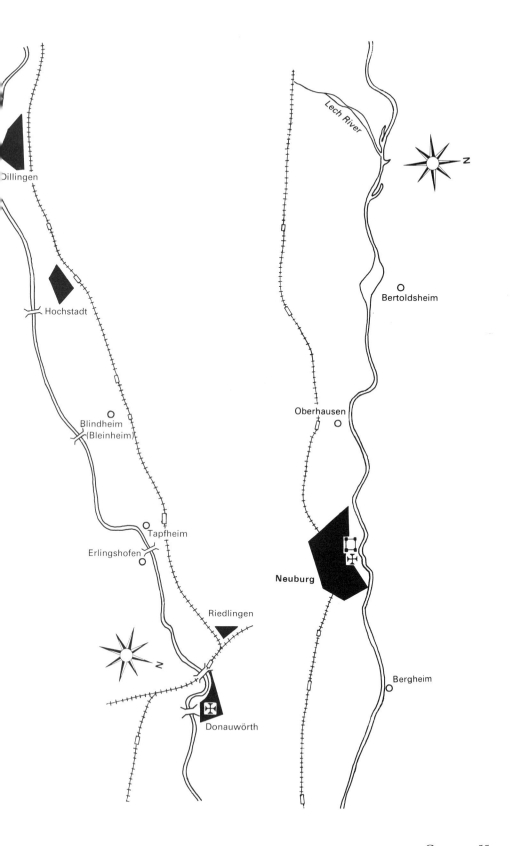

Dillingen

Hochstadt

Blindheim
(Bleinheim)

Tapfheim

Erlingshofen

Riedlingen

N

Donauwörth

Lech River

N

Bertoldsheim

Oberhausen

Neuburg

Bergheim

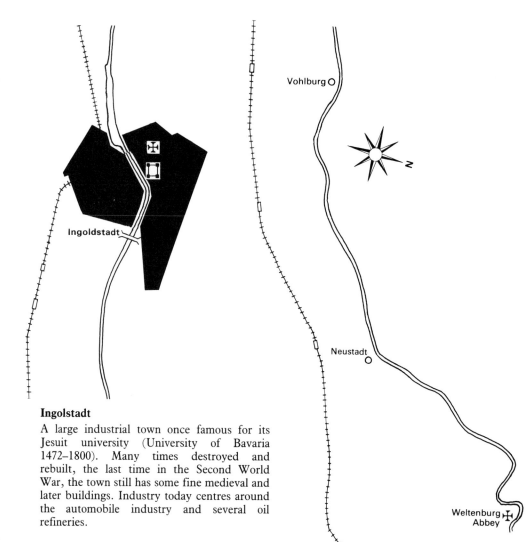

Ingolstadt

A large industrial town once famous for its Jesuit university (University of Bavaria 1472–1800). Many times destroyed and rebuilt, the last time in the Second World War, the town still has some fine medieval and later buildings. Industry today centres around the automobile industry and several oil refineries.

Km 2411
Kelheim

A small town on the confluence of the Danube and the Altmuhl. A former seat of the Duke of Bavaria. Above the town is the massive *Befreiungshalle*, the Liberation monument, a large dome supported by buttresses, built by Ludwig I to commemorate the liberation of Germany from Napoleonic rule.

From Kelheim boat trips sometimes run upstream through a rocky gorge to Weltenburg abbey. Kelheim is at the southern end of the Altmuhl which, when canalised, will be where the Rhine-Main-Danube canal joins up with the canalised Danube.

Bad Abbach

Barrage and lock. The town is a renowned spa with sulphurous water that has been in use for some 500 years.

Km 2379
Regensburg

Originally a Roman garrison town, Ratisbon, it became a bishopric in the 5th century and capital of Bavaria in the 6th. It continued as ducal capital and became an Imperial free city in 1245. From 1663 it was the seat of a perpetual diet of the Holy Roman Empire, but declined in importance and power shortly afterwards. Napoleon was wounded under its walls and strangely it has not been touched by war since this time. Its stagnation in the 18th and 19th centuries and the absence of damage in the Second World War have preserved intact the medieval centre of the city.

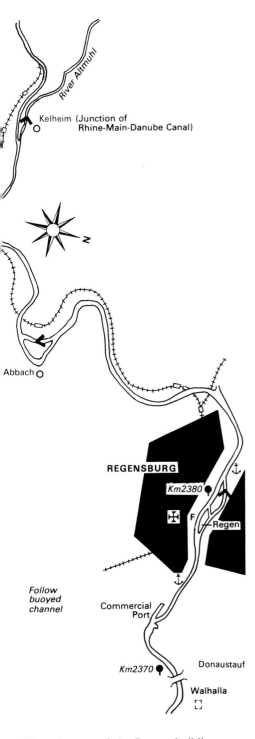

Kelheim (Junction of
Rhine-Main-Danube Canal)

River Altmuhl

N

Abbach

REGENSBURG

Km2380

Regen

Follow
buoyed
channel

Commercial
Port

Km2370

Donaustauf

Walhalla

Though parts of the Roman buildings survive, it is the medieval buildings lining the narrow streets, 13th and 14th century tower houses reminiscent of northern Italy, which dominate. There is also a medieval salt

warehouse, the medieval bridge still in everyday use, and the *Wurstküche*, the oldest sausage house in Germany. The family of Thurn und Taxis, which until 1867 held the German postal monopoly, at one time owned most of Regensburg. The museum at Regensburg contains paintings by Albrecht, Altdorfer and others of the Danube school. On the left bank is the museum ship *Ruthoff*, an old paddle-wheel tug that has been lovingly restored, with exhibits on early navigation on the Danube. Downstream of the town is the commercial port, the largest in Bavaria.

Day-trips around the river and a ferry to Passau on Sundays, conditions permitting.

The Ruthoff museum ship The *Ruthoff* is a paddle-wheel tug that has been restored with exhibits and models down below depicting early navigation on the river. The tug represents Regensburg's own early links with the river. It was built in 1922/23 in the Regensburg-Ruthoff shipyard as a state-of-the-art paddle-wheel steamer incorporating the latest developments in steam technology. It may seem an anachronism to use paddle-wheel propulsion as late as 1923 when propellers had long ago eclipsed the paddle-wheel, but a paddle-wheel has significant advantages over the propeller for river navigation. A propeller needs to have an undisturbed flow of water around it to be hydrodynamically efficient, a condition that is not fulfilled when there is insufficient depth. When the depths in the Danube are low propeller driven craft become inefficient whereas paddle-wheels remain efficient whatever the depth. As long as there is enough water to float the ship, paddle-wheels will drive it. In the early 20th century there were still numerous sections of the river where it was fast-running and shallow, with whirlpools and overfalls that often wrecked craft. In these sections the paddle-wheel coped better than the propeller. In fact paddle-wheel powered craft were built right up until the beginning of the Second World War. Not until the development of steerable propellers enclosed in a cylinder so that a jet of water was squirted out, a system that can cope with disturbed and shallow water, did the paddle-wheel lose its advantage.

The *Ruthoff* worked the middle Danube until one June day in 1944 when she hit a mine near Ersekcsanad in Hungary and sank. It was not until twelve years later that the tug was salvaged and rebuilt by the Hungarian state shipping company MAHART and renamed the *Ersekcsanad*. She served in the Hungarian shipping line until the mid-1970s when she was pensioned off and in 1979 was purchased to be restored as a museum ship in Regensburg.

Down below there are interesting exhibits showing navigation on the river in past centuries and into the 20th century. Before the age of steam horses pulled barges upstream and several men quanted from the stern of the barge. A large rowing boat was required to take a tow to the opposite bank when it was impossible to continue the tow on the same bank. Going downstream for the barge was a matter of drifting with the current and steering with long sweeps from the bow and stern. Anchors were kept ready so emergency stops could be made. Only some commodities justified the expense of teams of horses towing a barge upstream and one of these commodities was salt. From upper Austria salt was brought down to the Danube below Linz and then ferried upriver. In 1772 Doctor Charles Burney made the following observation on the trade: 'We met this morning a gang of boats, laden with salt, from Salzburg and Passau, dragged up the river by more than forty horses, a man on each, which expense is so great, as to enhance the price of that commodity above four hundred per cent.'

Bavaria The Bavarian villages and towns and the Bavarians themselves tend to turn their backs on the river. The Danube is seldom mentioned and seldom with words of affection. It is regarded as a nuisance, something you have to cross to get to the land on the other side, something that floods the land near the banks, too swift and dangerous to swim in and only mildly interesting to look at. Most of the houses in the towns and villages face away from the river. The villages belong to the mountains and it these the Bavarians talk about affectionately and at length. For the Germans the Danube is not really important. The Rhine is the German river, the *Schicksalsfluss*, the 'river of destiny', the setting for the long epic poem the *Nibelungenlied* that traces the mythopoeic roots of the German race through the adventures of Siegfried. Most Germans know of the *Nibelungenlied* and the named places on the Rhine where the action happened. Few know of the sequel on the Danube where most of the line Siegfried established was wiped out.

Km 2378 – Left bank
Entrance to the by-pass canal and lock at the mouth of the river Regen.

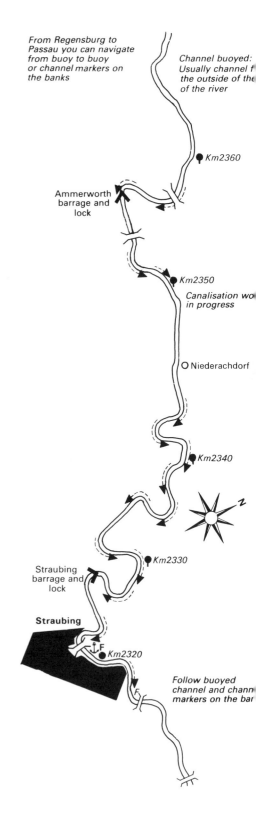

From Regensburg to Passau you can navigate from buoy to buoy or channel markers on the banks

Channel buoyed: Usually channel f the outside of the of the river

● Km2360

Ammerworth barrage and lock

● Km2350

Canalisation wo in progress

O Niederachdorf

● Km2340

● Km2330

Straubing barrage and lock

Straubing

● Km2320

Follow buoyed channel and chann markers on the bar

Twin spires of the Gothic church at Regensburg – the most perfectly preserved medieval town.

Km 2369 – Left bank
Walhalla

An incongruous Doric style temple constructed by Ludwig I in 1842 on the steep slopes above the Danube. It contains busts of 118 illustrious Germans whom Ludwig considered the founding fathers of Germany, and a large statue of Ludwig himself. Nearby are the ruins of Donaustaff castle.

Km 2354
Ammerworth barrage and lock.

Km 2325
Straubing barrage and lock.

Km 2320·5 – Right bank
Straubing

Small agricultural town in an area called the Gauboden, the granary of Bavaria. The medieval centre with gabled houses, turrets and towers, around a cobbled square still used as a market square, is an enchanting low-key place. On the outskirts of the town is St Peter's church with the chapel to Agnes Bernauer and to the macabre Dance of Death.

Agnes Bernauer Agnes was a beautiful young girl from Ausberg who Albert, son of the Duke of Bavaria, fell in love with. Alas, Agnes was a commoner and the Duke would not give permission for Albert to marry her. Undaunted the two lovers eloped and married secretly. When the Duke learnt of the secret union he was enraged and connived to send his son away on court business. In his son's absence he had Agnes tried for witchcraft and thrown into the Danube. In the fashion of the times, if she didn't drown she was obviously a witch with evil powers which enabled her to survive and would have been burnt at the stake; if she drowned she was innocent. Poor Agnes drowned not far from Straubing and the chapel in St Peter's church nearby is dedicated to her.

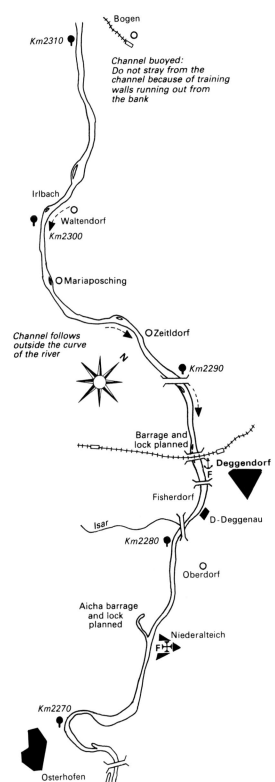

Km 2285 – Left bank
Deggendorf
Important port and railhead to the Danube
called the gateway to the Bavarian forest.
Numerous medieval buildings including the
Rathaus. It is said that the inhabitants around
here lived so sinfully that Satan was aroused
by the competition and decided to extinguish
the villagers. He brought a large rock with him
to drop on the village, but on hearing the
sweet music of the church bells, dropped it before he got there. The large rocky outcrop on
the right bank is called the 'Devil's Rock'.

Km 2276 – Left bank
Niederalteich
Niederalteich abbey overlooks the Danube. A
famous sacristy with many art treasures. A
small village below the abbey.

Km 2257 – Left bank
Hofkirchen
Small village on the edge of the Bavarian forest
dominated by its church.

Km 2248·5 – Right bank
Vilshofen
An old town first mentioned in 785, at the
mouth of the Vils and Wolfach rivers.

Km 2246 – Left bank
Windorf Markt
Small village on the slopes of the Bavarian
forest.

Km 2231
Kachlet barrage and lock. Built in the 1920s,
this lock was the first to International Waterways Standards and was the first step towards
the canalisation of the Danube in preparation
for the construction of the Rhine-Main-
Danube canal.

Km 2226 – Right bank
Passau
A border town between Germany and Austria,
known as the Venice of Bavaria from its situation on the confluence of three rivers: the
Danube, Inn and Ilz. Originally a Celtic settlement, Bojodorum, and later a Roman camp,
Castra Batava. It was established as a bishopric
in 739 by St Boniface, the 'Apostle of
Germany'. It quickly grew in size and power,
largely from its important position for trade on
the Danube, to become an Imperial free city in
the 13th century. The Bishops of Passau
managed to claim most of the Danube Valley
in Austria. In the 15th century the Oberhaus
on the left bank was built to defend the
wealthy town.

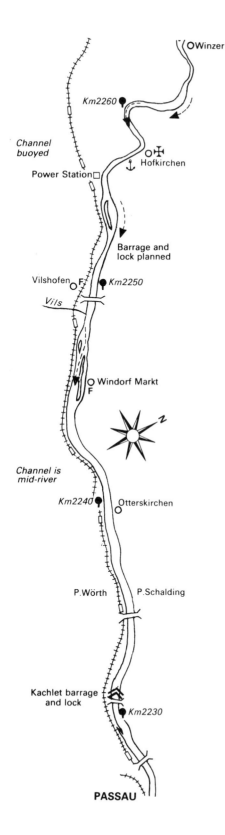

Fishermen on the upper Danube near Passau.

Much of Passau's wealth was derived from tolls on traffic on the river and storage of grain and salt brought upriver. The Italianate houses, churches and other buildings hemmed in by water on either side make it one of the most attractive towns in Bavaria. In the summer there is a music festival, 'The European Weeks', from June through to August.

Ferry to Regensburg on Saturday. Ferries twice a week as far as Straubing. Ferry to Linz and Vienna and numerous cruise ships leave from Passau.

The Inn

From the Oberhaus on the north side of the Danube you can look down on the roofs of Passau and the two rivers that join the Danube here: the Ilz and the Inn. The Ilz is a small river, but the Inn adds a substantial amount of water to the Danube. The force of the water brought down by the Inn is such that its brown waters can be seen pushing into the

DER BRAND VON PASSAU
AM 27. APRIL 1662

Von Passaus Dom fiel ich herunter
wobei mein schöner Leib zerbrach 1662
Bin trotzdem treu, wohlauf u. munter
und nur im Kopf noch etwas schwach

Passau was created anew after the disastrous fire of 1662 destroyed most of the town – here commemorated at the Rathaus.

Danube for several hundred metres before merging. Why is the Danube called the Danube below Passau when it looks as if the Inn is the bigger river? A check on the figures confirms the appearance: the Inn does carry a greater volume of water than the Danube.

In 1954 an abnormally mild spring thawed the Alpine snows at a faster than usual rate. The extra water brought down by the Inn raised the height of the water to such an extent that it cut across to the west of Passau to join up with the Danube, turning the town into an island with the ground floors of all the buildings submerged. The only way to get around was by boat. In the town square the heights of the various floods have been marked on the *Rathaus* wall. Only two other floods exceeded the 1954 level, those in 1501 and 1595. These are recorded as being approximately 10m, 33ft, above the normal level of the river.

Passau, a bit of baroque Italy transplanted to Bavaria.

III. Austria

PASSAU TO HAINSBURG

Km 2223 – Right bank
Border between Germany (State of Bavaria) and Austria

The valley the Danube has cut through the granite and gneiss of Upper Austria winds and loops back on itself under steep valley sides. After Passau the river runs along the frontier between Germany and Austria. The 'sausage equator' the Bavarians call it. Under Roman rule this stretch of the Danube was the northernmost limit of Roman territory. A Roman road to supply the frontier garrisons ran along the southern bank. At times the Romans gained a foothold on the northern side, but mostly they were content to keep the river between themselves and the fierce German tribes on the opposite side. Compared to the Germans, the Gauls and Celts were looked upon as tame stuff. While Rome conquered the Gauls and the Celts, in the end it decided to leave the German tribes to the east of the Rhine and north of the Danube alone. In the later years of the Empire, a few of the less fierce German tribes along the Danube such as the Hermunduri became Romanised and fought as mercenaries in the Roman army. The mad and sadistic Caligula even went as far as having a German bodyguard, though it has been suggested that this was purely in the hope that as they spoke no Latin, then they could not plot with his many enemies to end his demented reign. The garrison towns and forts of the Romans were replaced in turn by the castles and forts of subsequent conquerors.

Charlemagne strengthened the defences along the Danube after defeating the Avars in Hungary. Austria received its name from the Eastern March, the defensive line Charlemagne set up to protect his Empire. The Eastern March, *Ostmark*, becomes *Osterreich* in German, and bastardised into English we get Austria. (Though some scholars suggest that the name Austria is derived from *Hister*, the Greek and Byzantine name of the Danube, thus *Histerichi*, the people of the river *Hister*, which became *Osterichi*.)

Km 2215 – Right bank
Krempelstein Castle

Variously held by the Bishops of Passau and robber barons. Called the *Tailor's Castle* after a local story that relates how the poor tailor's goat died and when he flung the corpse into the river its horns caught in his clothing and dragged him in as well.

Krempelstein Castle, the 'Tailor's Castle' at km 2215.

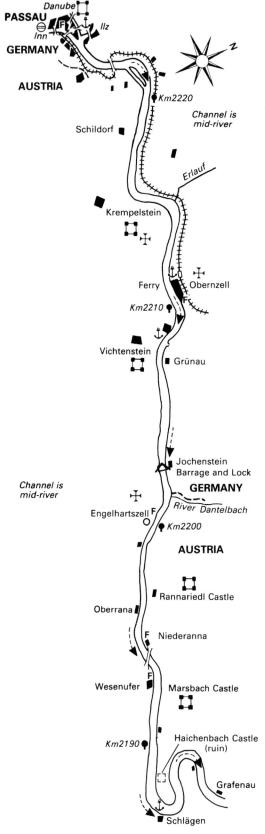

Km 2211
Obernzell
Small village, a centre of potting in the Middle Ages.

Km 2207 – Right bank
Vichtenstein Castle
Counts of Vichtenstein and Counts of Wasserburg, later the Bishops of Passau. A castle has existed here since the 11th century though the present castle was built in the 15th century.

Km 2203
Jochenstein
Barrage and lock. The barrage is built across from a rocky island where a *Lorelei*-like naiad, Isa, is said to reside. It is now topped by a Christian shrine to counter Isa's power.

Km 2201·7 – Left bank
Dantelbach River
Border between Germany and Austria.

Km 2200·5 – Right bank
Engelhartszell
Customs station. Originally a Roman garrison town. Later controlled by the Bishops of Passau, it grew prosperous on the trade along the Danube with various fairs from the 16th century for merchants to sell their wares. A toll station was established here in 1775. A Cistercian abbey was established in the 13th century and prospered until it was dissolved under Joseph II. It was re-established in 1925.

Km 2196·8 – Left bank
Rannariedl Castle
Mentioned in the 13th century, it passed to the Bishops of Passau in the 14th century. For some time it was in dispute between Bavaria and Austria and passed back and forth between various houses. In the 17th century it was a Bavarian stronghold but it finally passed to Austria in 1803.

Km 2193 – Right bank
Wesenufer
Small village. The castle is known as the *Grosser Keller* from its former use as a hostelry. In 1626 a detachment of 1000 men sent to quell a peasant rebellion were slaughtered as they slept, drunk on the good beer of the premises, by the peasants.

Km 2192 – Left bank
Marsbach Castle
Controlled by the Bishops of Passau, though like many of the other castles in this area there

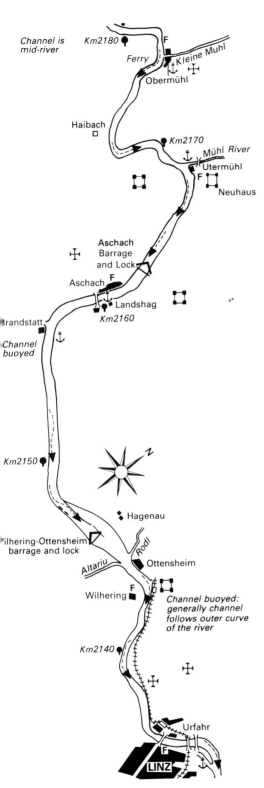

Channel is mid-river

Km2180

Ferry

Kleine Mühl

F

Obermühl

Haibach

Km2170

Mühl *River*

Utermühl

F

Neuhaus

Aschach Barrage and Lock

Aschach

F

Landshag

Km2160

Brandstatt

Channel buoyed

Km2150

Hagenau

Wilhering-Ottensheim barrage and lock

Rodl

Altariu

Ottensheim

Wilhering

F

Channel buoyed: generally channel follows outer curve of the river

Km2140

Urfahr

F

LINZ

was constant feuding going on with the bishopric. In 1486 Othmar Oberheimer, one of the last robber barons on the upper Danube, occupied the castle and terrorised the surrounding area. In 1520 the castle was taken by the Duke of Bavaria and Othmar was beheaded. Today it is a hotel.

Km 2188·5 – Left bank
Haichenbach Castle

Counts of Schaunberg, Counts of Nürnberg, Othmar Oberheimer, destroyed by Maximilian at the end of the 15th century. The Danube loops around the slopes the castle is built on. Various legends are attached to the castle, amongst them one which names it Cherry Tree Castle, *Kirschbäumer*. The story goes that the rightful occupant of the castle was captured and condemned to death. Before he died he spat some cherry stones over the wall from his cell and a cherry tree grew up. His young son who had been spirited away later returned to retake the castle. At night he climbed the cherry tree and entered the castle, opening the gates to let his men in, thus avenging his father.

Km 2178 – Left bank
Obermühl

Small hamlet. The Danube is hemmed in by steep slopes, heavily wooded mostly in pine, along this stretch of the river.

Km 2167·5 – Left bank
Neuhaus

Neuhaus Castle and small village.

Km 2163

Aschach barrage and double lock.

Km 2160 – Right bank
Aschach

A toll station from as early as the 10th century. Important market town with a charter from the 14th century. The toll station was transferred to Engelhartszell at the end of the 18th century. Many fine old houses are preserved. On the slopes above is Schaunberg Castle owned by the Counts of Schaunberg until the 16th century when it passed to the Counts of Starhemberg. The Starhembergs remain large landowners today.

Km 2147

Wilhering–Ottensheim barrage and lock.

Km 2144 – Left bank
Ottensheim

Toll station in the 12th and 13th century. Castle and village.

Km 2135
Linz

At Linz the Danube opens out after the bottleneck section upstream. It has been settled since the Bronze Age and later the Romans established an important garrison town, Lentia, here. It quickly prospered from the salt trade and shipping on the Danube. In the Middle Ages it was the largest market town on this section of the Danube, a meeting place for merchants from northern Europe and Mediterranean traders. Linz toll station was one of the most profitable in Austria through the Middle Ages and the city acquired much wealth until traffic on the Danube declined with the Ottoman advances on the lower Danube in the 16th century. Linz declined until the 19th century when the railways brought new prosperity to the city. River traffic also increased again on the Danube and Linz became an important industrial centre. During the Nazi annexation of Austria large steel and chemical industries were established to the south of the old city and these provided the basis for Linz's present prosperity.

The late medieval buildings, many with Baroque additions, around the Hauptplatz that encloses the old market square, are well worth a wander around. Three bridges cross the Danube from Linz to its suburb of Urfahr on the other side. Excursions can be made to the Abbey of St Florian where there is a good collection of the Danube School of painters.

Regular ferries upstream to Passau and downstream to Vienna.

Km 2131·5 – Right bank
Winter Harbour

From here down to km 2127 there is a string of industrial harbours serving the various industries on the banks. This was to be Hitler's industrial base in Austria refining ore for the Axis war effort. The smoking chimneys and piles of coal and ore can hardly be missed.

Km 2125 – Right bank
Traun River

Until the coming of the railways the Traun was used to transport salt from Upper Austria. On steep sections plank-lined water slides were used where the barges literally shot down the steep chutes when the retaining gates were opened.

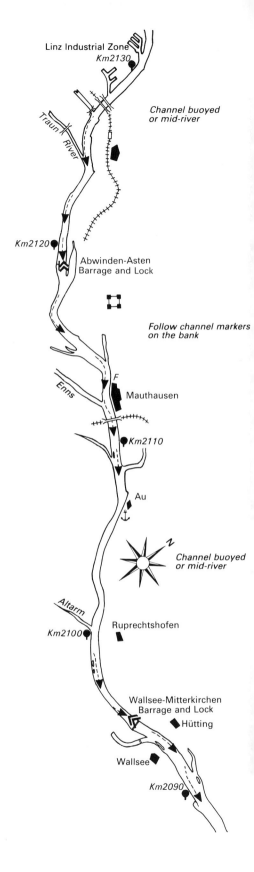

Grein: before the Danube was canalised all ships stopped here to take on a pilot. *Austrian National Tourist Office*.

Downstream Linz: hills of ore and coal and tall chimneys belching poisonous gases – the Danube in Austria is not all sleepy villages and vineyards.

The DDSG paddle-wheel ferry *Stadt Passau* at Obermühl.

Km 2119
Abwinden-Asten
Barrage and lock.

Km 2112 – Left bank
Mauthausen
Maut means a toll and it appears a toll station existed here from early on. The village was razed by the Emperor Frederic Barbarossa in 1189 when the villagers demanded tolls for his crusaders en route to the Holy Land. The Nazis erected a concentration camp in a quarry nearby where some 335,000 prisoners were kept. The name Mauthausen acquired a sinister reputation for brutality and death, the prisoners forced to work in the quarries until they dropped, and the site has been preserved as a monument to those who died here.

Km 2112 – Right bank
Enns River
Formerly used for shipping timber to the Danube. From 1945 to 1956 it was the frontier between the American and Russian zones during the partition of Austria.

Km 2095
Wallsee–Mitter Kirchen barrage and lock.

Km 2093·5 – Right bank
Wallsee
Settled by the Romans and later the site of a castle. It passed to a branch of the Habsburgs in the 19th century. It was here that the American General Patton and the Russian Marshal Tolbuchin celebrated their victory over the Nazis.

Km 2084 – Left bank
Dornach Castle
August Strindberg, the Swedish playwright and author lived here for a while. This is the start of the gorge known as the Strudengau.

Km 2081 – Left bank
Grein
Grein has been a river port from early times. Boats would stop here for the crews to say mass and take on a river pilot for the tricky section with whirlpools and overfalls down river. The old town has numerous medieval and later buildings, many of them decorated with reliefs or murals depicting river life.
The Strudengau Rapids Before the construction of the dams and locks that hold back the river and tame the current, all ships stopped at Grein to take on a pilot. The rapids and whirlpools below Grein claimed ships and lives

and acquired names and myths. Grein stands at the entrance to the valley and if the river was considered too dangerous to run a boat down, goods were taken overland to be reloaded at Vienna. The most dangerous of the rapids and rocks had stories of menace and doom attached to them. The *Schwalleck*, 'whirlpool corner', was a rock cliff projecting at right angles into the water. The acute deflection of the current caused a whirlpool at the tip of the rock which would throw a boat out of control and into the cliff-face. It was slowly blasted away, bit by bit, from the 18th to the 19th century, to make navigation safer. Two kilometres on from *Schwalleck* is the *Strudel* which means a whirlpool or vortex, not the sugar coated pastry normally associated with the word. At Haussten more rapids and whirlpools existed. In an old tower above the rapids lived the 'black monk' and whoever sighted him knew that death was not far away. A couple of emperors and a bishop met their death soon after sighting him, so the tale goes.

Much of the work to remove these dangers was undertaken during the reign of Maria Theresa and continued under Joseph II. Maria Theresa is often considered to be the founder of modern Austria. She created a central bureaucracy with Vienna as its centre rather than the scattered alliances to the Habsburgs that had previously made up the Empire. Vienna became the power centre rather than just the home of the Habsburg Empire. No doubt the work to improve navigation on the river was essential for communications with Vienna. She authorised the Baroque architect Bernard Fischer von Erlach to draw up plans and provided funds to carry out the work. Her son Joseph II continued the work using tons of explosive to blast away the cliffs to straighten the river and remove underwater rocks. This section of the river was finally tamed with the construction of the Ybbs-Persenbeug barrage, completed in 1959, which holds the water back and slows its passage over the rocky bottom.

Km 2078·6
Schwalleck
The first of the three major rapids in the Strudengau.

Km 2076·8
Struden
The second whirlpool called the *Strudel*.

Km 2076·5
Isle of Woerth
An islet just over a kilometre in length that divides the Danube into two arms.

Km 2076 – Left bank
Werfenstein Castle
Mentioned in the *Nibelungenlied*.

Km 2075 – Right bank
Hausstein
The third of the rapids after Grein.

Km 2072·8 – Left bank
Sarmingsten
Old shipping town.

Km 2069·8 – Right bank
Freyenstein Castle

Km 2061
Persenbeug
Barrage and lock. Persenbeug Castle immediately down river of the barrage was originally built in the 10th century and passed through various families including the Habsburgs. In 1800 Francis I acquired it again for the Habsburgs and it remains Habsburg property to this day. Karl I, the last of the Habsburgs to rule, was born here in 1887. It was an important shipping town and a number of wealthy ship owners lived here until the age of steam made horses and horse-drawn barges redundant.

Km 2059 – Right bank
Ybbs
A small Roman settlement and later an important trading town in salt and iron. It prospered under the Habsburgs and became an important market town. It was by-passed by the railways in the 19th century and subsequently declined. From Ybbs to Melk the river is the setting for various episodes from the second part of the *Nibelungenlied*.

Km 2049·5 – Left bank
Marbach
A ferry has crossed the Danube here since the 14th century. There has been a market town here since the Middle Ages dealing largely in wine. The church of Maria Tafel on the slopes behind has long been venerated for a miracle working Virgin, the object of pilgrimages since the 15th century.

Km 2044·5 – Right bank
Pöchlarn
Settled since Neolithic times. The Romans built a fort here and called the place Arelape. The Roman Danube flotilla was moved to the mouth of the Erlauf River just upstream (km 2046) from Tulln (Comagenis) after the Pro-

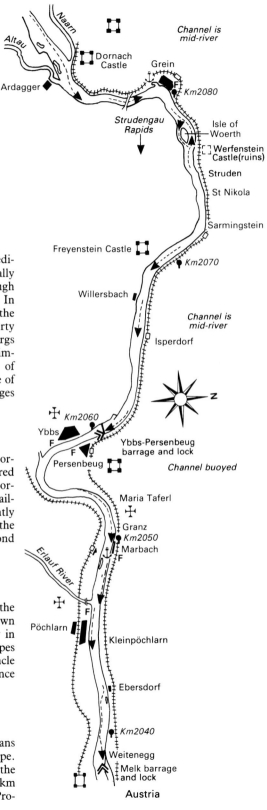

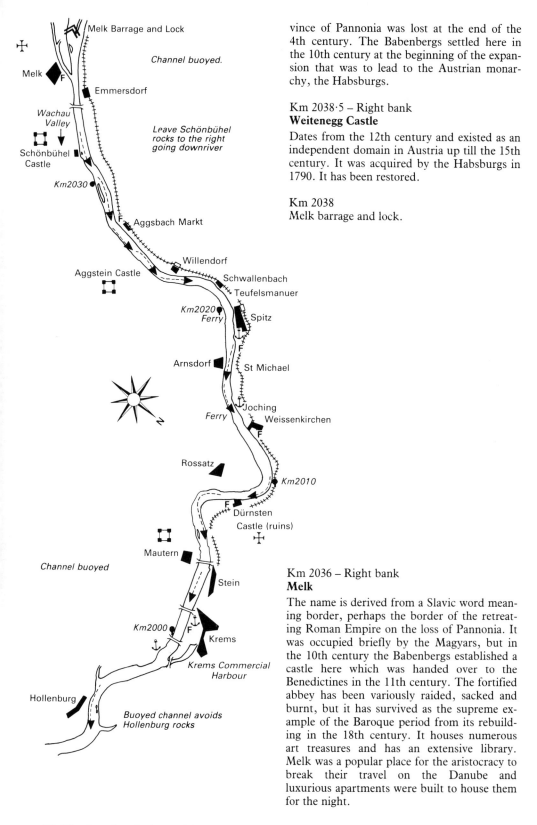

vince of Pannonia was lost at the end of the 4th century. The Babenbergs settled here in the 10th century at the beginning of the expansion that was to lead to the Austrian monarchy, the Habsburgs.

Km 2038·5 – Right bank
Weitenegg Castle

Dates from the 12th century and existed as an independent domain in Austria up till the 15th century. It was acquired by the Habsburgs in 1790. It has been restored.

Km 2038
Melk barrage and lock.

Km 2036 – Right bank
Melk

The name is derived from a Slavic word meaning border, perhaps the border of the retreating Roman Empire on the loss of Pannonia. It was occupied briefly by the Magyars, but in the 10th century the Babenbergs established a castle here which was handed over to the Benedictines in the 11th century. The fortified abbey has been variously raided, sacked and burnt, but it has survived as the supreme example of the Baroque period from its rebuilding in the 18th century. It houses numerous art treasures and has an extensive library. Melk was a popular place for the aristocracy to break their travel on the Danube and luxurious apartments were built to house them for the night.

Map labels:
Melk Barrage and Lock
Channel buoyed.
Melk F
Emmersdorf
Wachau Valley
Leave Schönbühel rocks to the right going downriver
Schönbühel Castle
Km2030
F Aggsbach Markt
Willendorf
Aggstein Castle
Schwallenbach
Teufelsmanuer
Km2020 Ferry Spitz
F
Arnsdorf St Michael
Joching
Ferry Weissenkirchen
F
Rossatz
Km2010
F Dürnsten
Castle (ruins)
Mautern
Channel buoyed
Stein
Km2000 F
Krems
Krems Commercial Harbour
Hollenburg
Buoyed channel avoids Hollenburg rocks

Melk. *Austrian National Tourist Office.*

The Wachau At Melk the Wachau Valley begins, commonly described as the most picturesque section of the Danube in Austria. The valley closes in on either side and were it not for the barrages holding the river back, it would as it once did, hurtle down the gorge in a collision of water on rock before spewing out over the flat land around Vienna. The Strudengau is more spectacular, but the Wachau is more picturesque with its gentler slopes dotted with small villages and castles.

While the Rhine has its *Lorelei*, the Rhine maidens, the Danube has Noeck, the Prince of the Danube and his daughters, the *Donauweibchen*. Noeck is an ill-made hybrid of an old man and a giant fish. He lives in a palace on the bottom of the Danube and entices travellers with promises of jewels and gold, then drowns them in the swift flowing current. The *Donauweibchen*, as if to make up for his ugliness and unnatural ways, are comely maidens who like to fraternise with mortals when they can.

Spitz from Hinterhaus castle. *Austrian National Tourist Office*.

Krems. The old part of the town has fine medieval buildings. *Austrian National Tourist Office*.

Km 2032 – Right bank
Schönbühel Castle

Dates from the 9th century though the present structure dates from the early 19th century. It stands on a smooth rock mound, a spectacular site by the Danube.

Km 2026 – Right bank
Aggstein Castle

A castle was built here in the 12th century and became a principal residence for the Lords of Kuenring in the 13th and 14th centuries. This powerful family founded numerous towns to the northwest. Their power brought them into conflict with the Babenbergs and Habsburgs who finally took the Kuenring lands in the 14th century. Aggstein was taken by the Habsburgs in 1430. One of the subsequent Lords of Aggstein, Jörg Scheck vom Wald, known as *Schreckenwald*, 'Terror of the Forest', acquired a notorious reputation for ill treatment of his subjects. Prisoners were said to be marooned on a rocky ledge and given the choice of starving or jumping to their death. The castle has been restored and can be visited.

Km 2024 – Left bank
Willendorf

Has been settled since Neolithic times. It is known amongst archaeologists for the *Willendorf Venus*, a small stone statue dating from 25,000 years ago, that can be seen in the Natural History Museum in Vienna.

Km 2020 – Left bank
Teufelsmauer

The devil's wall, a high cliff-like projection that has attracted various legends. Its said that the devil tried to put a dam across the Danube but abandoned construction prematurely when a cock crowed early.

Km 2019 – Left bank
Spitz

An old town with many fine medieval buildings preserved. Hinterhaus Castle standing behind was held by the Kuenrings for some time until the Habsburgs acquired it.

Km 2017 – Left bank
St Michael

A church existed here in the 10th century, the present fortified church dates from 1500.

Km 2013 – Left bank
Weissenkirchen

Known as the heart of the Wachau and famed for its vineyards. A fine fortified church was built in the 15th century with extensive fortifications to keep out the Turks.

Km 2009 – Left bank
Dürnstein

Old fortified town with the ruins of Dürnstein Castle on the craggy slopes above. Dürnstein is one of the most evocative places in the Wachau with the story of Richard the Lionheart adding romantic atmosphere, at least for English visitors. The castle was built around 1150 by the Lords of Kuenring. In 1193 Richard was imprisoned here by Leopold V. The castle was blown up at the end of the Thirty Years War in 1646.

If only one castle replete with myth was to be mentioned in any English account of the Wachau, it would be Dürnstein. It is the obvious choice for guidebooks and anyone else travelling on the Danube. When Frances Trollope, the adventurous mother of her more famous son Anthony Trollope, voyaged down the Wachau in the 1830s, she saw Dürnstein and vowed to return before leaving Austria. She travelled overland from Vienna to get back to Dürnstein and wrote 'I am now writing to you from a spot whence I truly believe, no English letter was ever written before...'; whether it is true or not doesn't matter. From the late 19th century on, the craggy ruins at Dürnstein became a pilgrimage the English had to make in Austria. If the Danube weather holds true the ruins of Dürnstein appear out of the misty rain as they would in any old film of *Dracula* or *Frankenstein*. It is smaller than I had imagined, but the setting is right and the ruins convey the proper imagery for the tale of Richard the Lionheart and his faithful minstrel Blondel.

If anyone came close to the medieval idea of romantic chivalry, of the good and true king who was a courageous leader of men, yet who loved the arts, who was just, humorous and wise, then it was Richard Coeur-de-Lion. Though much elaborated and adorned, the tales of Richard contain some truth. He was described by the chroniclers as a gifted man, endowed with a handsome physique, a mane of blond hair, a sharp wit, a leader of men who was always at the forefront of his knights, and an astute general. He loved poetry and music. He could drink as much as any of his men. He had a bad side as well that can be gleaned from between the lines of the chroniclers. A hasty temper that would often result in cruel and

Durnstein, one of the most evocative of the towns in the Wachau with the story of Richard the Lionheart and his faithful minstrel Blondel woven through its ruins. *Austrian National Tourist Office.*

barbarous behaviour. A sadistic streak that was probably seen as realism in those times. When he believed that Saladin was not keeping his word after a truce had been agreed, he marched two and a half thousand Moslem prisoners out and slaughtered them, by the sword or hanging, in front of Saladin's army.

It was on his crusade to the Holy Land in the late 12th century that Richard's men committed a sleight that was to lead to his capture and imprisonment at Dürnstein. After a long siege Richard, along with the French King Philip and Leopold V, the Duke of Austria, succeeded in capturing Acre. It had been largely Richard's battle and when Leopold hoisted his standard next to the English and French standards, some of Richard's knights promptly hauled it down and threw it into the moat, leaving it to be trampled in the mud. It

was an insult which Leopold never forgave. Philip and Leopold left the Holy Land soon after and Richard, fearful that the French king would try to take his lands while he was absent, followed after agreeing a treaty with Saladin.

Richard sailed from Acre in October 1192. On the voyage up the Adriatic his ship was wrecked at Aquilea, at the head of the Adriatic on Leopold's doorstep. To escape detection he travelled through Austria in disguise, but in Vienna he was recognised and taken prisoner. Leopold imprisoned him in a secret place which, as subsequent events revealed, was Dürnstein on the banks of the Danube. The popular tale is that Richard's faithful minstrel Blondel wandered far and wide in search of his master, singing his favourite songs. At length he came to Dürnstein and heard his master join in the refrain of his favourite song. So Richard was found, a ransom paid and Richard returned to England. Certainly agents would have been sent out to discover where Richard was when news of his capture reached

The Wachau near Dürnstein. *Austrian National Tourist Office.*

England, and the size and details of the ransom discussed. He remained in Dürnstein for nearly two years until he was moved to the Castle of Trifels in the Rhineland. Here a huge ransom was paid to secure his release. History doesn't record what happened to Blondel. Richard returned to England and secured his kingdom. He died in northern France five years later from an arrow wound which went gangrenous. Dürnstein was reduced to ruins after the Swedes blew it up in 1646 at the end of the Thirty Years War.

There is not a lot to see at Dürnstein. But the walk up to the ruins and the few remaining walls and towers convey an impression of brutality and harshness that go beyond their physical bulk. Partly it is the rocky crags the castle was built on. And it may be that the stories of Richard's imprisonment coloured my perception, and why not. The intrepid Frances Trollope wrote that she thought Dürnstein was chosen 'in the hope that the unequalled desolation of the scene might appal the lion's heart... even while his imprisoned body was suffered to live', and Dürnstein does have this effect. The castle has a solitary forbidding feel even amongst the babel of different languages heard around its walls.

Km 2003·5 – Right bank
Mautern

The site of an old Roman garrison camp called Favianis. In the Middle Ages it was a small market town.

Km 2003 – Left bank
Stein und Krems

Krems and Stein were originally separate towns until an 'und' joined them into one. This leads to various Austrian jokes along the lines of 'Stein Und Krems are three towns' – I imagine the locals are tired of it by now. The area has been inhabited since Neolithic times and the Romans constructed a fort at Stein. During the Middle Ages the towns prospered, Stein was a toll station on the river, and today both towns have numerous well preserved medieval buildings, some of the finest along the river. The area is one of the centres of wine production in the Wachau.

From Stein und Krems Gottweig abbey high above the right bank can be clearly seen. It was founded in the 11th century and totally rebuilt in the early 18th century after a fire. The resulting abbey is an outstanding example of Austrian Baroque.

Km 1998 – Left bank
Krems Commercial Harbour

Km 1994 – Right bank
Hollenburg

Castle and old market town.

Km 1980

Altenwörth barrage and lock.

Km 1976 – Right bank
Zwentendorf Nuclear Power Station

The power station is complete and could be operational, but after being built a referendum voted for its closure.

Km 1964 – Right bank
Tulln

An important Roman garrison town, then called Comagenis, where they based their Danube flotilla. It was occupied variously by the Avars and the Magyars before coming under the Dukes of Austria. In the *Nibelungenlied* it is here that Kriemhilde and King Etzel met.

Km 1950

Altenberg barrage and lock. This is the last barrage and lock before the Iron Gates on the border of Yugoslavia and Romania.

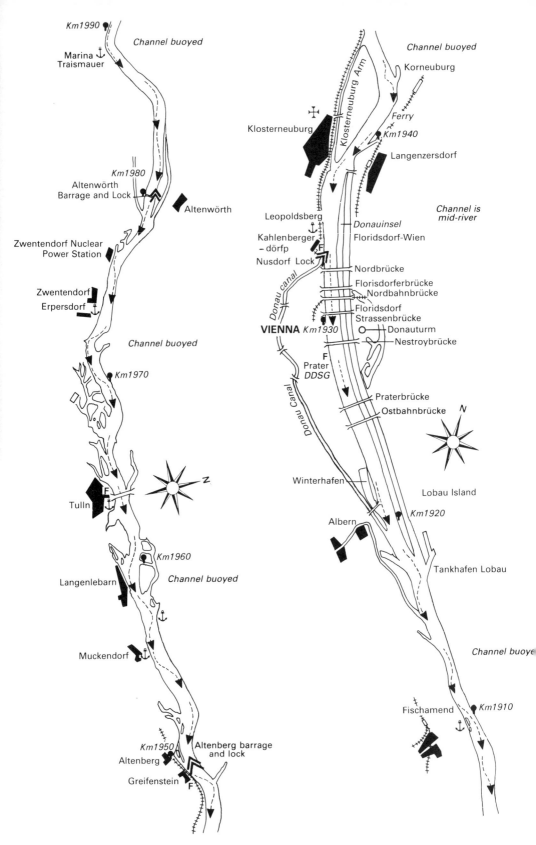

Km1990

Channel buoyed

Marina ⚓
Traismauer

Km1980

Altenwörth
Barrage and Lock

Altenwörth

Zwentendorf Nuclear
Power Station

Zwentendorf

Erpersdorf ⚓

Channel buoyed

Km1970

F
⚓
Tulln

Km1960

Langenlebarn

Channel buoyed

⚓

⚓

Muckendorf ⚓

Km1950

Altenberg

Greifenstein
F

Altenberg barrage
and lock

Klosterneuburg Arm

Channel buoyed

Korneuburg

Ferry

Klosterneuburg ✠

Km1940

Langenzersdorf

Leopoldsberg

Donauinsel

*Channel is
mid-river*

Kahlenberger
– dörfp
F

Floridsdorf-Wien

Nusdorf Lock

Donau canal

Nordbrücke

Florisdorferbrücke

Nordbahnbrücke

Floridsdorf

VIENNA Km1930

Strassenbrücke

Donauturm

Nestroybrücke

F
Prater
DDSG

Donau Canal

Praterbrücke

Ostbahnbrücke

N

Winterhafen

Lobau Island

Albern

Km1920

Tankhafen Lobau

Channel buoye

Fischamend

Km1910 ⚓

Km 1949 – Right bank
Greifenstein Castle

A castle on the steep slopes of the Weinerwald: the wood of Vienna.

Km 1943 – Left bank
Korneuburg

Korneuburg was probably originally built on an arm of the Danube, though the main arm has now moved away. A large shipyard builds vessels for the Danube.

Km 1939 – Right bank
Klosterneuburg

Originally a Celtic settlement and later a Roman garrison town. The large abbey was founded in the 12th century and became a centre of learning and research. It was redecorated and rebuilt in the 17th century in the Baroque style. The abbey's library is one of the largest in Austria. On the left bank Bisamberg Hill is the northernmost of the Alps.

Km 1936 – Right bank
Leopoldsberg and Kahlenberg

Now outer suburbs of Vienna. In 1683 the Imperial army descended these slopes to engage Kara Mustapha's Ottoman army. The defeat of Kara Mustapha marked the decline of the Ottoman Empire as it retreated slowly down the Danube.

Km 1933·8
Entrance to the Donaukanal

The Donaukanal is the old arm of the Danube flowing close to old Vienna. The present main channel of the Danube is an artificial diversion. The 19th-century regulation of the river was an attempt to stop it flooding over the low land to the east and over parts of Vienna. New works are currently in progress to further regulate the river, although some of the proposals have run into problems with conservation groups who say it will destroy important areas of marsh and certain rare species of plants that grow there.

Km 1928·9
Reichsbruecke

The original bridge collapsed into the Danube on August 1st 1976. No one is quite sure why the bridge collapsed, luckily it happened in the early hours of the morning so there were few casualties.

Praterkai, Vienna, with the new bronzed glass offices of the oldest steamship company on the Danube, the DDSG, behind.

Km 1929
Praterkai: Vienna

Vienna, like Linz, has long been a crossroads settlement where river-borne and overland trade intersected. The 'amber road' from the north and the 'spice road' from the east met here. Salt came down the river from Upper Austria. The site was settled by the Illyrians and the Celts before the Romans established the garrison of Vindabona. Marcus Aurelius died here in 180AD while defending Pannonia from the Teutons and the Slavs. The first vines were planted around the Wienerwald during the Roman period. After the Romans retreated the town was repeatedly pillaged until the 12th century when the Babenbergs secured the area. The first Duke of Austria, Heinrich II Jasomirgot set up his court here and Vienna began to prosper. In 1246 the male line of the Babenbergs died out and in 1278 the first of the Habsburgs, Rudolf von Habsburg, was made Duke of Austria.

The Donau Canal where the Danube comes closest
to Vienna.

Under the Habsburgs the city expanded and
many new and grandiose buildings were
started. Leopold I redecorated in the Baroque
style in the 17th century and many new Baroque buildings were built as well. The city expanded through the rule of Maria Theresa,
Joseph II and Franz II. It was occupied by
Napoleon in 1805 but reverted to the
Habsburgs after Trafalgar. The accession of
Franz Joseph was the beginning of a period of
marking time for the Habsburgs until the
Empire was carved up after the First World
War. Hitler occupied Vienna in 1938 and after
the war Austria was divided into four sectors
controlled by the Americans, Russians, British
and French. In 1955 Austria was given neutral
status. Vienna staged a spectacular economic
recovery and much rebuilding of its monuments and buildings was carried out.

From the river there is little to see of old
Vienna and its heritage. On the east bank
there are modern suburbs dominated by the
concave curves of steel and glass of the United
Nations buildings and the slender tower of the
Donauturm. On the west bank there are the
buildings of various shipping firms and
warehouses with a few old buildings surviving.

In the Donau Canal that cuts down from
just below Kahlenbergerdörfp and cuts off
Leopoldstadt and the Prater from the rest of
Vienna, the Danube comes closest to old
Vienna. Originally the canal was one of the old
courses the Danube took when it spread out
from the Wachau over the flat plain around
Vienna. In 1875 the Danube was diverted to
the new course it now takes to the east of
Vienna. The banks were built up and the river
was largely stopped from spreading out over
the countryside and turning the whole area
into a maze of tributaries and lagoons and
muddy islands. The massive diversion stopped
parts of Vienna being flooded. Old pictures
show the inhabitants of Leopoldstadt getting
about the streets by boat, merchants delivering
goods, floating market stalls. Craft of all des-
criptions are tied up along the bank selling
fruit and vegetables, pots and pans, sheep and
cows, timber, bricks, beer and bread. Vienna
was on the axis of the trade route between the
east and west. In the past goods had come
down the river directly into the heart of
Vienna, but after 1875 the river and river commerce moved away from old Vienna to the outer suburbs. Rail and road transport bit deeply

Viennese busker.

Der Donau

The Blue Danube waltz is most people's reaction to mention of the Danube. It was originally a choral work Strauss composed for the Viennese Men's Choral Association and was first performed as a waltz in the Diana Baths on the edge of the Danube. The building no longer exists, only a plaque in front of the new building, the IBM centre. It didn't catch on at first, and only later, after the French had adopted it, did Vienna take it back. It still has that gay lilt to it that attracted the Viennese to it, but it has been heard so often no-one listens to it anymore. It is most often used now as *muzak* in restaurants, hotels, on tours and it is often played at state occasions. It even has some sickly words penned for it by Franz Gerneth in 1890.

into river transport and it declined except for traditional river cargoes such as coal and ore.

Kaffeehaus

Coffee is just not coffee in Vienna. I usually ordered a *kleinen mokka*, a small strong black expresso, or a *melange*, half milk and half coffee. It took me a while to translate *kapuziner* into *cappucino*. A *braunen* is coffee with just a dash of milk and a *Turkischen* is strong Turkish coffee. I had to try an *enspänner* just for the sound of the name and got coffee with a hefty dollop of whipped cream on top. Coffee is an integral part of Vienna and the famous *Kaffeehäuser* still exist. The history of the *Kaffeehaus*, so the story goes, started when a Hungarian opened *Zum Roten Kreuz* in the Domgasse with coffee beans left behind by the defeated Turkish army in 1683. The *Kaffeehäuser* prospered and became the place to be seen for wealthy socialites and a place out of the cold for the less well off. Different *Kaffeehäuser* became meeting places for artists, musicians, writers, students, depending on their location. Many of the famous old *Kaffeehäuser* such as the *Hawelka* still exist.

The Pestsäule, a monument to Vienna's deliverance from the plague in 1679.

Stefansdom, St Stephen's cathedral, in the heart of Vienna. From the top (522 steps up) there is an unrivalled view, though now restricted by iron bars because of the high number of suicides in the past.

Danube so blue,
You flow straight through
The meadows and dales
Vienna now hails
Your silvery stream
With glist'ning gleam,
For hearts that are happy
Beat on your shores and sweetly dream
From the forest black
To the sea you track,
You give blessing while caressing,
And while flowing East,
You have never ceased
Joining shore to shore
Forever more.
Castles from on high
Watch you passing by,
Send a fleeting
Joyful greeting
And the mountain peak
On which sun beams streak,
Is reflected in
Your waves unique.

Fishermen's cabin on the Danube near Vienna.

Perhaps it sounds less saccharine sweet and banal in German. Whatever the lyrics this one waltz is known worldwide to millions, often the only association that can be made with the Danube. It pairs Vienna with the Danube and like the line that describes the Danube as blue, this bonding of Vienna to the river is no longer true either.

Km 1920–1915 – Left bank
Lobau Island
A heavily wooded island which became the centre of a controversy when it was planned to flood it in the canalisation work on the Danube. The plans have now been abandoned.

Km 1919·3 – Right bank
Southern entrance of the Donaukanal

Km 1918–1914
Commercial harbours

Km 1909 – Right bank
Fischamend
Old river village.

Km 1902 – Left bank
Orth
Orth Castle and village. The castle houses a fisheries museum.

Km 1890 – Right bank
Petronell
The ancient Roman settlement of Carnuntum. One of the Danube legions, around 10,000 men including auxiliaries, was stationed here. Marcus Aurelius made it his base during his Danube campaign. The place was deserted for a considerable time after the Romans left and not until the 11th century was it resettled. The castle here has a Museum on the Danube.

Km 1887 – Right bank
Bad Deutsch-Altenburg
Old spa town with fine medieval buildings.

Km 1884 – Right bank
Hainburg: Austrian customs post.
The eastern outpost of the Bavarian-Austrian Empire guarding the entrance to the *Porta Hungarica*. It was a fortified city, invariably the first of the Austrian possessions to be attacked by invaders from the east. In 1683 the city refused to surrender to the Turks so that when they eventually took it, the entire population, over 8000 souls, was slaughtered. It has fine medieval buildings and fortifications.

The Danube upstream of Vienna. *Austrian National Tourist Office.*

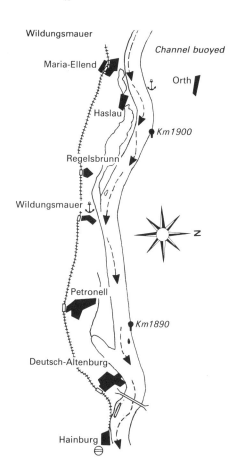

Upper Austria.

IV. Czechoslovakia

HAINBURG TO KOMARNO

Winston Churchill is credited with inventing the phrase the 'Iron Curtain' in his Fulton speech in Missouri on the 5th March 1946: 'Nobody knows what Soviet Russia and its communist international organisation intend to do in the immediate future, or what are the limits, if any, to their expansive and proselytizing tendencies about the present position in Europe... From Stettin, in the Baltic, to Trieste, in the Adriatic, an Iron Curtain has descended across the Continent. Behind that line all the capitals of the ancient states of central and eastern Europe – Warsaw, Berlin, Prague, Vienna, Budapest, Belgrade, Bucharest and Sofia – all these famous cities, and the populations around them, lie in the Soviet sphere, and all are subject, in one form or another, not only to Soviet influence, but to a very high and increasing measure of control.' It was in fact used a year earlier than this in February 1945 when Josef Goebbels said that if Soviet Russia occupied eastern Europe, an Iron Curtain would drop across Europe and 'Behind this curtain there would then begin a mass slaughter of peoples, probably with acclamation from the Jewish press in New York.' Count von Krosigk and Lord Conesford amongst others also used it around this time. The earliest reference to the Iron Curtain was made in 1920 when Ethel Snowdon employed it to describe the consequences of the Bolshevik revolution in Russia.

I have a cartoon strip cut from a magazine pinned above my desk. In it two characters are peering out of a plane window looking for the 'Iron Curtain'. 'I don't see it! Where is the bloody thing?' one of them says. 'There!' says the other. 'That's not it! That doesn't look like an 'Iron Curtain'! I was expecting something a bit more spectacular than that! Just shows you what's in a name!' He continues in exasperation, '...I mean it wouldn't be the same if Churchill had christened it the 'Iron

Roller Blind' or the 'Iron Wardrobe' would it?' The musing continues, 'And suppose Churchill had been called 'Boggis'? The entire face of history might have been different...' 'Or not...,' the other replies.

Now the events of 1989 have brought the 'Iron Curtain' down and linked eastern Europe to the west, at least in freedom of movement and expression if not in material terms. Yet I suspect many in the west have a psychological curtain erected against this 'foreign' part of Europe, *Mitteleuropa* and the eastern states, and that the effects of the 'Iron Curtain' and the isolation it engendered will be with us for longer than we think.

Km 1880·3 – Left bank
River March
Border between Austria and Czechoslovakia. On the right bank it is still Austria for a short distance downstream.

Km 1880
Porta Hungarica
Historically the door to Hungary though now it is in Czechoslovakia. And the eastern door to Austria. On the left bank Mount Theben is at the southern end of the Carpathians and on the right bank another hill, Hundsheimer Kogel, form an entrance between them, the gateway to the east, to what used to be the Austro-Hungarian Empire and is now Czechoslovakia. The natural gateway was fortified by the Romans and later by the Hungarians. The castle guarding the entrance was destroyed in 1809 by the French.

Km 1872·7– Right bank
Border between Austria and Czechoslovakia.

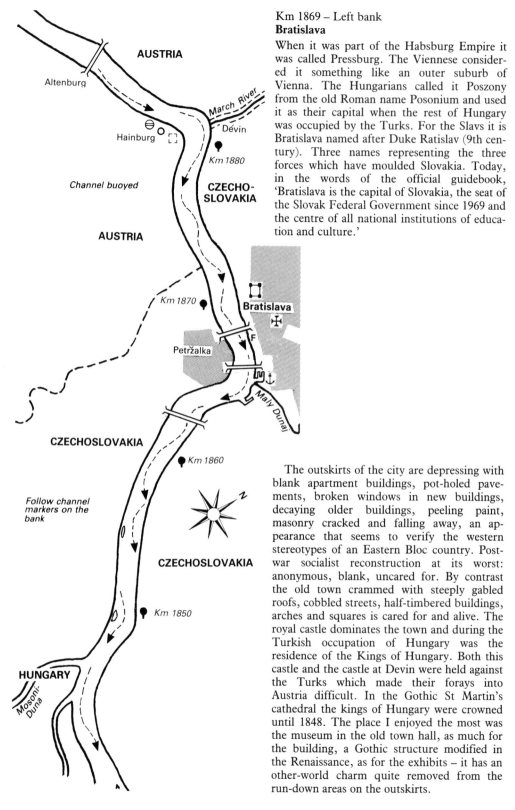

AUSTRIA

Altenburg

March River

Hainburg

Dévin

Km 1880

Channel buoyed

CZECHO-
SLOVAKIA

AUSTRIA

Km 1870

Bratislava

Petržalka

F

Malý Dunaj

CZECHOSLOVAKIA

Km 1860

N

Follow channel
markers on the
bank

CZECHOSLOVAKIA

Km 1850

HUNGARY

Mosoni-
Duna

Km 1869 – Left bank

Bratislava

When it was part of the Habsburg Empire it was called Pressburg. The Viennese considered it something like an outer suburb of Vienna. The Hungarians called it Poszony from the old Roman name Posonium and used it as their capital when the rest of Hungary was occupied by the Turks. For the Slavs it is Bratislava named after Duke Ratislav (9th century). Three names representing the three forces which have moulded Slovakia. Today, in the words of the official guidebook, 'Bratislava is the capital of Slovakia, the seat of the Slovak Federal Government since 1969 and the centre of all national institutions of education and culture.'

The outskirts of the city are depressing with blank apartment buildings, pot-holed pavements, broken windows in new buildings, decaying older buildings, peeling paint, masonry cracked and falling away, an appearance that seems to verify the western stereotypes of an Eastern Bloc country. Postwar socialist reconstruction at its worst: anonymous, blank, uncared for. By contrast the old town crammed with steeply gabled roofs, cobbled streets, half-timbered buildings, arches and squares is cared for and alive. The royal castle dominates the town and during the Turkish occupation of Hungary was the residence of the Kings of Hungary. Both this castle and the castle at Devin were held against the Turks which made their forays into Austria difficult. In the Gothic St Martin's cathedral the kings of Hungary were crowned until 1848. The place I enjoyed the most was the museum in the old town hall, as much for the building, a Gothic structure modified in the Renaissance, as for the exhibits – it has an other-world charm quite removed from the run-down areas on the outskirts.

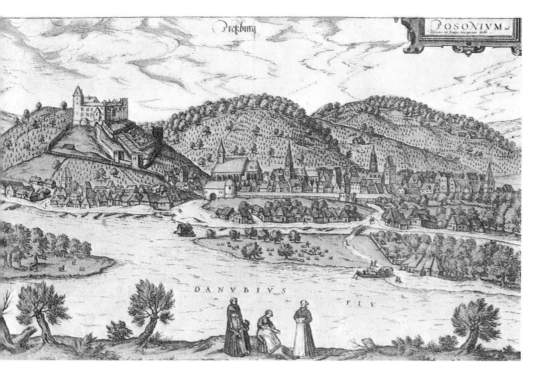

Pressburg, now Bratislava. From an engraving, 1593.

A hydrofoil runs daily from Bratislava to Vienna. Down river are the commercial docks, the largest on the Danube in Czechoslovakia. In the future it is planned to link Bratislava with Prague using the River Oder.

A yachting tale from the Communist days In Bratislava harbour I came across *Kondor* in my pre-'89 voyage. Apart from the dull grey it was painted, the yacht looked much like any fifteen metre ocean-going yacht you might run into anywhere in the world, a little too rugged and practical to be called a beauty, but beautiful to any cruising sailor's eye. I had heard of *Kondor* before, of the owner Zdenek Polasek, of his labour of love building this boat.

I met Zdenek when he returned late at night. I went on board and somehow, through my primitive German and sign language aided by squiggles and figures on a note pad, we understood each other. Zdenek was a miner, and *Kondor* represented his dream fuelled by years of hard work. He showed me a photograph of the launch of *Kondor*, the two masts stepped in schooner rig, sails bent on, bedecked with flags. As I looked over the boat finished in loving detail, I realised everything that could be was made from steel. Cleats, davits, hand-

rails, the wind generator aft, stanchions, dorade boxes and cowls. Even the masts and booms were steel as Czechoslovakia does not produce the sort of aluminium extrusion used in mast construction. The engine was a marinised truck engine in an immaculate engine room. Anything Zdenek could not make or modify he imported at vast cost. To buy his autopilot Zdenek had to work for two years.

In the saloon of *Kondor* over a bottle of wine I asked him the inevitable question: when was he going to head down river to the sea?

Pressburg (Bratislava) with an Ulm Box in the foreground, 1815.

Zdenek's face hardened. He went over to a locker and pulled a pile of papers out and handed them to me. It took a while before I deciphered what he was saying. The authorities would not give him a visa to leave. He showed his repeated applications for a visa and then showed me some more papers. When I understood what he was saying I realised why he was close to tears. Five years before his son had attempted to escape across the border into Germany. He had been shot before he got across. Not only had Zdenek lost his son, he also lost the right to leave. The authorities had denied him permission to leave because his son had attempted to leave without it. Catch 22. 'Why not just go?' I asked. He explained that while he wanted to sail to all the places in the world he had read about, to the Indian Ocean, the Pacific Islands, the Caribbean, the Mediterranean, he wanted to return to Czechoslovakia. It was his country. He did not want to be an exile from the country of his birth. 'And what if they never give you permission?' I asked, 'What will happen to *Kondor*?'. Zdenek hoped that his beloved yacht would remain a testament to the will of a man who hoped. 'When I die, *Kondor* will remain.'

I wonder what Zdenek is doing now. Sailing around the Mediterranean in my own yacht *Tetranora* after the 'velvet revolution', I kept looking in every harbour for a battleship-grey yacht flying the Czechoslovakian flag, but I didn't see Zdenek. Neither of us sitting in the saloon of *Kondor* that night could have dreamed of what was to happen so dramatically and so quickly, though I have the feeling Zdenek knew something would happen. When I asked if there was anything I could do for him, plead his case in London or write to the newspapers, he asked me to hold off for a bit, he would write to let me know if he thought that course of action was necessary. I remember being puzzled and asked Zdenek if something was in the air, did he have other options? He had smiled and indicated there was a possibility.

The Slavs

The Slavs trickled down from the northeast penetrating into Europe over centuries. Always portrayed as backward, lowly, unintelligent, the essential peasant, they were subjugated and seemed to disappear as eastern Europe was overrun by the Huns, the Avars and the Magyars, only to reappear as great ink blots across large parts of Europe. In my historical atlas the Slavs are a striped enclave around Moscow in 360. By 400 they have

Shop window in Bratislava old town, known as Pressburg when it was part of the Habsburg dominions.

edged east to Poland and most of eastern Europe has been invaded by the Huns. By 450 the Huns occupy everything from the North Sea to the Caspian and the Slavs occupy an area smaller than they did in 360. Then in 500 the Huns are gone, back to the Steppes, and the Slavs occupy a huge chunk of eastern Europe. The pattern repeats itself with the Avars who displace the Slavs in 550, but by 650 the Slavs occupy most of eastern Europe again. Only the Magyars split the Slavs into two, occupying the great Hungarian plain leaving a group of Slavs in the north and another in the south.

Like swamp peasants, like guerrilla farmers, the Slavs always seem to be around to mop up the country when the invaders have tired themselves out and to colonise it by just being there. The Magyars marooned the Slavs of the north from their cousins in the south and in the process trapped pockets of Slavs in their territory. The Habsburgs incorporated the region into their Austro-Hungarian Empire.

Not until 1918 was Slovakia, the southern half of newly made Czechoslovakia, given back to the peasant stock who had always occupied it.

It was no wonder that the old Habsburg aristocracy from Vienna to Budapest was incensed about the decisions made in Paris at the end of the Great War. To give part of Europe to the Slovaks, to the peasant stock, was a taste of things to come after the next world war. The old order was crumbling at the edges long before the new order arrived. In 1934 Patrick Leigh Fermor was told, 'You should have seen it before the War,' by his aristocratic host in Bratislava. For the Austrian and Hungarian aristocrats who remained in the city its great days were long gone and would never be seen again. The men from the steppes had finally triumphed after a thousand years of being here and there were few who had a good word for the new owners of Slovakia. After the Second World War and the Sovietisation of Czechoslovakia there were even fewer.

Circus coming to town: Bratislava.

Km 1866
After Bratislava the Danube splits into a huge watery expanse with numerous channels and islands. The northern channel, the Maly Dunai, and the main channel, flow around a large island over 90km long, called the Ostrov. A number of rivers empty into the northern channel adding to the volume of the Danube. There is also a southern channel, the Mosoni Duna, cutting off another island, the Szigetköz.

Km 1847 – Right bank
Border between Czechoslovakia and Hungary.

Km 1768 – Left bank
Komárno
The Czechoslovakian half of the old Hungarian Komárom on the opposite bank. It is primarily an industrial port town with a large shipbuilding industry. I rate it for the best ice-cream in Czechoslovakia.

The dam
For some time now work has been proceeding on a huge dam being built jointly between Czechoslovakia and Hungary. The dam will back water over the flat marshes and islands as far as Bratislava, making navigation on this swiftly flowing stretch of the river much easier and at the same time generating a considerable amount of hydroelectric power. The conservationists have argued that the dam will destroy a unique habitat and the hundreds of species of flora and fauna, some of them very rare, in it.

Even before the events of 1989 there was a powerful lobby in Hungary urging the government to back out of the project. Eventually the Hungarians decided to abandon the project despite Czechoslovakia demanding compensation amounting to billions of dollars which Hungary with its huge debt problems was in no position to pay. Austrian companies which had large contracts for the construction also waded into the debate campaigning against what they call *ecotourismus*. The Austrian companies badly needed the contracts after the scheme to construct a dam at Hainburg on the Austro-Czech border was abandoned after a successful campaign against it by Austrian conservationists and there is the smell here of sneaky politics and dumping your own dirt in the neighbour's backyard.

Czechoslovakia has now put the project on hold after the overthrow of the Communists. For me the conservation issue is complicated by the fact that presumably both Hungary and Czechoslovakia will have to build coal-fired or

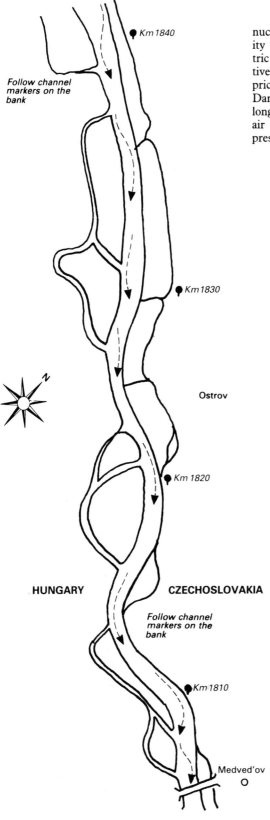

nuclear power stations to generate the electricity that would have come from the hydroelectric scheme, so that air pollution and radioactive waste from these stations becomes the price for conserving the habitat around the Danube. Conservationists will have to think long and hard on the tricky equation between air pollution and radioactive waste and preserving rare habitats.

● Km 1840

Follow channel markers on the bank

● Km 1830

Ostrov

● Km 1820

HUNGARY   **CZECHOSLOVAKIA**

Follow channel markers on the bank

● Km 1810

Medved'ov
○

V. Hungary

KOMÁROM TO MOHÁCS

Km 1768 – Right bank
Komárom
The Hungarian customs post on the right bank of the river. It is a sleepy place compared to the bustle in the commercial port of its sister town Komárno on the opposite bank. Until 1919 Komárno was Hungarian, part of Komárom, but the Treaty of Trianon gave the larger part of the town to Czechoslovakia.

Km 1763 – Right bank
Szöny
The new commercial port created after the loss of Komárno. The important Roman garrison town of Brigecium was located near here.

Km 1718·5 – Right bank
Esztergóm
At Esztergóm the Hungarian Central Massif rise up abruptly from the flat plain that stretches back to Bratislava. Esztergóm is dominated by its cathedral, modelled on St Peter's in Rome, standing on a hummock overlooking the Danube. Around it are the remains of the old Hungarian Royal Palace and the old buildings of Esztergóm. The place now has an air of tranquillity, a quiet river town with a few tourists wandering around, but a thousand years ago it was the centre of the infant Hungary.

The Celts had a settlement here from the 4th century BC. In the 2nd century BC the Romans established a garrison called Strigonium and built towers on the surrounding hills. A town, Salva Mansio, grew up beside the garrison. The philosopher emperor Marcus Aurelius spent some time here in the 2nd century when he was attempting to secure the Empire south of the Danube and no doubt some of his *Meditations* were written here. At the end of the 10th century Prince Géza established his seat at Esztergóm and for nearly 300 years the kings and queens of Hungary lived in

Stefan, the perfect gentleman of Esztergóm.

the palace. In the 12th century under King Béla III many new buildings were erected and Esztergóm had a Byzantine air to it, a legacy of the time Béla III spent in Constantinople. King Béla IV moved the Hungarian court to Buda and Esztergóm declined in power, though it remained the ecclesiastical centre of

Nagybajcs

Km 1800

Follow channel markers on the bank

CZECHOSLOVAKIA

Mosoni-Duna

Gönyü

Km 1790

HUNGARY

Channel buoyed

Km 1780

heavy it seems impossible that the puffy fingers of a prelate could lift them; bishops' robes embroidered in gold thread and weighted down with precious stones; mitres with more gold thread; crosiers so embellished that a strong man would have to lift them into place for a frail Bishop; ornamental crosses so decorated with filigree and precious stones that the shape of the cross is nearly lost; a Carolingian rock crystal cross – the oldest artifact in the collection dating from 870; the skull of a saint in a bejewelled casket; and a Byzantine silver gilt plate with an ebony cross worked into the centre, at the intersection of the cross a piece of the true cross – though later I discovered that the piece of the true cross had been stolen long ago and the piece now there was simply representational. Much later I saw an exhibition of medieval reliquary at the British Museum, the exhibits coming from all over Europe, and though it was impressive it did not compare with the exhibition in the crypt at Esztergóm. The place reeks of the medieval see and its Middle Age bishops.

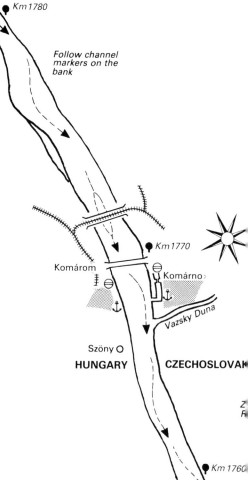

Follow channel markers on the bank

Km 1770

Komárom

Komárno

Vazsky Duna

Szöny

HUNGARY   **CZECHOSLOVAK**

Km 1760

Hungary with the See of the Archbishops located here. In 1543 it fell to the Turks and it remained under Turkish occupation for almost 150 years. The bishops returned in 1820 and construction began on the huge cathedral, the largest in Hungary.

The cathedral stands in the old royal palace of which only parts remain. It is a muscle-pounding heart-thudding circular climb to the huge copper dome on the top. The bells inside peal with a deafening din when sounded and if you clap your hands, the noise is amplified several times and echoes around inside the dome. You can walk around the bottom of the dome on a rickety walk-way with views along the Danube and across to the other side into Czechoslovakia. The ruins of the bridge which used to cross the Danube at Esztergóm to Czechoslovakia can be seen; it was not rebuilt after it was destroyed in the Second World War. In contrast to the old world elegance of Esztergóm, in Czechoslovakia there is industry with high chimneys belching poisonous fumes.

Down below in the crypt of the church there is a collection of medieval relics that is utterly fascinating: chalices worked in filigree of a fineness that seems impossible; filigree drinking horns adorned with animals from a medieval bestiary; plates of silver and gold embossed in fine design and studded with precious and semi-precious jewels; bishops' rings with chunky precious stones and gold clasps so

When I arrived at Esztergóm for the second time I was greeted at the pontoon by a wiry gentleman who seemed like something out of one of the old aristocratic Hungarian estates. He bowed stiffly from the waist and said, 'My name is Stefan – welcome to Esztergóm.' He had an old world charm and a dignity that contrasted vividly with anything I had encountered in Czechoslovakia. He was more Habsburg than anyone in Vienna. He directed us to a fish restaurant up the arm of the Danube where a fish meal was served up that was absolutely superb. Hungary is like this, full of pleasant surprises that, even before the 'Iron Curtain' fell, turned stereotypes of Eastern Bloc countries around and forced you to look at the country and its people with unblinkered eyes.

The Danube Bend After Esztergóm the Danube, the Duna in Hungarian, flows east for a while before abruptly changing direction and turning south. Appropriately enough it is called the Dunakanyar, the Danube Bend, a section of the river that with the high land of the Hungarian Massif rising abruptly up from it lends comparison to the Wachau in Austria, the Hungarian Wachau. In fact the river and the scenery are much different here, the Danube is slower without the whirlpools and overfalls of the Wachau, and the land is more gentle. This part of the river is the watery playground for the landlocked Hungarians who will be seen swimming, canoeing, fishing, sailing, or just messing about in boats. The shores and slopes are dotted with holiday houses.

If you are travelling down river on the hydrofoil from Vienna you don't see much of the Danube Bend as the hydrofoil whizzes by. Similarly the cruise boats don't always stop here. From Budapest there are day cruises up to Esztergóm and back again or there are coach tours of the important places along the river. Having travelled along here by hydrofoil, pleasure boat and on a coach, strangely enough you will see more from the coach trip than from the river since many of the places are difficult to get to by boat.

Km 1708·2 – Left bank
River Ipoly
Border between Czechoslovakia and Hungary on the left bank.

Km 1706·5 – Left bank
Szob
Border town with customs post for rail travellers.

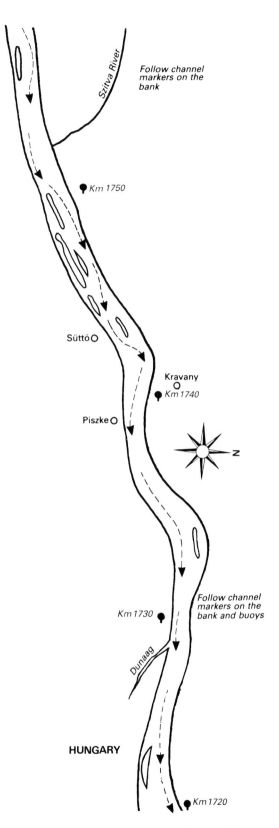

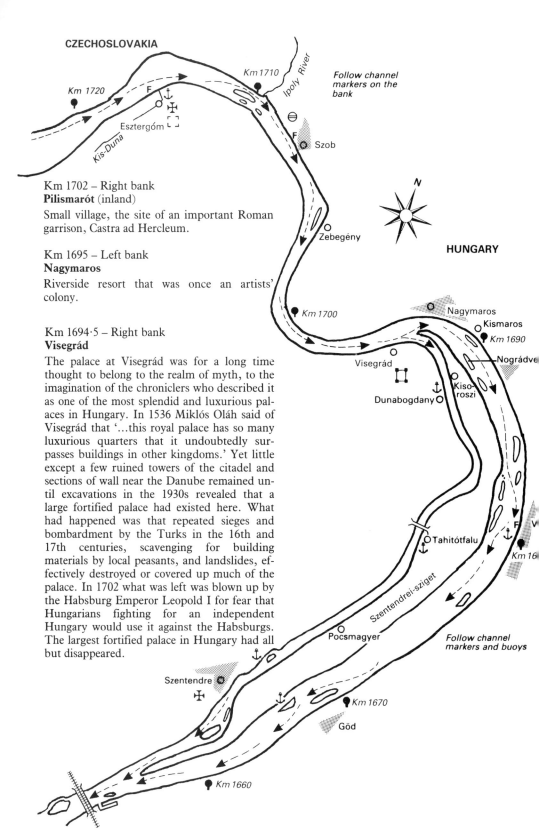

CZECHOSLOVAKIA

Km 1720

Km 1710

Ipoly River

F

Esztergóm

Kis-Duna

Follow channel
markers on the
bank

Szob

Zebegény

Km 1700

N

HUNGARY

Nagymaros

Kismaros

Km 1690

Nográdve

Visegrád

Kiso-
roszi

Dunabogdany

Szentendrei-sziget

Tahitótfalu

F V

Km 16

Pocsmagyer

Follow channel
markers and buoys

Szentendre

Km 1670

Göd

Km 1660

Km 1702 – Right bank
Pilismarót (inland)

Small village, the site of an important Roman
garrison, Castra ad Hercleum.

Km 1695 – Left bank
Nagymaros

Riverside resort that was once an artists'
colony.

Km 1694·5 – Right bank
Visegrád

The palace at Visegrád was for a long time
thought to belong to the realm of myth, to the
imagination of the chroniclers who described it
as one of the most splendid and luxurious pal-
aces in Hungary. In 1536 Miklós Oláh said of
Visegrád that '...this royal palace has so many
luxurious quarters that it undoubtedly sur-
passes buildings in other kingdoms.' Yet little
except a few ruined towers of the citadel and
sections of wall near the Danube remained until excavations in the 1930s revealed that a
large fortified palace had existed here. What
had happened was that repeated sieges and
bombardment by the Turks in the 16th and
17th centuries, scavenging for building
materials by local peasants, and landslides, effectively destroyed or covered up much of the
palace. In 1702 what was left was blown up by
the Habsburg Emperor Leopold I for fear that
Hungarians fighting for an independent
Hungary would use it against the Habsburgs.
The largest fortified palace in Hungary had all
but disappeared.

The site was occupied by the Romans in the 2nd century BC who established a garrison town, Pone Navata, by the Danube. After the Romans left the Roman fort was settled by the Slavs and the name they gave to the settlement, Visegrád, meaning 'High Castle', is the name used today. When the infant Hungary turned to Christendom a monastery was built here. A lower castle was begun in 1250 after the Mongol invasion, when the combination of the craggy site and the energy of King Béla IV produced one of the strongest castles in Hungary. In 1316 Charles of Anjou took up residence at Visegrád and he set about making the fortress more comfortable. His successors, Louis I and Sigismund, continued the extensions until Visegrád was one of the largest and most luxurious castles in Hungary. Some estimates reckoned it covered an area of forty acres.

Today some of the lower castle remains, but the partially reconstructed citadel high above the Danube is the most impressive part of the original complex. From here there is a view over the Danube in both directions where it curves around a sharp 180° corner towards Budapest.

Postcard depicting the Serbian Orthodox Church in Szentendre.

Km 1691·8 to 1657·5
Szentendre-sziget

A long narrow island, also called Andrew Island, that splits the Danube into two until nearly to Budapest. Most commercial traffic uses the left channel although some smaller barges and pleasure craft use the right hand channel, the Szentendre-Duna. The island is fertile and extensively cultivated along its length. At the beginning of the island the Danube swings abruptly to the south and runs more or less south from here after its predominantly eastern course until Vukovar in Yugoslavia when it turns east again.

Km 1680 – Left bank
Vác

The site was a minor Roman garrison that was often under siege from the indigenous tribes inland. It developed into a small town and was made a bishopric in the 11th century. The Mongols overran the town in 1241 and in 1544 the Turks took the town when they occupied Hungary. Not until the 19th century, with increased transport on the Danube, did Vác recover, and most of the buildings date from this time.

Km 1666·5 – Right bank
Szentendre

The small town looks as if it has been transplanted from the eastern Mediterranean, and in a way it has. Although it was a Roman camp, it did not survive the Dark Ages and not until the 12th century did the newly arrived Hungarians resettle the area. The town was all but deserted during the Turkish occupation, but at the end of the 17th century, refugees displaced from the east settled at Szentendre. Eight hundred Serbian, Albanian, Bosnian, Dalmatian and Greek families set up house and the town soon prospered. With the Danube on the doorstep the merchants and artisans exported goods to the west and east. The orthodox faith they brought with them is reflected in the elaborate baroque orthodox churches they built.

In the 18th and 19th centuries Szentendre stagnated because of its proximity to Budapest, and to an extent the town has remained locked in time for some 200 years. It has the appearance of Mediterranean or Balkan village transported into the middle of Hungary, complete with pastel washed houses and a number of well preserved orthodox churches – a taste of things to come further down the Danube. The town is now preserved as a historical monument.

Km 1665·8 – Left bank
Ruins of the Trajan bridge built built in the 2nd century AD.

Km 1654 to 1651·3 – Right bank
Obuda Island

Km 1653 – Left bank
Commercial harbour

Km 1651·5 to 1648·8
Margitsziget
Margaret Island. It is named after the daughter of King Béla IV whose daughter went into a Dominican convent on the island and remained there for the rest of her life. The enlightened authorities have kept the island as a huge recreation park, right in the middle of

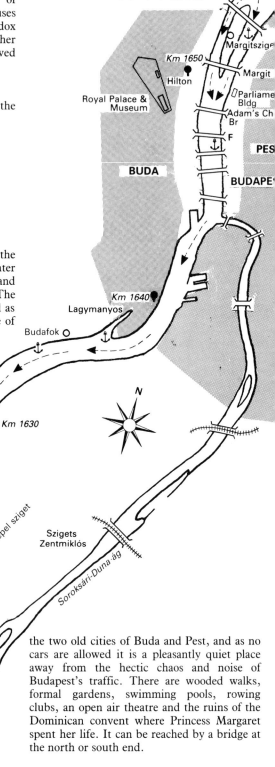

the two old cities of Buda and Pest, and as no cars are allowed it is a pleasantly quiet place away from the hectic chaos and noise of Budapest's traffic. There are wooded walks, formal gardens, swimming pools, rowing clubs, an open air theatre and the ruins of the Dominican convent where Princess Margaret spent her life. It can be reached by a bridge at the north or south end.

Adam Clark's Chain Bridge: Budapest.

Km 1647
Budapest

More than any other city, Budapest is **the** city of the river, the queen city of the Danube if you like. Vienna sits away from the Danube and turns her back to it. Belgrade has a nodding acquaintance with the Danube but belongs more to the Sava River that joins the Danube there. Budapest sits squarely across the Danube, acknowledges it, and accepts the river as an intrinsic part of everyday life. Numerous bridges cross the river, including the famous chain suspension bridge built by a Scot, Adam Clark, in the 1840s; riverside walks stretch the length of Buda and Pest; ferries criss-cross up and down the river and the Houses of Parliament look out over it; Fisherman's Bastion in Buda was built to provide views downstream; and Margaret Island sits in the middle of the river. If you arrive overland it is possible to wander around Vienna or Belgrade and never catch sight of the Danube. In Budapest that is impossible.

Until 1873 Budapest did not exist. Buda on the west side of the Danube and Pest on the east were separate cities, and until Clark's chain bridge of 1840, were linked only by ferries or by barges tied to each other to form a floating bridge. The tempestuous nature of the Danube, icing up in the winter and the thaw and consequent floods in the spring and early summer, when ferries and floating bridges could not be employed, effectively cut off the two cities until the chain bridge and subsequent bridges enabled the unification of 1873. Such was the Hungarians' respect for the task carried out by the Scots engineer – the bridge cost the prodigious sum of half a million pounds and involved a labour force culled from Scotland, England, Italy and local Slavs – that a square close by the bridge is named *Clark Adam tér* in his honour.

The two sides of the river are quite different. At Buda the last hills of the Hungarian Massif drop steeply down to the river. On the other side at Pest the great Hungarian Plain, the *Puszta*, begins. When the Romans arrived they had no trouble deciding where to build a garrison. The eastern side of the river had no natural protection at all, whereas the western side offered every natural advantage for easy defence. At Obuda just north of Buda, the Romans established one of their largest garrisons, Colonia Septima Aquincum, on the Danube flank. At Buda itself there was a civilian settlement. Later on the Romans became worried that an amphibious attack could be mounted across the Danube, and established a garrison, Contra-Aquincum, on the eastern side. When the Romans departed they left behind large numbers of lime-kilns and brick-kilns and the Slavs who moved into Contra-Aquincum called it *Pec* from the kilns, later Pest. The medieval town on the east bank flourished from trade on the Danube and was fortified by thick walls at some period. The west bank also had a small settlement, but it was not until after the Mongols swept across the *Puszta* and destroyed Pest that Béla IV again fortified the steep western slopes in the 13th century. Buda, protected by the river and fortifications, prospered and became the seat of Hungarian royalty from the 14th century. An imperial castle was built and the kings and queens of Hungary were crowned in the cathedral. In 1526 it all came to an end with the disastrous battle at Mohács where the Turks defeated the Hungarian army. In 1541 Buda became a Turkish city and fort and they were to hold it until 1686 when Charles of Lorraine freed the city. In the 18th century, as part of the Habsburg domain, the city flourished and there was a positive frenzy of building in the baroque style. Under the Habsburgs Budapest became the centre, as much as Vienna, of eastern Europe, until the disastrous consequences of the First World War, when Hungary was on the losing side. Under the right wing Admiral Horthy Hungary was sluiced into the Second World War on the wrong side again and the consequences for Budapest were disastrous.

Before the Red Army reached Budapest, the Germans and an extreme right wing organisation led by Ferenc Szálasi determined to hold the city at whatever cost. All the bridges across the Danube and many other key structures were blown up. By the time Budapest was finally liberated on the 13th February 1945, only one in four of the buildings was standing. In the Royal Palace above Buda that now houses the Museum of History, the National Gallery and the Museum of the Hungarian Working Class, there are a series of photographs showing Budapest at the end of World War II. The devastation is complete and the Royal Palace, where the Germans dug in for a last ditch defence, is a flattened bed of rubble. The palace and many of the other old buildings in Budapest have been totally rebuilt to the original plans. In the case of the palace, old passages and rooms dating from the 14th century and unknown before the war were uncovered during the reconstruction and have been incorporated into the present museum. The scale of the reconstruction of Budapest is staggering and says something about the almost frenetic energy of the Hungarians.

Budapest: hot in the summer but in the winter it rains, even on the statues.

Today Budapest is simply the most delightful city along the Danube. It is more urbane, sophisticated, unregimented, hedonistic, than you could ever believe. Ironically you get more of a feeling of what the Habsburgs were about here than you do in Vienna. It is a warmer city than Vienna, which has an air of cold haughtiness about it. It has the only Hilton Intercontinental I have seen that does not irrevocably scar the landscape. It has the Fisherman's Bastion, a Disneyesque creation of the early 20th century, a folly built solely to enhance the views of Buda and to provide views of the Danube. It has Turkish baths left over from the Ottoman occupation. In Vaci utca the shop windows are full of fashionable clothes, jewellery, fashion accessories and the sort of shops that sell knick-knacks for the home and kitchen which look useful but turn out to be utterly useless. At Gerbeaud's in Vörösmarty square there are cakes and sorbets to rival anything in Vienna. To get about you can take the trams or buses or a taxi. Budapest

Budapest: the city of the Danube. Whereas Vienna turns her back on the river and Belgrade faces the River Sava rather than the Danube, Budapest sits squarely across it.

is the only place in Europe where you can flag down a taxi and know it will cost little to go anywhere, even if the driver goes by a roundabout route. There is so much to see and do that it requires a large guidebook to document it all and in Budapest that is no trouble at all. The city has had a printing press since the 1470s, some thirty years after Gutenberg first printed his Bible, and has always considered itself to be the publishing centre of Europe, so there are numerous guides available, many of them translated into English.

The Magyars and Hungary Like the other tribes, the Slavs, the Avars and the Bulgars, the Magyars filtered in from the northeast, but unlike the others, the Magyars managed to hold on to the huge flat plain they eventually called the *Puszta*. The first Magyars to conquer the area did so sometime around the end of the 9th century. Others of this tribe with their unpronounceable agglutinative language worked their way up to what is now Finland

and today Finnish and Estonian are the only languages related to Hungarian, both part of the Finno-Ugric group. On Christmas Day AD 1000 the first king of Hungary, Stephen I, was crowned. His father Prince Géza had adopted Christianity, and Stephen likewise accepted the new faith and was eventually to attain sainthood. In 1241 the new nation was overrun by the Mongols under Ghenghis Khan and after the hordes had departed King Béla IV set about strengthening the defences of the land.

The Arpád dynasty that had ruled Hungary since Stephen I ended in 1301 with the death of Andrew III. A series of foreign kings, drawn from the royal register of Europe, ruled Hungary for 150 years. In 1456 a national leader emerged in the shape of János Hunyadi. He led the massed armies of the west against the Turks and defeated them at Nándorfehérvár (now Belgrade, which is a good deal easier to pronounce), a victory that was celebrated all over the Christian world. The son of Hunyadi, Matthias Corvinus, was crowned king and for thirty years Hungary enjoyed a native ruler once again and a period of prosperity. It was to end in 1526 when the Turks defeated the Hungarian army at Mohács. The Turks did not so much destroy Hungary as allow it to fall into a state of disrepair and when they were finally ousted 150 years later the Hungarians had much to rebuild.

Under the Habsburgs there was order and time to rebuild, but many Hungarians resented the stern administration from Vienna. In 1703 a revolt was led by Ferenc Rákóczi which was finally quelled in 1711. In 1848 another rebellion was led by the poet Sánfor Petöfi and this too failed though the anthem he wrote for it – the last line 'We swear, that we will no longer be slaves' conveys the general drift of the whole – is known by most Hungarians to this day. Hungary was by and large ruled by aristocratic landowners who controlled huge estates farmed in the feudal style by serfs who had few, if any, rights. This medieval system existed right up to the 20th century when the calamitous events of the Great War changed the face of Europe.

The Austrians dragged Hungary into the war with them and at the end of it the country was devastated, its economy in ruins and its politics in disarray. In 1919 the right wing Admiral Miklós Horthy took power and began a purge of left wing politicians and sympathisers. In 1920 the Treaty of Trianon stripped Hungary of two thirds of its former territory, now parts of Romania, Yugoslavia

Looking across to Buda from Pest.

Ferry dock: Budapest.

Communist poster of 1918 depicting the bloody demise of the double-headed eagle and the Habsburg crown. Author's collection.

Geriatric busker at Fisherman's Bastion.

Budapest: advertising style and elegance.

Communist poster of 1919.

Where the water came up to in the floods of 1838, sign on one of the oldest restaurants in Pesti Barnabas utca, in Pest.

and Czechoslovakia. This loss of territory is still a sore point with Hungarians who believe that the terms of the treaty were too harsh by far and that fellow Hungarians, especially those in Romania, are discriminated against. After the Second World War Hungary became a People's Republic and slowly got back to rebuilding the war-torn country. In October 1956 an uprising which proclaimed Hungary a neutral state and withdrew it from the Warsaw Pact was brutally crushed by Soviet troops and tanks ten days after it was declared. The Hungarians were once again under a foreign power and despite their efforts to break free, were destined to be trodden underfoot. The Hungarians joke that only they can lose a war and call the defeat a triumph for independence.

Hungary was one of the first to explore just what Gorbachov's *perestroika* meant for the Warsaw Pact countries. Hungary had always been less authoritarian than some of its neighbours, allowing private enterprise to co-exist with state controlled industry and letting its nationals travel abroad, though the weakness the *forint* always made this difficult. As early as September 1987 there was a call for a new constitution guaranteeing freedom of expression and in May 1988 there was a reshuffle in the Communist Party to accommodate the demands for greater freedoms. In February 1989 the Communist Party agreed to hold multi-party elections. In May 1989 the barbed wire fence between Hungary and Austria was dismantled and in September the government did nothing to stop East Germans crossing into Austria from Hungary. In March 1990 parliamentary elections were held for the first time in 45 years and at last Hungary may become truly independent.

Km 1642 – Left bank
Ráckevei (Soroksári) Duna

An arm of the Danube that describes a huge arc to rejoin at km 1586. It encloses the large island of Csepel, some 56km long. At the northern end the island is largely an industrial satellite of Budapest.

Km 1637·5 – Right bank
Budafok

Small village renowned for its wine.

Km 1586 – Left bank
Ráckevei Duna rejoins the main stream at the southern end of Csepel Island.

Km 1578 – Right bank
Dunaújváros

A huge purpose-built industrial town constructed along Soviet lines in 1949. The enormous steel and iron mill and the other processing plants are all in the south separated from the apartment blocks for the workers by a low hill. Sadly the smoke and fumes drift over to the apartments when the wind is in the wrong direction, coating them in soot and dust, and the whole place has a melancholy and drab air to it.

Km 1561 – Right bank
Dunaföldvár

A small pleasant farming town on the edge of the *Puszta*. It is connected by a bridge to the other side of the river and consequently is a busy little place. There are only two such bridges connecting Transdanubia with the *Puszta* across the Danube between Budapest and the Yugoslavian border, the other bridge being at Baja.

The Puszta

It has been described as the dullest place in Europe. Its life, it has been said, is as grey as its dust. Even Hungary's celebrated poet and leader of the rebellion of 1848, Sánfor Petöfi, who gathered the peasants of the *Puszta* into his raggle-taggle army, found the Great Plain depressing '...my trip was preceded by 10, yes ten, days of rain, and on top of that it rained in torrents for two days of the journey. Now you can imagine what a jolly time I had – but no, you can't, not by any means, even if you were to burst with effort. True, my cart had a canvas top, but so much mud clung to the wheels that in the truest sense of the word we were forced to stop every hundred paces and scrape the sticky black buttery stuff off the spokes' (1847). From the Danube this drabness is not evident as the banks are frequently lined with thick stands of willow and ash which stops the horizon short and you will have to venture ashore to experience the monotony of the flat landscape.

The Great Plain covers more than half of Hungary stretching from the Danube to the foothills of the Carpathians in Transylvania. The word *Puszta* which now is used to describe the Great Plain (strictly speaking it is Az Alföld) also describes its evolution. In the Middle Ages the plain was fenland with wooded areas. The flooding of the Danube and the Tsiza River which meanders across it further east made it a lonely place where villages could be cut off for months during the winter thaw and a place where whole armies could disappear without trace. The demand for timber for ship-building during the Middle Ages stripped much of the *Puszta* close to the Danube of timber – to build a fighting galley required 50 beech trees, 300 pines and 300 mature oaks. During the Turkish occupation much timber was felled to build small forts and much of the rest was burned off to deny cover for the *Hajdúk* – the Hungarian groups fighting the Turks. The Great Plain became the badlands of Hungary, depopulated, desolate, uncared for and bleak. This is when the word *Puszta* was used to describe it; *Puszta* means abandoned, and for centuries after the Turks left this is how it remained.

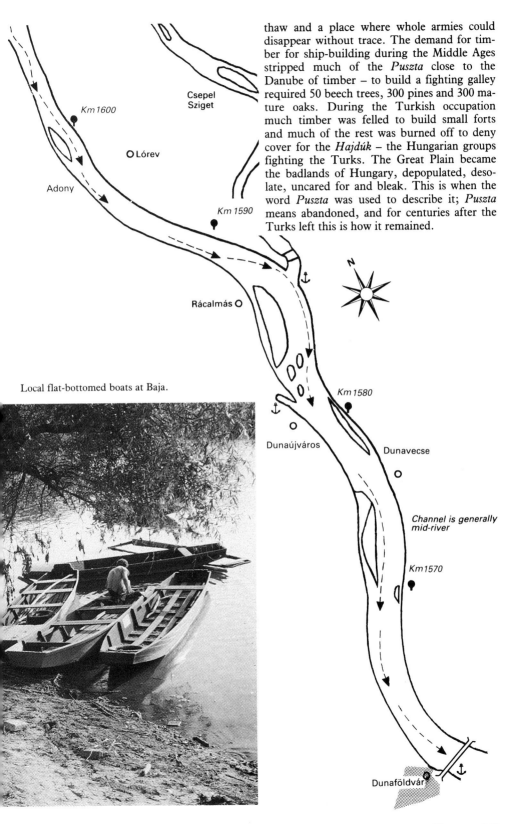

Csepel Sziget

Km 1600

O Lórev

Adony

Km 1590

N

Rácalmás O

Local flat-bottomed boats at Baja.

Km 1580

Dunaújváros

Dunavecse

Channel is generally mid-river

Km 1570

Dunaföldvár

Not until the 19th century did the character of the *Puszta* change. Flood regulation work on the Tsiza and the Danube drained huge areas and grass grew readily on the rich soil. Cattle and sheep were grazed and Hungary's cowboys, the *csikos*, roamed the new grasslands tending huge herds of cattle and flocks of sheep. The land around the *Puszta* villages was turned into market gardens and irrigation channels were dug to water them. *Puszta* now came to mean the way of life on the plain. Most of the peasants worked on vast estates owned by aristocratic families and these hard-worked people formed the core of Sánfor Petöfi's rebellion against the landowners. The nationalisation of the land by the Communists in 1949 appeared to offer the peasants a new life, but the huge collective farms they were herded into were to prove just a variation on their plight of the previous 150 years. In the 1960s the farm workers, Stalin's euphemism for peasants, were allowed to cultivate private

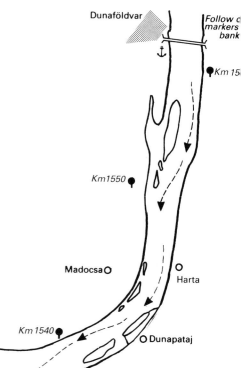

plots and keep whatever they grew. Times were undoubtedly better for the inhabitants of the *Puszta*, and today many of the villages appear to be quite prosperous, at least by eastern European standards. Now the huge collective farms are to be divided up, though those with long memories must hope that this will not mean a return to the old estates owned by a few.

Km 1546 – Left bank
Harta

A large agricultural village.

Km 1531 – Right bank
Paks

Not to be confused with Pécs. A large agricultural and industrial town. Before the regulation of the Danube this whole area was prone to flooding. When Maxwell and Taylor went down the Danube in the eighteen foot *Walrus* in 1905 they got lost in the flooded channels which extended for miles to either side. 'It was clear often that the *Walrus* had quite lost her way. She was evidently travelling over what under normal conditions would be pastures, for every now and then she would strike a bush or find herself in distressing circumstances among the trees of an island.'

Eventually the pair found the main channel again after having been lost for several days. For them this stretch of the river was almost deserted and it is interesting to reflect that most of the settlements that now exist are comparatively new, built after regulation of the river made it possible to build next to it without the danger of flooding. Old settlements by the river are mostly on higher ground where the flood levels did not reach.

Km 1515 – Left bank
Kalocsa

A town some five kilometres inland from the river. It is noted for its folk-art, particularly the floral decoration of houses and furniture, and its embroidery along similar floral themes. The town has an ancient pedigree, King Stephen is supposed to have established a bishopric here in the 11th century, and there are numerous old buildings including the 18th-century cathedral. There is a good museum of folk-art in the town.

Km 1507 – Left bank
Fajsz

Small agricultural town noted for its wine and black tobacco.

Km 1479 – Left bank
Baja

A commercial port and river resort. Numerous channels and canals wind up to and around the town. It is a sleepy pleasant place with numerous old buildings. The orthodox church was having a new copper cupola put on when I was there and this was the centre of the town's attractions for days – when would the crane arrive to hoist it aloft? There is a small museum on the Danube though all the exhibit labels are only in Hungarian, a pity as it has numerous interesting exhibits on old fishing methods and transport.

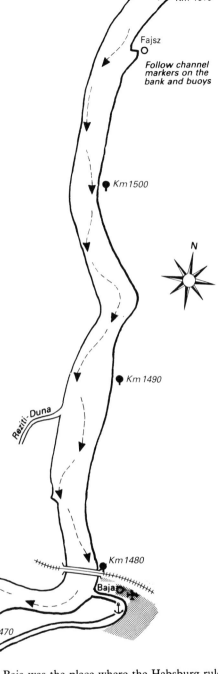

Baja was the place where the Habsburg rule in Hungary came to an end in November 1921. Charles, the last crowned emperor of the Habsburgs, attempted to regain Hungary, but after a minor battle, a footnote in history, he and the Empress Zita were evacuated by a British gunboat from Baja and taken to Madeira, their chosen place of exile.

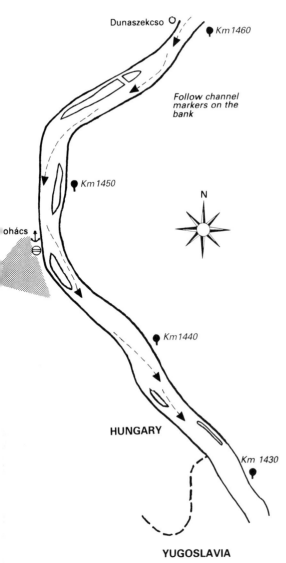

Dunaszekcso Km 1460

Follow channel
markers on the
bank

Km 1450

N

ohács

Km 1440

HUNGARY

Km 1430

YUGOSLAVIA

Km 1447 – Right bank
Mohács

This sleepy little town by the Danube is remembered for the battle that was lost here when the Turks beat Louis II and his Hungarian army. The defeat at Mohács in late August, 1526, was to determine the fate of Hungary for the next 150 years when the Turks ruled over the country and were to reach as far as the gates of Vienna. The Ottoman Empire in the 16th century was as great as any that the Greeks, Alexander, the Romans, Byzantium, or Charlemagne ever put together – covering an area that reached from Vienna to Aden and the Persian Gulf and stretched along North Africa to Algeria.

When the advancing Turks took Belgrade, Louis II on the throne of Hungary knew he had to raise an army to stop them overrunning his kingdom. Hungary at this time was in a weak state, with the nobles arguing amongst themselves and with the king. When Louis II gathered his army, most of the nobles did not contribute men or arms and the young king largely relied on a group of German mercenaries he had recruited. He probably knew the small army was doomed to defeat – before he departed he left instructions for the dispersal of his household and ordered his hounds to be cared for. The Hungarian force met the Turkish army in the swamps at Mohács. At first things seemed to go well for Louis, but while his mercenaries were looting the fallen Turkish soldiers the Turks counter-attacked and routed the Hungarian army. Most of the 25,000 strong army were killed in the fetid swamps. Louis himself died when his horse fell and crushed him in a small stream, the Cesle. The nobles who had refused to help Louis were still unable to form a united resistance to the Turks and in a short time Budapest had fallen.

At Mohács a group of rudely carved wooden figures commemorates the battle. There is little else and were it not for the bridge across the Danube you get the feeling that Mohács would quietly fade away into the humid waterland around it. The customs post for the border with Yugoslavia just down river is here.

Km 1433
Border between Hungary and Yugoslavia.

VI. Yugoslavia

BATINA TO PRAHOVO

Km 1425·5 – Left bank
Tisza or Velike Bačka Canal
In 1802 a canal was built from the Tisza River to the Danube. However the course of the Danube moved steadily west through the 19th century and so the canal had to be continually extended. Bezedan lock, built at the then entrance to the canal in 1856, is said to be the first concrete lock in Europe. The canal has had as many names as extensions: the Franzenscanal, Ferenc canal, King Peter I canal and finally the Velike Bačka canal. It was largely developed for flood control and irrigation, navigation being a secondary consideration, but in the late 19th century a substantial amount of cargo was being carried as far as Szeged. Another canal, the Ferenc-Josef, Alexander I, or Mali canal, also ran from here to Novisad in an attempt to cut out a difficult section of the Danube. Neither canal is used today as the dimensions are too small for most barges although John Marriner used the Mali Canal in 1967 when he took his motorboat *September Tide* up the Danube.

Km 1425
Batina on the right bank and Bezdan on the left bank suffered heavy damage in the Second World War. A victory statue by the Yugoslav sculptor Antun Augustincic commemorates the resistance of partisans in the war. The customs post for entry into Yugoslavia.

Km 1401 – Left bank
Apatin
An old Danube town originally settled by Germans. It has a brewery founded in 1756 by the settlers and a large shipyard. The town has long been known for its sailors and for its hemp ropes, which were used on sailing ships from various European countries. Today it is a sports fishing centre for the watery wilderness around it.

Fishing cabin in the waterland after the border with Hungary.

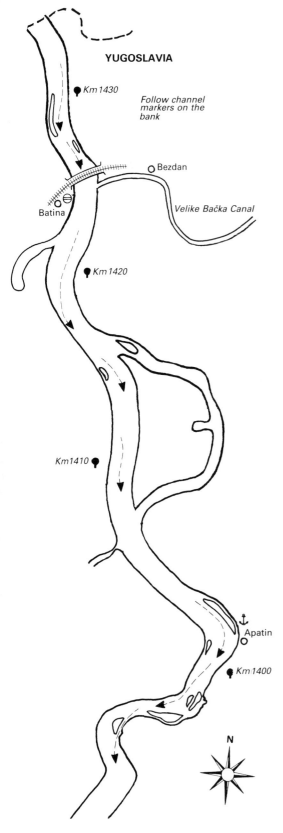

YUGOSLAVIA

Km 1430

*Follow channel
markers on the
bank*

Bezdan

Batina

Velike Bačka Canal

Km 1420

Km 1410

Apatin

Km 1400

N

Waterland From the border with Hungary to Vukovar the Danube spreads out over a watery area up to 20km. Numerous channels branch off and the main arm is dotted with islands. The humid climate encourages thick almost jungle-like growth which coupled with the white sandy beaches of the islands and shore, gives the appearance of the tropics trapped in the middle of Europe. Bird and fish life is prolific, with white egrets, cormorants, herons, hoopoes, storks and birds of prey like the osprey everywhere. The Yugoslavs come here to camp on the islands and fish in the channels. Pottering through here it was possible to get lost if the channel markers weren't closely followed though finding a place to stop for the night was easy; just choose an island and anchor in its lee.

Km 1382·5 – Right bank
Drava River

An important tributary supplying a large volume of water to the middle Danube, second only to the Sava River in Yugoslavia. It used to be navigable for 138km. Osijek a short distance up the Drava is an important commercial port.

Syrmia The rich fertile land of this region in Upper Serbia, the land between the Danube and the Sava, was called Srem by the Serbs and Syrmia by the Hungarians. It has long attracted settlers from all over Europe. Numerous Germans and Saxons settled here as well as Romanians, Hungarians and Ruthenians. Today the region has five official languages, Serbian, Hungarian, Slovak, Romanian and Ruthenian, making parliamentary business a polyglot nightmare and official publications a bulky affair. Tucked away in the countryside are assorted nationalities speaking another dozen or so languages, or dialects, as well as a variety of religious sects and groups. Local newspapers and journals are produced in Hungarian and Serbian. Somehow the diverse mixture of cultures coexists amicably, probably because this is one of the richer regions of troubled Yugoslavia.

The hills on the right bank of the river, the Fruska-Gora, are renowned for their vineyards and orchards, the latter producing the plums necessary for Yugoslavia's national tipple, *sljivovica*, plum brandy. Tucked away on the slopes are numerous monasteries, many of them belonging to the esoteric Kalugermonasteries, a Byzantine order devoted to St Basilius. There are also numerous Serbian orthodox monasteries, this orthodox belt marking a difference between the Balkans with

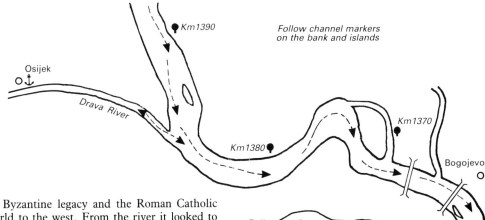

its Byzantine legacy and the Roman Catholic world to the west. From the river it looked to me like part of Austria, churches and monasteries perched on bluffs above the river, cultivated fields, vineyards, small villages tucked into the folds of the valleys – and in a way it is.

Km 1333 – Right bank
Vukovar

A very old site where a Bronze Age settlement existed and later the capital of Roman Lower Pannonia. It takes its present appearance from the arrival of German settlers in the 18th century. The surrounding area is very fertile and the German colony prospered. Until 1920 Vukovar belonged to Hungary but the Treaty of Trianon awarded this area to Serbia. Many of the older buildings have a distinctly northern European look to them, particularly the old residence of the Counts of Eltz who owned most of the town. The modern buildings are built along the banks of the Danube and next to the new Hotel Duna is what looks like an old lighthouse with 1913 inscribed on it.

There are a lot of snakes in this part of the Danube. At Vukovar I spotted one swimming on the surface of the river and a little later another swam up to the bank and snapped up one of the numerous frogs with a casual gulp. They were a greenish olive-grey with a zig-zag diamond pattern, the Viperine water snake, I decided, and though said not to be venomous, I didn't go near them. A Yugoslav I met at Vukovar said that in the Iron Gates snakes were caught to be milked of their venom and that I would certainly encounter a lot more of them there. In fact I saw no snakes at the Iron Gates, nor for the rest of the Danube.

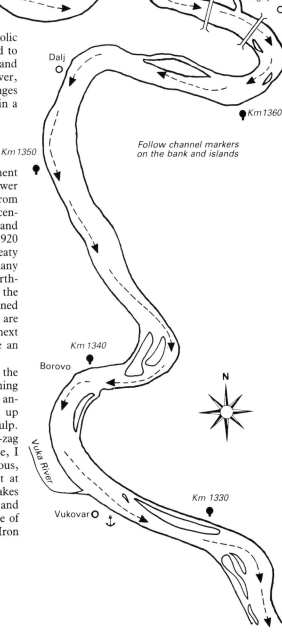

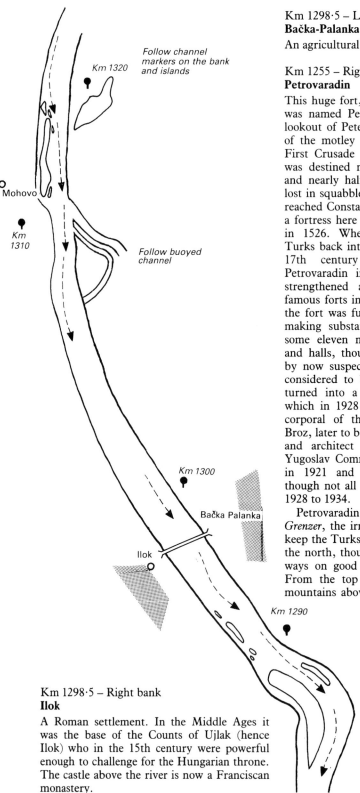

Follow channel
markers on the bank
and islands

Km 1320

Follow buoyed
channel

Mohovo

Km
1310

Km 1300

Bačka Palanka

Ilok

Km 1290

Km 1298·5 – Left bank
Bačka-Palanka
An agricultural town opposite Ilok.

Km 1255 – Right bank
Petrovaradin
This huge fort, the 'Gibraltar of the Danube', was named Peterwardein, the watchtower or lookout of Peter, by Peter the Hermit, leader of the motley armed mob who made up the First Crusade of 1096. The ill-fated crusade was destined never to reach the Holy Land and nearly half of the initial force had been lost in squabbles with local rulers before Peter reached Constantinople. The Hungarians built a fortress here which was taken by the Turks in 1526. When Prince Eugene forced the Turks back into the Balkans at the end of the 17th century he determined to make Petrovaradin impregnable and had the fort strengthened along the lines of Vauban's famous forts in France. Under the Habsburgs the fort was further modified, Maria Theresa making substantial additions to it including some eleven miles of underground passages and halls, though its military usefulness was by now suspect. By the 19th century it was considered to be a military dinosaur. It was turned into a military barracks and prison which in 1928 received a famous prisoner, a corporal of the 25th regiment called Josip Broz, later to become Marshal Tito, the unifier and architect of post-war Yugoslavia. The Yugoslav Communist party had been banned in 1921 and Josip Broz was imprisoned, though not all the time in Petrovaradin, from 1928 to 1934.

Petrovaradin was the headquarters of the *Grenzer*, the irregular force that was set up to keep the Turks out of the Habsburg Empire to the north, though the Habsburgs were not always on good terms with this border force. From the top of the Adriatic to the Banat mountains above Belgrade this line of soldier-

Km 1298·5 – Right bank
Ilok
A Roman settlement. In the Middle Ages it was the base of the Counts of Ujlak (hence Ilok) who in the 15th century were powerful enough to challenge for the Hungarian throne. The castle above the river is now a Franciscan monastery.

settlers, mostly Serbs, formed a living frontier line. The force was divided into three: one third were active soldiers on duty, one third were ready to take arms, and the remaining third tilled the soil. They were free peasants, paying no taxes, but owing a loose allegiance to the Christian forces to the north. They lived together in groups of thirty to fifty, in large families called *zadruga*, as the Slav clans always had. Like the Romans before them, they used the Danube and the Sava as part of the defensive line. The boatmen of the force, who were often river-pilots as well as soldiers, were called *Chaikists* after their boats, the *chaikas*, fast, tar black punts probably similar to those seen on this stretch of the river today, though brightly coloured fibreglass boats are fast replacing them. The *Grenzer* were formally disbanded by Franz Josef in 1881 because he feared the power of these fiercely independent Serbs on his southern flank.

Km 1255 – Left bank
Novisad

The Turkish occupation of the region around Novisad forced most of the indigenous population to leave, and not until after after the Turks had been pushed back by Prince Eugene was it resettled, with much of the land around Novisad awarded to faithful generals and soldiers of the Habsburg army. Settlers were also brought in from Germany, Hungary, Slovakia, Romania and the Urals to farm the rich land, along with the Serbs who had been displaced here by the Turks. In 1748 Maria Theresa gave it a royal charter and the Latin title of Neoplanta, which in Serbian became Novisad. The city gradually developed into a cultural centre for the Serbs, with the major Serbian publishing houses established here in the 19th century, and came to be known as the 'Athens of the North' attracting artists and writers from all over Serbia.

The city still has a lively cultivated air to it though most of publishing houses have departed to Belgrade. In the local tourist office I was plied with information and apologies for the scarcity of literature in English on the town – with five official languages of their own I considered it a miracle they had anything at all. Unlike many other Yugoslavian cities and towns, Novisad has a spruceness and tidiness to it, and best of all it does not appear to be in a constant state of reconstruction.

At Novisad the bridge connecting Petrovaradin and Novisad is the lowest bridge on the Danube and can make navigation difficult when the river is high. On the cruise boats the enclosed steering position on the top deck,

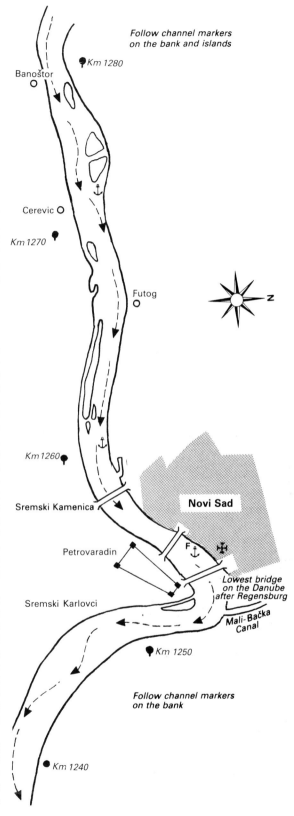

Follow channel markers on the bank and islands

Km 1280
Banoštor

Cerevic

Km 1270

Futog

Km 1260

Sremski Kamenica

Novi Sad

Petrovaradin

F

Lowest bridge on the Danube after Regensburg

Sremski Karlovci

Mali-Bačka Canal

Km 1250

Follow channel markers on the bank

Km 1240

Crossing the Danube with elegance, the new bridge at Novisad.

the highest structure, can be completely dismantled, folding flat like a cardboard box, in order for the boat to clear the low bridge. Sometimes even this measure does not suffice and passengers and baggage must be transshipped to another cruise boat on the other side of the bridge in order to continue the trip.

At Novisad there is the lowest bridge across the Danube. Cruise boats and tugs fold down the upper wheelhouse or lower it on a hydraulic jack in order to pass safely under it.

Km 1254·4 – Left bank
Mali-Bačka Canal

This canal connects up with the Velike Bačka Canal and the other irrigation channels to the north.

Km 1244 – Right bank
Sremski Karlovici

The German name for the town was Karlowitz and it was here in 1699 that the Treaty of Karlowitz, between Austria, Poland, Venice and Turkey, in which the Turks relinquished any rights to Hungary and Transylvania, was signed. The treaty effectively made Austria and the Habsburgs the most important power on the Danube, controlling navigation on the river from Bavaria to the Balkans. A circular building commemorates the treaty.

Km 1215·5 – Right bank
Stari Slankamen

An old spa town whose hot springs have been used since Roman times. Here the battle in 1691 between the Habsburg forces under Louis of Baden and the Turks effectively ended Turkish control of Serbia. It is famous for its vineyards – *slankamen* means grape – and so for its wines, particularly the reds.

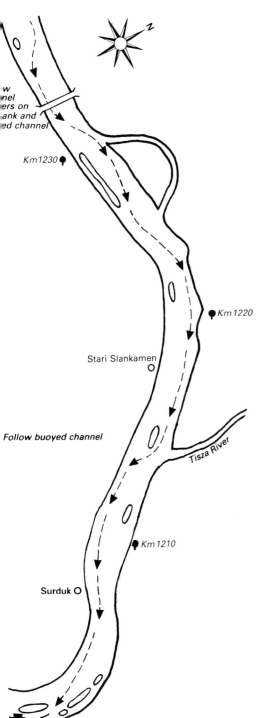

w
nel
ers on
ank and
ed channel

Km1230 ●

Km1220 ●

Stari Slankamen ○

Follow buoyed channel

Tisza River

Km1210 ●

Surduk ○

● Km1200

Km 1214·5 – Left bank
Tisza River

The longest tributary emptying into the Danube. The Tisza has its origins in the Carpathians in the Ukraine and flows down across the Hungarian *Puszta* and northern Yugoslavia for a distance of nearly 1000km before it reaches the Danube. The Tsiza was navigable at least as far as Szeged, a steamer made a regular run to the city in the 1850s, and in 1913 nearly half a million tonnes of cargo was carried on the river.

Km 1173 – Right bank
Zemun

A satellite of Belgrade on the opposite bank of the Sava. The Romans had a colony, Taurunum, here, and the Slavs moved in after the Romans, calling it Zemljin, hence Zemun. Until the Treaty of Karlowitz in 1699 which made the Sava River the border between Hungary and the western limit of the Ottoman Empire, it was not of great account. As a border town on the eastern edge of the Habsburg Empire it was an important quarantine town. All travellers coming from the east had to spend ten days in the quarantine station, though the period could be extended up to forty days if the plague or other infectious disease were known to have broken out to the east. As the Hungarian border town it prospered from commerce on the Danube and the Sava, and unlike much of Belgrade, the waterfront has remained more or less intact – from the river the old buildings of Zemun predominate though the new blank apartment blocks built after the Second World War surround the old centre. Zemun remained Hungarian until after the First World War when the borders were redrawn and Hungary lost its territory along 240km of the Danube.

Km 1170 – Right bank
Belgrade

Belgrade, or more properly Beograd, is a city that belongs as much to the Sava River as to the Danube. Its site on the confluence of the two rivers made it the logical place to build a settlement or defend a kingdom and every invader who has come through this way, from the east or the west, has determined to take and hold Belgrade. It is said of the city that the most amazing thing about it is that it exists at all: from the Romans up until the Second World War it has been destroyed and rebuilt so many times it is difficult to keep track of how many Belgrades there have been. For myself that is no great loss as Belgrade is one

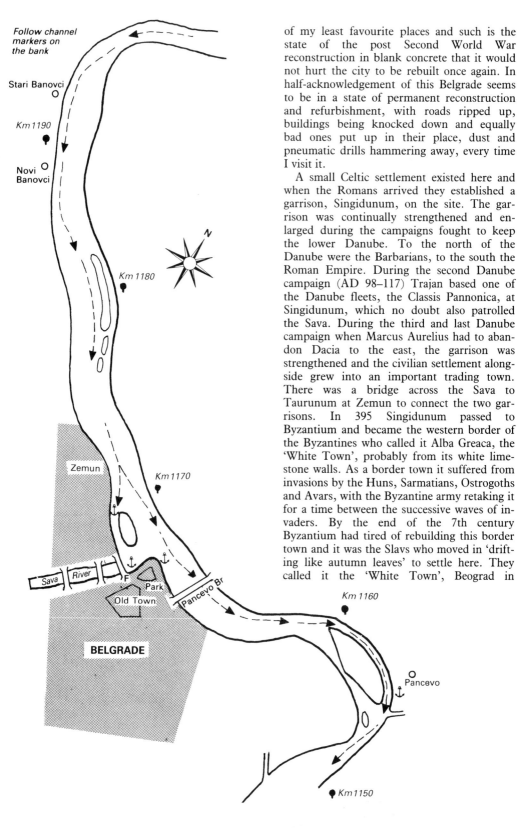

Follow channel markers on the bank

Stari Banovci ○

Km 1190 •

Novi ○
Banovci

Km 1180 •

N

Km 1170 •

Zemun

Sava River

F
Park

Old Town

Pancevo Br

BELGRADE

Km 1160 •

○
Pancevo

Km 1150 •

of my least favourite places and such is the state of the post Second World War reconstruction in blank concrete that it would not hurt the city to be rebuilt once again. In half-acknowledgement of this Belgrade seems to be in a state of permanent reconstruction and refurbishment, with roads ripped up, buildings being knocked down and equally bad ones put up in their place, dust and pneumatic drills hammering away, every time I visit it.

A small Celtic settlement existed here and when the Romans arrived they established a garrison, Singidunum, on the site. The garrison was continually strengthened and enlarged during the campaigns fought to keep the lower Danube. To the north of the Danube were the Barbarians, to the south the Roman Empire. During the second Danube campaign (AD 98–117) Trajan based one of the Danube fleets, the Classis Pannonica, at Singidunum, which no doubt also patrolled the Sava. During the third and last Danube campaign when Marcus Aurelius had to abandon Dacia to the east, the garrison was strengthened and the civilian settlement alongside grew into an important trading town. There was a bridge across the Sava to Taurunum at Zemun to connect the two garrisons. In 395 Singidunum passed to Byzantium and became the western border of the Byzantines who called it Alba Greaca, the 'White Town', probably from its white limestone walls. As a border town it suffered from invasions by the Huns, Sarmatians, Ostrogoths and Avars, with the Byzantine army retaking it for a time between the successive waves of invaders. By the end of the 7th century Byzantium had tired of rebuilding this border town and it was the Slavs who moved in 'drifting like autumn leaves' to settle here. They called it the 'White Town', Beograd in

Zemun: from the river the old buildings of the town and the park predominate, behind are the ubiquitous apartment blocks of new Belgrade.

Slavonic. In the 10th century the Byzantines again controlled the town though the new rivals, Hungary and Bulgaria, had arrived on the scene. Serbian rule began in 1284 with Dragutin, a vassal of the Hungarians, and the Serbs quickly moved into Belgrade and the surrounding area. However the Hungarians feared Serbian power and destroyed Belgrade in 1319.

In 1521 the Turks took the city and it was to remain Turkish for 346 years until it was handed back to the Serbs in 1867. Contrary to popular history, Belgrade enjoyed some considerable prosperity during part of the Turkish rule, being a bridgehead for trade on the Danube. It became the centre of Serbian life and was rebuilt, for the 20th or 30th time. After the First World War and the Hungarian occupation, Belgrade was returned to the newly formed Kingdom of Serbs, Croats and Slovenes, the kingdom that was to become Yugoslavia in 1928, and rebuilt again. In 1941 the Germans sent wave after wave of bombers to flatten it, and succeeded. When the city was liberated in October 1944 rebuilding started again and modern Belgrade, the city of Socialist realist architecture that we see today, had arrived.

I'm not alone in my opinion of Belgrade. In 1924 Negley Farson had this to say of the capital of the diverse nationalities of the Kingdom of Serbs, Croats and Slovenes.

'It is one of the ugliest cities imaginable, repulsively so! It is absolutely devoid of charm! The squalor or sordidness is not that of the Waza in Cairo, the slums of Whitechapel, or the lower east side of New York – the result of great poverty and unavoidable congestion – it is the nightmare of rotten bad taste. The worst eyesores have been built since the war.'

From the Danube one of the reasons for the neglected appearance of Belgrade is that it faces the Sava and belongs to this river rather than the Danube. When I arrived here in *Rozinante* the only place I found to berth was in an abandoned basin, with urine yellow industrial effluent trickling into the black mud, surrounded by dismembered cranes and warehouses with broken windows, yet only a short walk from down-town Belgrade. At Belgrade the Danube is a river fronted by commercial harbours, cranes and gantries, a river for the factories to empty industrial effluent and waste into, a river that is a convenient backyard tip and looks like it. A short distance up the Sava the front yard of Belgrade is more presentable; restaurants and bars face onto it, and it is here the cruise and trip boats come to.

Cruise boats going up and down river can be picked up in Belgrade and there are hydrofoil day-trips to the Gorge of Kazan. The Sava is stated to be navigable for 595km as far as Sisak, though large barges cannot get much above 100km up it. No canalisation of the Sava has been carried out and it is little used today except by small pleasure craft.

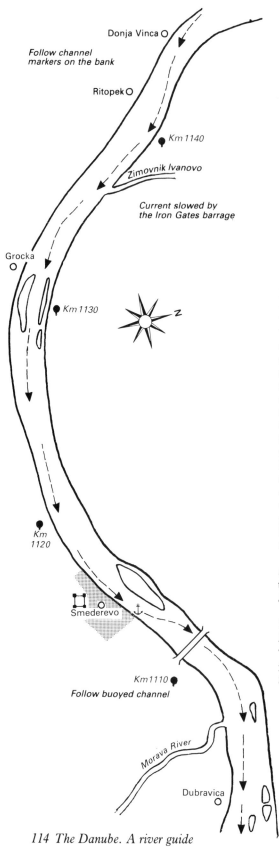

Km 1154 – Left bank
Pancevo

An old town now industrialised. Two old disused lighthouses mark the entrance to the harbour. The Yugoslav authorities, like the Bulgarians and worst of all the Romanians, have the least respect of all the Danube countries for the river in terms of dumping effluent and waste in it. From Belgrade the Danube becomes visibly more polluted and the invisible pollutants, acid waste, organic solvents, heavy metals and the like combined with fertiliser run-off and pesticides from agriculture around the river and its tributaries adds up to a deadly cocktail that is only now beginning to attract international attention.

Km 1116 – Right bank
Smederevo

In 1427 Smederevo was made the capital of Serbia and in 1430 the fortress of Smederevo was built in a single year to defend it against the advancing Turks. The stories behind its construction by the despot Djuradj Brankovic relate that the starving peasants who constructed it had to supply eggs to mix with the mortar as this made it set harder and that anyone who died in the construction was bricked up inside. It is a colossal fortress with walls up to 17ft (5m) thick and is said to have twenty-five defensive towers though I could only count the remains of less than half this number. The Turks had a difficult time taking it and it was not until 1459 that they had total control which they were to keep for the next 400 years. It remained in a good state of preservation until 1941 when it was being used by the Germans as an ammunition dump and mysteriously blew up.

The town of Smederevo, with the usual apartment blocks standing behind the old town, is known for its vineyards, producing *Smederevka* wines.

Km 1103·2 – Right bank
Morava River

The longest river in Serbia, some 500km long, flowing down from the western side of the Stara mountains.

Serbs

The popular idea of the Serbs and Serbia is derived largely from the brief episode when the Archduke Franz Ferdinand was assassinated in Sarajevo by a student from a small band of anarchists who wanted to draw world attention to the plight of Bosnia and the Serbs. Instead it started the Great War which in the end would give Serbia the independence it had wanted and struggled to get for centuries. To our grandfathers, who were more familiar with the Balkans than we are today, the Balkans were 'the tinder-box of Europe' and Serbs were a quarrelsome bunch, always making wars or feuding.

The Serbs are one of the tribes of the Slavs, cousins of the Slovaks, who migrated out of southern Russia in the sixth century and over further centuries established themselves in the Balkan valleys and highlands. The Slavs were not a nation, but a loose association of tribes and clans, some closer than others through marriage or the necessity to defend their lands from other invaders. In the 11th and 12th centuries a Serbian state of sorts established itself with a capital at Prizren. As with so many of the other nations and kingdoms along the Danube, the invading Turks interrupted things. The Serbs met the Turks at Kosovo, an upland plain in the south of Serbia, on St Vitus's Day in 1389, a date etched in Serbian folk memory. The Serbs were defeated by the Turks and for nearly 500 years were ruled by them, often brutally.

There were numerous uprisings by the Serbs, though these were often thwarted by the Serbs themselves who were given to much internecine bickering and feuds which lasted for generations. In 1804 the first concerted rising under Black George, a prosperous pig farmer, used guerrilla tactics with great effect. The uprising was punctured by a rival leader, Milosh Obrenovitch, who captured and beheaded Black George. Nonetheless he made part of northern Serbia autonomous, though owing allegiance to the Turks. His successor, Michael, was killed in the vendetta with the Black George clan, but the dynasty carried on with Alexander Obrenovitch on the Serbian throne at the turn of the century. The Russians, who had aspirations in the Balkans, sought out one Peter Karageorgevitch of the Black George clan, and in 1903 helped him to take power in a bloody coup. Bernard Newman heard an eye-witness account of the bloody events years later which he relates in *Balkan Background*.

'At a given signal – the raising of a blind in the Russian Legation – a group of officers rushed into the palace. Among their leaders was Colonel Maschin, brother-in-law of the queen: the guards were in the plot and did not resist. Alexander and Draga attempted to hide in a linen closet, but were dragged out and slashed to pieces – as bloody a murder as ever graced Balkan annals. The remnants of their bodies were laid out in the kitchen, and servants cleared up the mess while the new King Peter Karageorgevitch walked in to take possession of the palace.'

Things were still not straightforward, for there was another actor on the Serbian stage at this time, Nikola Pastitch, who had been fighting for Serbian autonomy since the 1880s. He controlled an organisation that used terrorism as an instrument of control, popularly known as the Black Hand, and it is this organisation that was responsible for the assassination of the Archduke Franz Ferdinand at Sarajevo. The Serbs came out on the winning side of the war they had ignited and the Kingdom of Serbs, Croats and Slovenes was formed, to become Yugoslavia, the Land of the South Slavs, in 1928.

It is still dominated by the Serbs; Serbia is the most prosperous part of the diverse regions making up the country, and Serbs to a large extent control what goes on. On my second trip through here there was much dissent over the fact that Serbia, one of the richest provinces, was supporting the poorer provinces. Workers went on strike, there were marches in Belgrade, and the Serbs threatened to declare a quasi-independent status if their living standards were not improved even if that meant they were living better than others in Yugoslavia. The Serbs were at it again. From the events at the turn of the century when the Serbs and others were bickering amongst each other we get the verb, 'to Balkanise', meaning to divide a region up into small antagonistic states, always unstable and corrupt, likely to erupt into civil war at any time. Yugoslavia is a country made up of diverse groups: Catholics, Orthodox and Muslims; Serbs and Croats who can understand each others language, but not read it, as the Serbs use the Cyrillic and the Croats the Roman alphabet; the Slovenes who have difficulty understanding Serbo-Croat though their language has the same roots; and the Albanians and Montenegrins in the south who have separate cultural roots. Now Tito, the man who unified the diverse parts of Yugoslavia for so many years, has gone, and the rumblings of the different cultures can be heard again, Serbia louder than the others.

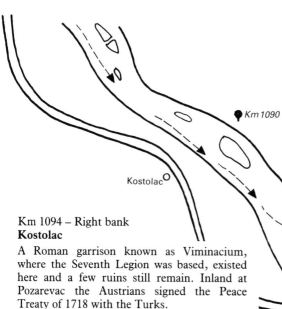

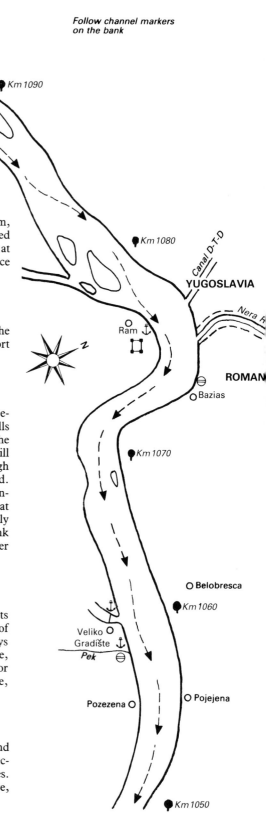

Km 1094 – Right bank
Kostolac

A Roman garrison known as Viminacium, where the Seventh Legion was based, existed here and a few ruins still remain. Inland at Pozarevac the Austrians signed the Peace Treaty of 1718 with the Turks.

Km 1077 – Right bank
Ram

Near the village there are the ruins of the castle of Ramski Grad, originally a Roman fort called Armata.

Km 1075 – Left bank
Nera River

The Nera is the border on the left bank between Yugoslavia and Romania. The foothills of the Banat Mountains rise here towards the Carpathians in the northeast. Watchtowers will be seen along both sides of the river though they are more often than not unmanned. Yugoslavia continues on the right bank for another 220km until the border with Bulgaria at km 845. (The rest of this chapter will deal only with the right bank. Romania on the left bank of the Danube will be dealt with in Chapter VIII.)

Km 1059 – Right bank
Veliko Gradiste

The Yugoslavian customs station for boats crossing from Romania. It lies at the mouth of the River Pek, a gold-bearing river in days gone by. The Romans had a fort here, Punicum, and it is said that the Emperor Trajan built a bridge across the Danube, though no traces of it remain.

The Iron Gates

From here until Kladovo at kilometre 934 and Turnu Severin on the Romanian side, this section of the Danube is known as the Iron Gates. In Yugoslavian it is called the Djerdap Gorge,

tion of taking a craft of this size through a whirlpool. It is neither more nor less. It is like a succession of mechanical disasters – as if something has gone wrong with the ship. She strains, the steering gear doesn't answer, and the engine goes crazy. We swung round to face an engine-turned strip of grey water, on which I saw the Danube towing-steamer – broadside to me in the stream – cutting for the Roumanian shore.'

Negley Farson and *Flame* were whooshed through the Iron Gates and managed to avoid the rocks and reefs that have wrecked so many craft. Coming upstream against the current was a problem that the engineers attempted to solve in a number of ways. At km 949 a short canal by-pass was built for 2½km in 1891–1896 so that ships could avoid this section where rapids and rocks made navigation especially difficult. The Sip canal didn't lessen the current greatly, with the 600hp tug *Thommen* taking over an hour to get up with a single loaded barge on the inauguration run. A cable-tug, the *Vaskapu*, was installed which hauled itself up on a chain laid along the bed of the canal. Eventually it was replaced by a railway line along the side of the canal with a powerful locomotive to haul barge-tows up the canal on a long cable. The *Vaskapu* was moved upstream to the Greben area where a chain was laid so it could help vessels past this difficult section. In 1967 the old cable-tug was still in place and helped John Marriner to get his yacht *September Tide* up the Danube.

'Ahead in the now strong daylight I could see a very odd ship. Two funnels abreast each other, a wide beam and smoke pouring from her, the elderly tug *Vaskapu* seemed stationary in the Danube...What, I had wondered, had she been stationed there for? Now I knew. *Vaskapu*, built I do not care to think how many years ago, wood burning, contemptuous of time, was the mariner's friend. Without her, none but the very exceptionally strong could ever get by the current of Cape Greben. Operated by the joint Yugoslav-Romanian river authority, she sat in midstream clinging coyly to her underwater cable which stretched for a mile or so on the river bed. For *Vaskapu* was no ordinary ship; no sordid propellers for her, no paddles. She relied on the unusual, on her cable, for motive power.'

When I sailed *Rozinante* down this stretch of the river it had been tamed by the huge Iron Gates Dam. Now it is more like a huge inland lake, a piece of Switzerland or upper Austria transplanted to Yugoslavia. When the locks at the dam were closed the water backed up over

Old signal station at the entrance to the Gorge of Kazan which indicated the state of the river for navigation.

in German the Eisernes Tor, in Romanian the Portile de Fier, all meaning the Iron Gates or Gorge. Until the huge dam and lock complex at kilometre 944, built between 1960 and 1971, which backed the river up and slowed it down to a virtual stand-still, this section was the most difficult and dangerous of any on the Danube. Craft using this section of the river had to take on a pilot and barge-tows often had to be broken up and brought through one by one or utilise a second tug to get through. In 1925 Negley Farson described what it was like taking his small yacht down this section.

'*Flame* fought with her rudder like a horse trying to take over the bit. The engine slowed down almost to stopping, and then raced as if our stern were sticking out in the air. *Flame* wobbled and shook, and then straightened out to streak past five red buoys. This is the sensa-

this section submerging islands, towns, villages, farms, old forts and castles, forests and fields. Most of the old perils of the Danube were also submerged and now there are virtually no dangers to navigation in the buoyed channel. Most of the towns and villages were rebuilt and some of the ancient monuments were moved to safety higher up, though a few seem to have gone missing despite the assurances of Romanian officials charged with their care. In the dammed up section at low water the top branches of the trees on the islands stick up out of the water, whole forests on some of the islands, creating a surreal aspect and a danger to small boats. In the section around Golubac I got lost in *Rozinante* amongst the treetops of a submerged forest and feared that there might be more just under the water that could rip a hole in the bottom of the boat. Eventually I found a way out and moored up in a tiny cove further on by the simple expedient of dropping anchor on top of a partially submerged tree and taking a line to one of its branches.

Km 1040·5 – Right bank
Golubac Castle
The castle stands next to the Danube on a rocky bluff, though it must have been much higher above the river before it was flooded. The town of Golubac was rebuilt higher up as is evident from the new construction of the houses. The castle occupies the site of a Roman castle called Columbarium, the 'dovecote', and was built sometime in the 14th or early 15th century only to be captured by the Turks in 1428. They were to hold it for 260 years until abandoning it in 1688. Its name is derived from the Serbo-Croat for a dove, *golub*, echoing the Roman name. Today it is an impressive structure with nine towers around thick ring walls.

There are numerous stories attached to the castle. The caves around the castle were said to be the breeding ground of huge mosquitoes and biting flies. The mosquitoes were said to come from a dragon slain near here by a knight, inevitably a George, who after his valiant deed tried unsuccessfully to throw the body of the dragon in the Danube. The rotting carcass was the source of the pestilent mosquitoes who hereafter plagued the area. Presumably DDT removed the creatures as there were few mosquitoes here compared to further downstream. Under Turkish control the myths did not dry up. A beautiful Turkish girl, Zuleika, part of the harem of the Governor of Moldova, had an affair with a Hungarian noble. Her punishment for adultery was to be tied to the rock in the mid-

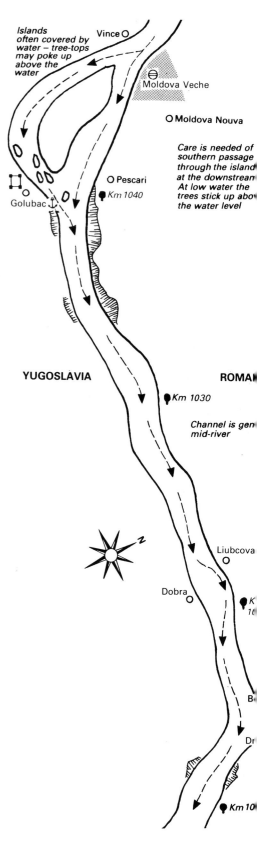

dle of the Danube until she had repented of her sin, in Turkish 'Ba-ba-kai' means 'Repent of thy sin', which is the name of the rock to this day. She was rescued by the Hungarian noble who later taunted the mortally wounded governor with his Zuleika who, even worse, was by now a Christian. A variation on the story relates how a beautiful Christian girl was kept prisoner in Golubac and was punished for trying to escape by being chained to the rock where she died.

Today only treetops remain to show where Babakai and the other islands around it used to obstruct the channel. Like stelai telling an ancient story, the tree tops, blackened limbs with the bark peeling off, reach up just above the surface when the water levels are low, an eerie submerged world remembering the tales of Golubac and Babakai.

Km 1039 to km 1035·5

The Danube enters a steep-sided gorge where the mountains drop precipitously for 600m (nearly 2000ft) down to the river which is squeezed into a 150m (nearly 500ft) gap. Before the dam this was a stretch of rapids and rocks. This is a silent place where every sound, a bird call, a dog barking, the occasional car or truck, can be heard echoing from cliff to cliff.

Km 1029
Stenka Channel

In the 1880s a channel was blasted through the rocks for three kilometres to make a safe channel to get river traffic through this once difficult section. Although it was often called the Stenka Canal, it was not a purpose-made waterway like the Sip Canal downstream, but a channel cleared of most the dangers to navigation.

Km 1021·5 – Right bank
Dobra

A small village rebuilt higher up after the flooding of the valley. It was once a Serbian guard post. Boats going downstream had to take on a pilot here until Kladovo.

Km 1012 to km 999
Upper Klissura

The Danube enters the second narrow section, called the Upper Klissura, with steep cliffs on either side. Klissura is a Romanian word derived from the Greek *kleisoura* meaning a crevice or a crack. This was formerly also a difficult section with rapids and rocks making navigation dangerous. An old chart of the

Danube, before it was tamed by the dam, shows rocks obstructing the river so that the channel winds from side to side. At kilometre 1003 the channel hugs the Serbian shore to avoid rocks obstructing most of the river though if you go too close there are also rocks close to the Serbian side. It was a navigator's nightmare and it is no wonder that pilots were required for this section.

Km 1011 – Right bank

Commemorative tablets to the Emperor Tiberius could be seen on the bank here, but with the flooding of the valley they were removed.

Km 1004·3 – Right bank
Lepenski Vir

Near here a significant archaeological discovery has been made which may upset the whole theory that man learnt to become a farmer, a settled animal rather than a hunter and gatherer, around the Mesopotamian area from whence the new culture spread to other parts of the world. A well laid-out town with 59 houses dating from 8000 years ago has been excavated and if the dating is correct, this settlement is as old or older than the Mesopotamian settlements. This means that all those civilizing influences thought to have developed in the Middle East probably developed simultaneously and independently here and that Neolithic civilization spread from the Danube throughout Europe. The discovery is revolutionary and if further finds reinforce it, the archaeological textbooks will have to be rewritten.

Km 999
Greben

The rock at Greben marked another of the difficult stretches on the Danube before the dam was built. It was to here that the cable-tug *Vaskapu* was moved from the Sip Canal to help barges over this dangerous section. When John Marriner came up to the Greben with *September Tide* he would not have got past this section without the *Vaskapu*.

'Now we were in the thick of it again. *September Tide* was making virtually no headway. I kept both motors at maximum revs and looked constantly at the houses in Greben village ashore. No progress.'

Marriner got a tow from the *Vaskapu* and so got past this section though he needed the skills of Alexander, a Romanian pilot, to keep out of the main force of the current so some headway could be made and to avoid the numerous underwater rocks.

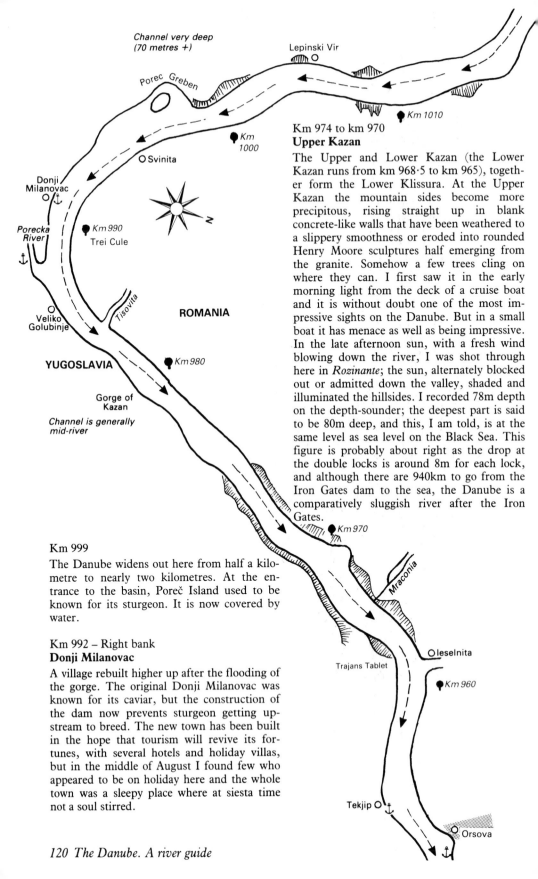

Channel very deep
(70 metres +)

Porec Greben

Lepinski Vir

Km 1010

Km 1000

Svinita

Donji
Milanovac

Porecka
River

Km 990
Trei Cule

Tisovita

ROMANIA

Veliko
Golubinje

YUGOSLAVIA

Km 980

Gorge of
Kazan

Channel is generally
mid-river

Mraconia

Km 970

Ieselnita

Trajans Tablet

Km 960

Tekjip

Orsova

Km 974 to km 970
Upper Kazan

The Upper and Lower Kazan (the Lower Kazan runs from km 968·5 to km 965), together form the Lower Klissura. At the Upper Kazan the mountain sides become more precipitous, rising straight up in blank concrete-like walls that have been weathered to a slippery smoothness or eroded into rounded Henry Moore sculptures half emerging from the granite. Somehow a few trees cling on where they can. I first saw it in the early morning light from the deck of a cruise boat and it is without doubt one of the most impressive sights on the Danube. But in a small boat it has menace as well as being impressive. In the late afternoon sun, with a fresh wind blowing down the river, I was shot through here in *Rozinante*; the sun, alternately blocked out or admitted down the valley, shaded and illuminated the hillsides. I recorded 78m depth on the depth-sounder; the deepest part is said to be 80m deep, and this, I am told, is at the same level as sea level on the Black Sea. This figure is probably about right as the drop at the double locks is around 8m for each lock, and although there are 940km to go from the Iron Gates dam to the sea, the Danube is a comparatively sluggish river after the Iron Gates.

Km 999

The Danube widens out here from half a kilometre to nearly two kilometres. At the entrance to the basin, Poreč Island used to be known for its sturgeon. It is now covered by water.

Km 992 – Right bank
Donji Milanovac

A village rebuilt higher up after the flooding of the gorge. The original Donji Milanovac was known for its caviar, but the construction of the dam now prevents sturgeon getting upstream to breed. The new town has been built in the hope that tourism will revive its fortunes, with several hotels and holiday villas, but in the middle of August I found few who appeared to be on holiday here and the whole town was a sleepy place where at siesta time not a soul stirred.

Donji Milanovac II, rebuilt higher up the slopes after the old village was flooded.

Trajan's Tablet, moved higher up to a new position after the valley was flooded. Much of the inscription has been lost, but the first three lines can still be deciphered.

Km 968·5 to km 965
Lower Kazan

Km 964 – Right bank
Trajan's Tablet

This tablet set into the cliff-face in a small inlet records the achievement of Trajan. Only part of the original inscription is left, which reads:

T A B U L A T R A I A N A
IMP. CAESAR DIVI NERVAE F
NERVA TRAIANV AVG. GERM
PONT. MAXIMV. TRIBI OT
RIAE O

The expanded inscription originally read:

Imperator Caesar divi Nervae filius – Nervae Trajanus Augustus Germanicus – Pontifex Maximus tribunitae potestatis quartum – Pater patriae consul quartum – montis et fluviis anfractibus – superatis viam patefecit.

The Emperor Caesar son of the divine Nerva – Nerva Trajan Augustus Germanicus – High priest and for the fourth time Tribune – Father of the country and for the fourth time Consul – overcame the hazards of the mountain and the river – and opened this road.

Before the flooding of the gorge the tablet was set at a point lower down where the Emperor Tiberius (14–37AD) started a road around the cliffs which was finished by Trajan (98–117AD) around 103AD. It was constructed by drilling holes in the cliff-face and supporting a road of planks on beams sticking out of the cliff. It was roofed over to stop attacks from the cliff-top. Until the gorge was flooded the holes that had supported the beams were clearly visible and Trajan's tablet commemorating the construction of the road served as a handy fireplace for Serbian fishermen, its inscription blackened from countless fires and despoiled by Serbo-Croat graffiti. Trajan marched his legions along this road to the bridge he had built across the Danube to Turnu Severin for the campaigns against Decebalus, king of the Dacians. The campaign was fought for the gold mined in the hills of Transylvania and to secure the territory on the western side of the Black Sea. The Emperors Vespasian and Domitian were to follow him until the tribes on the north side of the Danube proved impossible to contain and Rome retreated to the southern shore and then upriver to Belgrade.

Km 956·5 – Right bank
Tekjip

Another of the villages rebuilt in the gorge after the old village was submerged.

Km 952 to Km 950

Until the gorge was flooded the island of Ada Kaleh existed here, a piece of Turkey forgotten when the Congress of Berlin of 1878 took the island from the Turks, but neglected to give it to anyone else. The Austrians had held the island for a while, calling it New Orsova, and built a citadel here that they were forced to hand over to the Turks in 1739. From that time until the occupants were resettled in the 1960s as the Iron Gates dam neared completion, it was a predominantly Turkish settlement.

The island, whose name means 'Island Fortress' in Turkish, was probably settled by soldiers' families after the Turks obtained it in 1739. In 1878, after the Congress of Berlin divided the Balkans up, the Turks continued to live here. After the First World War it was given to Romania who left it pretty much as it had been and did not interfere with its way of life. When Patrick Leigh Fermor visited it in 1934 he found a piece of the Levant still sandwiched between the Carpathians and the Balkans in Middle Europe.

'Balconied houses gathered about the mosque and small workshops for Turkish Delight and cigarettes, and all around these crumbled the remains of a massive fortress...A pathway among pear trees and mulberries led to a little cemetery where turbanned headstones leant askew and in one corner lay the tomb of a dervish prince from Bokhara who had ended his life here after wandering the world, 'poor as a mouse', in search of the most beautiful place on earth and the one most sheltered from harm and mishap.'

He listened to the *imam* call from the mosque, which amusingly had been built in the former Austrian administration building, and heard the echo of Islam bounce around the hills of Kazan, an echo of the Empire which had once controlled all of this region.

With the flooding of the gorge the important buildings on the island were removed so that the mosque, baths and other structures could be rebuilt on Simian Island. The Turks were resettled in Constanţa on the Black Sea coast or returned to Turkey. Despite assurances from the Romanians, the dismantled buildings seem to have gone astray or, most probably, have been dumped somewhere, with the bulk probably still on Ada Kaleh under the water.

Km 949
Iron Gates

The narrow gorge that begins here is the Iron Gates proper, although the name now applies to the whole section of river between the Car-

The first lock of the double lock system at the Iron Gates dam.

pathians and Balkans from kilometre 1059 at Veliko Gradiste. Like many of the other sections, this stretch of the river was highly dangerous with underwater rocks and rapids making transit difficult. Since the building of the Iron Gates dam this section has become a wide trouble-free stretch of river with all the dangers some 40m and more deep. This contrasts vividly with what it was like when at extreme low water there could be less than a metre over some of the dangers in the channel.

Km 946·7 to km 944
Sip Canal
To get over the worst section of this part of the river the Sip Canal was built from 1891 to 1896. It was a narrow canal on the right bank, approximately 2½km long with 2m depth and a fall of 3·7m over the whole distance.

Km 943
Iron Gates Barrage and Double Lock
Officially the Djerdap Power Station, this huge dam and lock system – there are double locks on both the Yugoslavian side and the Romanian side – has drastically altered the landscape for more than a hundred kilometres upstream, creating a huge mountain lake, and radically changing the nature of navigation on the Danube. Before the dam opened it took 4½ days to transit a full barge train through the Iron Gates. Today it takes just 15 hours.

The earlier attempts at regulating navigation through the Iron Gates were only partially successful. The channel blasted through the rocks at Greben and the Sip Canal constructed in the late 19th century could only be marginally improved upon in the early 20th century and so after the Second World War, Yugoslavia and Romania decided on a definitive solution. Although improving navigation on the Danube was high on the agenda, more important to the two developing countries was the huge amount of power that would be generated by the hydroelectric stations, six turbines for Yugoslavia and six for Romania, that would be installed in the dam. The annual output of the power station was to be in the region of 10 to 12 billion kilowatts, which, shared between the two countries amounted to slightly less than the total annual output of Yugoslavia and to just over a third of Romania's total output when construction began on the dam in 1960.

The dam stretches for 1278m (4220ft) across the river and is over 70m (230ft) high. At each end the two locks are 310m (1023ft) long, 34m (112ft) wide, with a depth of 4·5m (14·85ft). The locks can accommodate one of the large pusher tugs and nine 1000-tonne barges or a small ship up to 5000 tonnes. In *Rozinante*, all nineteen feet of her, we were squeezed in with two barge tows each with four of the smaller 800-tonne barges, and another tug, and still there was room to spare. One difficulty which the engineers had not thought about was the effect of strong winds blowing downstream and straight into the first lock, making operation of the huge lock gates difficult and manoeuvring for large barge trains dangerous in the approach to the lock. I had to wait with several barge trains for a day because of gale force winds blowing down river, the wind funnelled to gusts of over forty knots through the Gorge of Kazan.

The banking up of the waters for over a hundred kilometres upstream meant that whole villages and towns had to be rebuilt higher up: some 8500 people in Yugoslavia and 14500 in Romania had to be resettled. In addition the road and railway line that ran along the river had to be reconstructed higher up along with electricity and telephone lines and other services. The dam was opened in 1972 with one double-lock open while work continued on the other. It is now fully operational and though the environmentalists may deplore the destruction of the valley upriver from the dam, the argument is a difficult one because river transport is the most energy efficient of all the systems and if power were not produced by the hydroelectric scheme then it would have to be produced using fossil fuels or nuclear power, with the certain and uncertain pollution from these sources of energy.

Km 934 – Right bank
Kladovo
An old Roman garrison town, now a modern dormitory town for the Iron Gates dam and its workers. It is the customs and immigration post for boats coming from Turnu Severin on the opposite bank.

Km 864
Barrage and lock
The Prahovo dam and lock, like the Iron Gates dam, has been built jointly between Yugoslavia and Romania. It is not on the same scale as the Iron Locks, but is still an impressive piece of engineering that has tamed the river and produces a useful amount of hydroelectricity.

The top lock of the double lock system at the Iron
Gates dam.

Fishing boats at Prahovo. Like all river boats powered by muscle they are long and slim so they can be easily rowed ag
the current, rather than short and fat for load carrying.

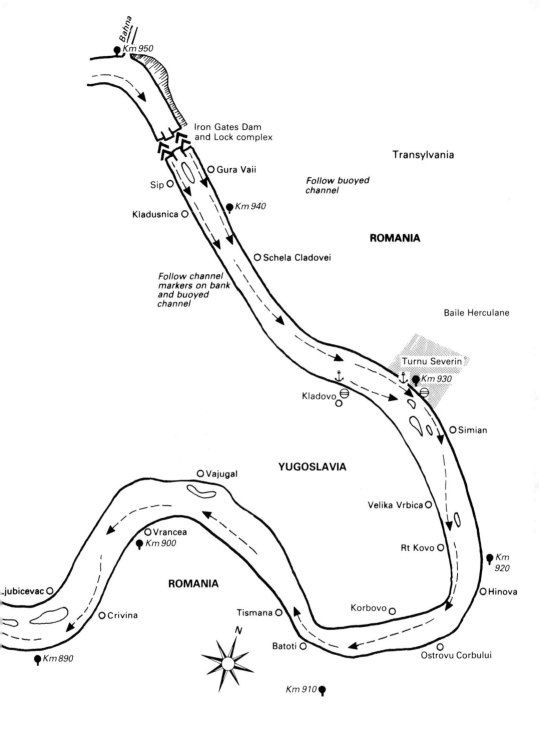

Bahna
Km 950

Iron Gates Dam
and Lock complex

Transylvania

Gura Vaii

*Follow buoyed
channel*

Sip

Km 940

Kladusnica

ROMANIA

Schela Cladovei

*Follow channel
markers on bank
and buoyed
channel*

Baile Herculane

Turnu Severin
Km 930

Kladovo

Simian

YUGOSLAVIA

Vajugal

Velika Vrbica

Vrancea
Km 900

Rt Kovo

Km
920

jubicevac

ROMANIA

Hinova

Crivina

Tismana

Korbovo

N

Batoti

Ostrovu Corbului

Km 890

Km 910

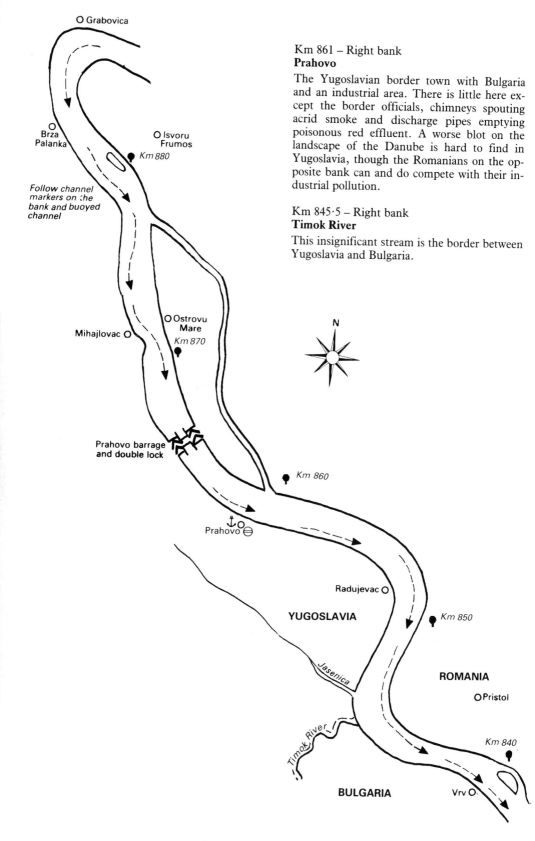

Km 861 – Right bank
Prahovo

The Yugoslavian border town with Bulgaria and an industrial area. There is little here except the border officials, chimneys spouting acrid smoke and discharge pipes emptying poisonous red effluent. A worse blot on the landscape of the Danube is hard to find in Yugoslavia, though the Romanians on the opposite bank can and do compete with their industrial pollution.

Km 845·5 – Right bank
Timok River

This insignificant stream is the border between Yugoslavia and Bulgaria.

Grabovica

Brza
Palanka

Isvoru
Frumos

Km 880

*Follow channel
markers on the
bank and buoyed
channel*

Mihajlovac

Ostrovu
Mare

Km 870

**Prahovo barrage
and double lock**

Km 860

Prahovo

Radujevac

YUGOSLAVIA

Km 850

Jasenica

ROMANIA

Pristol

Timok River

Km 840

BULGARIA

Vrv

N

VII. Bulgaria

VIDIN TO SILISTRA

Km 790 – Right bank
Vidin
Once described as a fairy-tale city with spires and cupolas and minarets, Vidin is now dominated by concrete high-rise buildings that obscure the old town and the fortress. The Romans built a fort here on the site of a Celtic settlement and called the place Bononia. After the Romans left the Bulgars moved in and called it Bidin, hence todays Vidin. In the 13th century the fort was enlarged by the Hungarians and by the 14th century was the capital of northwest Bulgaria. In 1398 the Turks occupied it and apart from a few brief periods they were here until the 19th century. Osman Pazvantoglu, whose tomb lies nearby, was a pasha with a yen for more power who for fifteen years (1792–1807) ruled Vidin and the surrounding region as an autonomous despot, making raids into Ottoman territory as far as Sofia. He considerably strengthened the fortress using French engineers sent by Napoleon who had ambitions in Bulgaria. On his death the Turks returned. The appearance of the fort and old town, with seven ring walls and a moat and twenty-five minarets, earned it the title of Baba Vida or 'Grandmother Vida', the name still used for the fort. When Bernard Newman cycled down the Danube he described it thus:

'From the top of one of the towers I got a wonderful view of the town and fortress of Vidin. The place is situated on a very slight elevation which, when the Danube is in flood, is almost an island, for behind the town, to the west, stretches a series of marshes which, in flood, attain a breadth of several miles. The water defences of the town were indeed unique for, apart from their natural strength, the moats which surrounded the old town could be filled at short notice with water from the Danube or its tributary Topolovitza.'

On the Bulgarian side of the Danube the white lime-stone cliffs force the Danube eastwards.

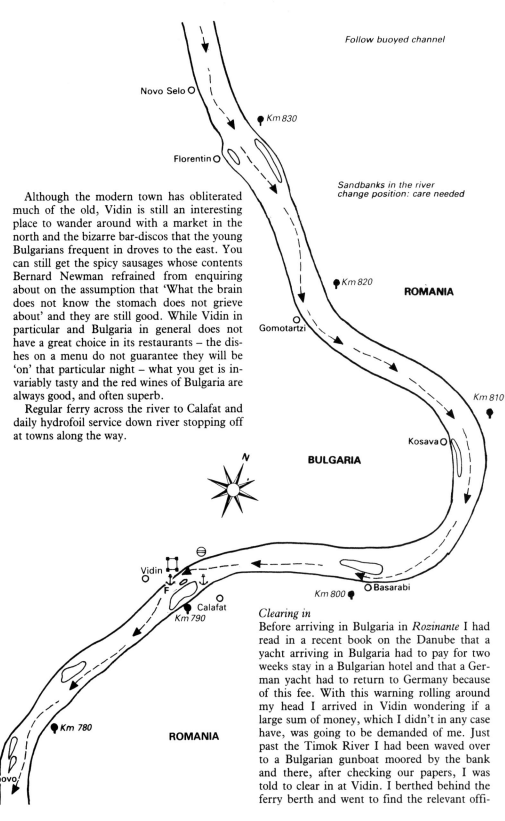

Follow buoyed channel

Novo Selo O

● *Km 830*

Florentin O

Sandbanks in the river change position: care needed

Although the modern town has obliterated much of the old, Vidin is still an interesting place to wander around with a market in the north and the bizarre bar-discos that the young Bulgarians frequent in droves to the east. You can still get the spicy sausages whose contents Bernard Newman refrained from enquiring about on the assumption that 'What the brain does not know the stomach does not grieve about' and they are still good. While Vidin in particular and Bulgaria in general does not have a great choice in its restaurants – the dishes on a menu do not guarantee they will be 'on' that particular night – what you get is invariably tasty and the red wines of Bulgaria are always good, and often superb.

Regular ferry across the river to Calafat and daily hydrofoil service down river stopping off at towns along the way.

● *Km 820*

ROMANIA

O Gomotartzi

Km 810 ●

Kosava O

N

BULGARIA

Vidin O

F

Calafat O
● *Km 790*

● *Km 800* O Basarabi

Clearing in

Before arriving in Bulgaria in *Rozinante* I had read in a recent book on the Danube that a yacht arriving in Bulgaria had to pay for two weeks stay in a Bulgarian hotel and that a German yacht had to return to Germany because of this fee. With this warning rolling around my head I arrived in Vidin wondering if a large sum of money, which I didn't in any case have, was going to be demanded of me. Just past the Timok River I had been waved over to a Bulgarian gunboat moored by the bank and there, after checking our papers, I was told to clear in at Vidin. I berthed behind the ferry berth and went to find the relevant offi-

● *Km 780*

ROMANIA

O
Simenovo

cials. In a dusty old office I found the harbourmaster, a grey-haired plump gentleman
who seemed distressed at my presence. In
pidgin German I understood that I was supposed to clear in at the port some two kilometres upstream. I got him to understand that
it would take me a good hour to get upstream
(the current in the Danube is still running at
3–4 knots off Vidin) and wheezing and sighing
in sympathy, we went back to his office to
phone the officials at the ferry port. Ten
minutes later they were in the harbourmaster's
office, smiles all round, a cursory check of the
contents of *Rozinante*, and I was issued with
papers to cruise the Danube in Bulgaria. No
two weeks' hotel costs. A good deal less paperwork than in neighbouring Yugoslavia. And a
politeness that made me feel welcome in Bulgaria, a welcome that remained wherever I
went.

Bulgaria is a bureaucratic country that can
be difficult to travel in, but the effort is often
rewarded. Everywhere in Bulgaria I found an
intense interest in *Rozinante's* trip down the
Danube and a friendliness and generosity that
turns many stereotypes of the country upside
down – which just goes to show that you can't
believe everything you read.

Km 769·5 – Right bank
Artchar
A small town that was once Ratiaris, Roman
capital of Upper Thrace, Dacia Repenisis,
which Trajan fortified during his Dacian
campaign.

Km 744 – Right bank
Lom
Situated by the Lom River (km 741·5), the
town is a rival to Vidin. It is said to be built on
the site of a Roman garrison, Almus. The
town is spread out along the banks of the
Danube, a characteristic which caused Bernard
Newman to call it an 'overgrown village… a
little place spread over a large area.' I know, I
had to walk five kilometres under a hot Balkan
sun to get petrol. Bulgarians are allowed to
have their own private plots to grow vegetables
and keep livestock, and every house has a
patch of land so intensely cultivated that the
green of growing vegetables, dotted with the
red of tomatoes and peppers is almost fluores-
cent. Many also have a small haystack for the
livestock fitted into the scheme of things –
mini farms lined up next to each other.

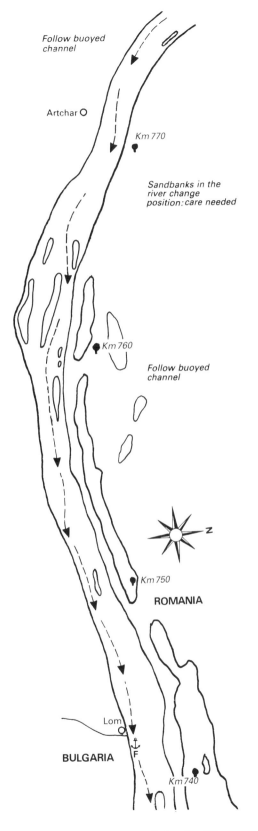

Follow buoyed channel

Artchar O

Km 770

Sandbanks in the river change position: care needed

Km 760

Follow buoyed channel

Km 750

ROMANIA

Lom

Km 740

BULGARIA

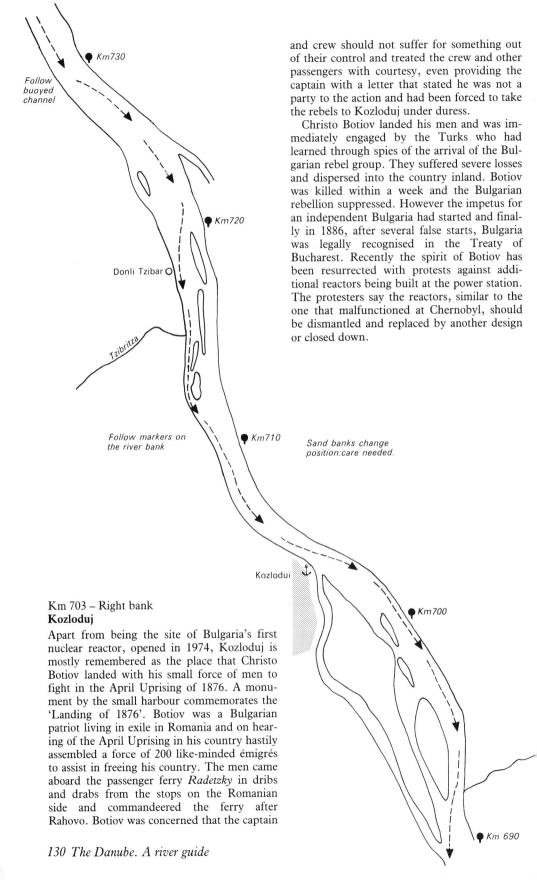

Km730

Follow
buoyed
channel

Km720

Donli Tzibar

Tzibritza

Follow markers on
the river bank

Km710

Sand banks change
position:care needed.

Kozlodui

Km700

Km690

and crew should not suffer for something out of their control and treated the crew and other passengers with courtesy, even providing the captain with a letter that stated he was not a party to the action and had been forced to take the rebels to Kozloduj under duress.

Christo Botiov landed his men and was immediately engaged by the Turks who had learned through spies of the arrival of the Bulgarian rebel group. They suffered severe losses and dispersed into the country inland. Botiov was killed within a week and the Bulgarian rebellion suppressed. However the impetus for an independent Bulgaria had started and finally in 1886, after several false starts, Bulgaria was legally recognised in the Treaty of Bucharest. Recently the spirit of Botiov has been resurrected with protests against additional reactors being built at the power station. The protesters say the reactors, similar to the one that malfunctioned at Chernobyl, should be dismantled and replaced by another design or closed down.

Km 703 – Right bank
Kozloduj

Apart from being the site of Bulgaria's first nuclear reactor, opened in 1974, Kozloduj is mostly remembered as the place that Christo Botiov landed with his small force of men to fight in the April Uprising of 1876. A monument by the small harbour commemorates the 'Landing of 1876'. Botiov was a Bulgarian patriot living in exile in Romania and on hearing of the April Uprising in his country hastily assembled a force of 200 like-minded émigrés to assist in freeing his country. The men came aboard the passenger ferry *Radetzky* in dribs and drabs from the stops on the Romanian side and commandeered the ferry after Rahovo. Botiov was concerned that the captain

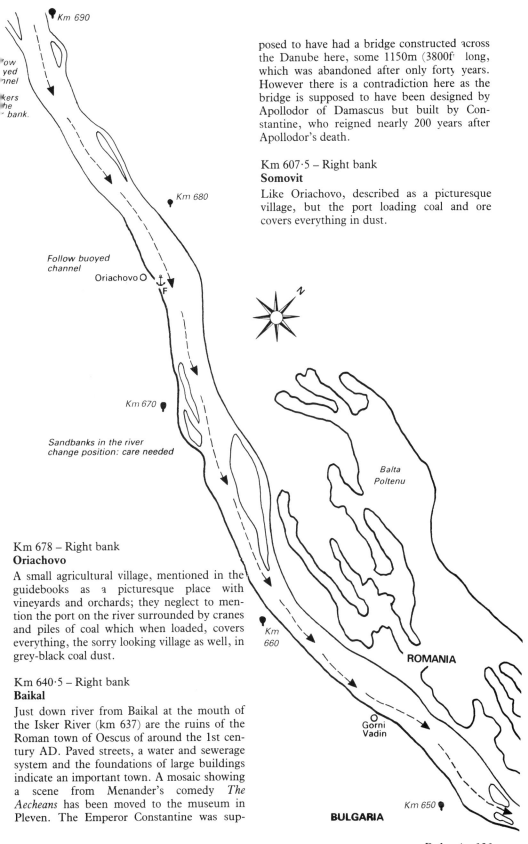

Km 690

ow
yed
nnel

kers
he
bank.

Km 680

Follow buoyed
channel

Oriachovo O ⚓
F

Km 670

Sandbanks in the river
change position: care needed

posed to have had a bridge constructed across the Danube here, some 1150m (3800f long, which was abandoned after only forty years. However there is a contradiction here as the bridge is supposed to have been designed by Apollodor of Damascus but built by Constantine, who reigned nearly 200 years after Apollodor's death.

Km 607·5 – Right bank
Somovit

Like Oriachovo, described as a picturesque village, but the port loading coal and ore covers everything in dust.

N

Balta
Poltenu

Km 678 – Right bank
Oriachovo

A small agricultural village, mentioned in the guidebooks as a picturesque place with vineyards and orchards; they neglect to mention the port on the river surrounded by cranes and piles of coal which when loaded, covers everything, the sorry looking village as well, in grey-black coal dust.

Km
660

ROMANIA

Km 640·5 – Right bank
Baikal

Just down river from Baikal at the mouth of the Isker River (km 637) are the ruins of the Roman town of Oescus of around the 1st century AD. Paved streets, a water and sewerage system and the foundations of large buildings indicate an important town. A mosaic showing a scene from Menander's comedy *The Aecheans* has been moved to the museum in Pleven. The Emperor Constantine was sup-

O
Gorni
Vadin

Km 650

BULGARIA

Bulgarian summers While the Romanian side of the Danube is virtually deserted, the Bulgarians use the river for recreation. In these lower reaches the river spreads out into marshy lagoons on the Romanian side and cuts into the white limestone of the Balkans on the Bulgarian side. Islands are dotted about the river with glaring white sandy beaches and thick green vegetation behind, like a vision of the Amazon and a quite incongruous geography for Europe. The channel winds in and out of the islands and sandbanks. The channel changes as parts of the river silt up and with scanty buoyage in places I often found I was navigating over the tops of submerged trees and bushes where I thought the channel should be according to charts of the river only five years old. Usually I retraced our course and waited until a barge tow came along so I could follow them along the main channel. In other places I took *Rozinante* up old channels and creeks to find quite idyllic spots where I could run the boat into the bank and spend the night in wonderful solitude or in a small village. The police never seemed to mind despite all the warnings about Bulgaria and its officials I had encountered before leaving.

In places the Bulgarian beaches look like something from the crowded shores of the south of France with bodies everywhere, in the water, lying in the sun on bright beach towels under bright sun umbrellas, pottering about in canoes and kayaks and occasionally small run-abouts. In other places you think the river bank is deserted until you spot a tent amongst the trees, a fisherman under the shade of a willow, a tar-black punt wedged into a nook in the bank. Washing is often brought down to the river and in places the bank is covered in multi-coloured squares of drying washing. Once you wave to someone on the bank a whole chorus of waves, shouts and whistles come back revealing that there are people out and about all along the river, their presence unsuspected.

Km 597 – Right bank
Nikopol
The village of Nikopol straggles up a limestone slope to the ruins of the fortress on the top. The Emperor Trajan built the first fort here after an important victory over the Dacians and called it Nikopolis, 'City of Victory'. The fort and town were rebuilt by the Byzantine Emperor Heraclios in 629 and it developed over the centuries into one of the strongest fortresses on the Danube. The advancing Turks took Nikopolis and strengthened it further – it is mentioned as having twenty-six massive towers at this time. The menace of the Turks pressing westwards prompted a Crusade to be mounted against them and, led by Sigismund of Hungary, the crusaders journeyed down the Danube and besieged the Turks at Nikopolis. The crusaders, drawn from all over

Once clear of the Iron Gates the Danube twists and winds through islands with white sandy beaches and Amazon-like vegetation.

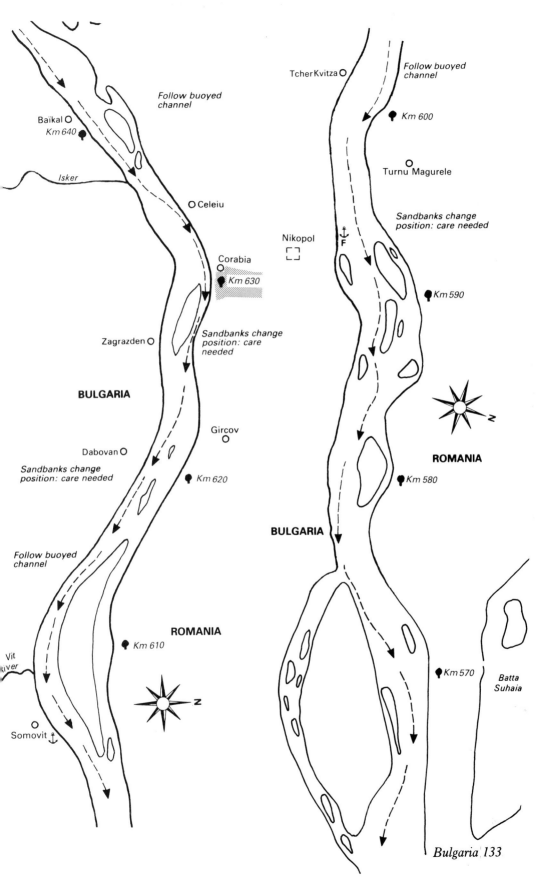

Follow buoyed
channel

Tcher Kvitza ○

● Km 600

Baïkal ○
Km 640 ●

Isker

Turnu Magurele ○

○ Celeiu

Nikopol

Sandbanks change
position: care needed

⚓ F

Corabia
○
● Km 630

● Km 590

Sandbanks change
position: care
needed

Zagrazden ○

BULGARIA

N

ROMANIA

Gircov
○

Dabovan ○

● Km 580

Sandbanks change
position: care needed

BULGARIA

● Km 620

Follow buoyed
channel

ROMANIA

Vit
River

● Km 610

● Km 570   Batta
              Suhaia

N

Somovit ○ ⚓

Tar-black fishing boats, Lom.

Europe, spent much time bickering, and could not agree on a strategy to take the fort, going off on forays of their own after the Turks. When Sultan Bajazet's army appeared the cavalry charged off after it only to be lured into a trap where their horses were impaled on hidden stakes and the riders slaughtered afterwards. The rest of the crusaders fled and the Turks' victory was complete and their occupation of the Balkans assured. Not until 1878 and the Russian-Bulgarian campaign against the Turks were they severely threatened again at Nikopol.

The present village hardly reflects the importance Nikopol once had, but it is a pleasant place with some well preserved old houses and a pleasant square. Unfortunately the Romanians have built a gigantic fertiliser works on the opposite shore which to the whoosh of gases escaping under pressure sends a nitric-red and sulphurous white miasmal haze over to the village from high chimneys. The noise and fumes completely destroy any

appreciation of the village, which is little helped by the hum of heavy machinery on the Bulgarian side.

Km 574
Belene Islands

The site of a large prison camp along the lines of Stalin's *gulags* which after the Second World War housed political prisoners, dissidents and criminals. Horrible crimes against the prisoners are reported to have been carried out and the prisoners were worked until they dropped from disease or malnutrition. It is still used today, though the atrocities are said to have been eliminated, and it is hardly surprising that a Bulgarian gunboat stopped *Rozinante* just off the islands to check our papers – however the captain and crew were not threatening, and after inspecting the papers waved us on our way.

Km 554 – Right bank
Svištov

A pleasant town which unfortunately, like many other Bulgarian towns, shows its worst face to the Danube. Described as picturesque, the view from the Danube is of an industrial port loading sand and red iron ore that stains the water all around. Situated on a section of the Danube that is easily crossed, the site has seen the coming and going of the Romans, Byzantines, Turks, Russians and the troops of Germany and Bulgaria which crossed the Danube here in 1916 to invade Romania. Its other claim to fame is a museum with the pierced heart of the Bulgarian poet and humourist Aleko Konstantinov, a much loved figure who was assassinated for his politics when he was 34 years old.

The Concrete Stork

At km 547 I nosed *Rozinante* up into an old arm of the Danube, mooring off the small village of Vardim for the night. We went ashore to find the usual gaggle of houses with private concentrated gardens and livestock with horses and carts much in evidence carrying things about. In the small shop we found hardly anything to buy, some bread, cheese and some lolly-water in *Coca Cola* bottles that tasted of little else except sugar. Most of the vegetables in these little villages change hands on a barter system and despite my best efforts, I couldn't buy any of the plump tomatoes or green peppers that could be seen everywhere in the back yards. Back at the boat I was surprised to be greeted in perfect English by the occupant of a kayak. Valetin came from Svištov and sur-

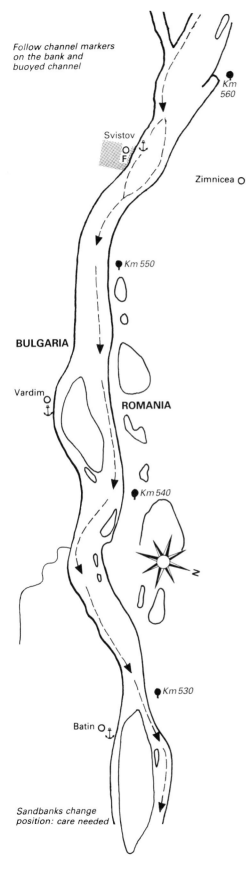

Follow channel markers on the bank and buoyed channel

Km 560

Svistov

Zimnicea

BULGARIA

Km 550

Vardim

ROMANIA

Km 540

N

Km 530

Batin

Sandbanks change position: care needed

prised me still further when he told me he was building a fourteen metre yacht there. Everything had to be made for it, the blocks, winches, brackets, bearings; like Zdenek and *Kondor* in Czechoslovakia, all the equipment was fashioned by Valetin or friends of his. He had designed the yacht himself and was building it in ferro-cement. He wanted to sail around the world and hoped to finish it in a year – if he has he should be sailing by now in *Kolombo Livia*, the 'Concrete Stork'.

Valetin returned a little later, bearing a huge watermelon, a bucket of tomatoes and a bottle of Bulgarian red. He wanted nothing and I had by now run out of yachting magazines to give away. I offered to post some to him but he was uncertain if they would arrive, customs officials have a predilection for glossy western magazines when they check parcels coming into Bulgaria.

Km 495 – Right bank
Rousse

Ruse, Ruschuk, Pysche, it has numerous names applied somewhat arbitrarily on recent maps. It is the fourth largest town in Bulgaria and the largest Bulgarian harbour on the Danube. Under the Romans it was also their largest harbour on this stretch of the Danube, called Sexanta Prista, 'the city of sixty ships', until the fleet was moved upstream as the Romans lost ground to the Dacians. The site declined in importance compared with others along the Danube until the Turks arrived and established a degree of order in these swamplands. Little remains of the Turkish fort except the Kyuntoukapu Gate. Rousse is the home of one of Bulgaria's numerous freedom fighters of the 19th century, Baba Tonka, Granny Tonka, whose house has been turned into a museum. The house was used to store arms and ammunition for the Bulgarian rebels and Granny Tonka led them through the surrounding swamps, organised raids along with other women, and raised her five sons and two daughters to be rebels. They were all hanged by the Turks for their activities and the skull of one of her sons, Stefan Karadzha, is on show.

The town itself is a delightful place full of neo-baroque 19th-century buildings, with the main street closed off as a pedestrian precinct. In the evening the locals come out for an evening stroll and the street resounds to noise and colour and the chink and rattle of glasses and cups in the numerous bars and cafés along the street. As Bernard Newman said when he visited it in 1934, 'it belongs to Europe and not to the Balkans.' For a while at the end of

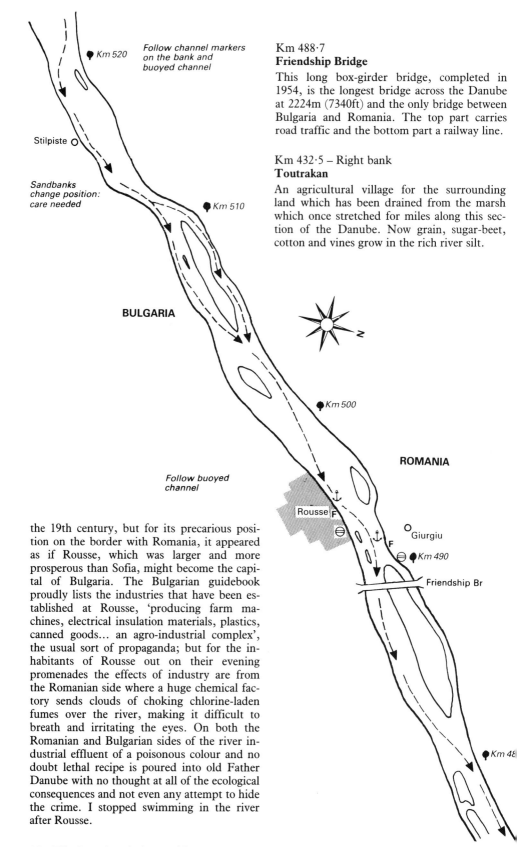

Km 520

Follow channel markers on the bank and buoyed channel

Stilpiste

Sandbanks change position: care needed

Km 510

BULGARIA

Km 500

ROMANIA

Follow buoyed channel

Rousse F

Giurgiu

Km 490

Friendship Br

Km 48

Km 488·7
Friendship Bridge

This long box-girder bridge, completed in 1954, is the longest bridge across the Danube at 2224m (7340ft) and the only bridge between Bulgaria and Romania. The top part carries road traffic and the bottom part a railway line.

Km 432·5 – Right bank
Toutrakan

An agricultural village for the surrounding land which has been drained from the marsh which once stretched for miles along this section of the Danube. Now grain, sugar-beet, cotton and vines grow in the rich river silt.

the 19th century, but for its precarious position on the border with Romania, it appeared as if Rousse, which was larger and more prosperous than Sofia, might become the capital of Bulgaria. The Bulgarian guidebook proudly lists the industries that have been established at Rousse, 'producing farm machines, electrical insulation materials, plastics, canned goods... an agro-industrial complex', the usual sort of propaganda; but for the inhabitants of Rousse out on their evening promenades the effects of industry are from the Romanian side where a huge chemical factory sends clouds of choking chlorine-laden fumes over the river, making it difficult to breath and irritating the eyes. On both the Romanian and Bulgarian sides of the river industrial effluent of a poisonous colour and no doubt lethal recipe is poured into old Father Danube with no thought at all of the ecological consequences and not even any attempt to hide the crime. I stopped swimming in the river after Rousse.

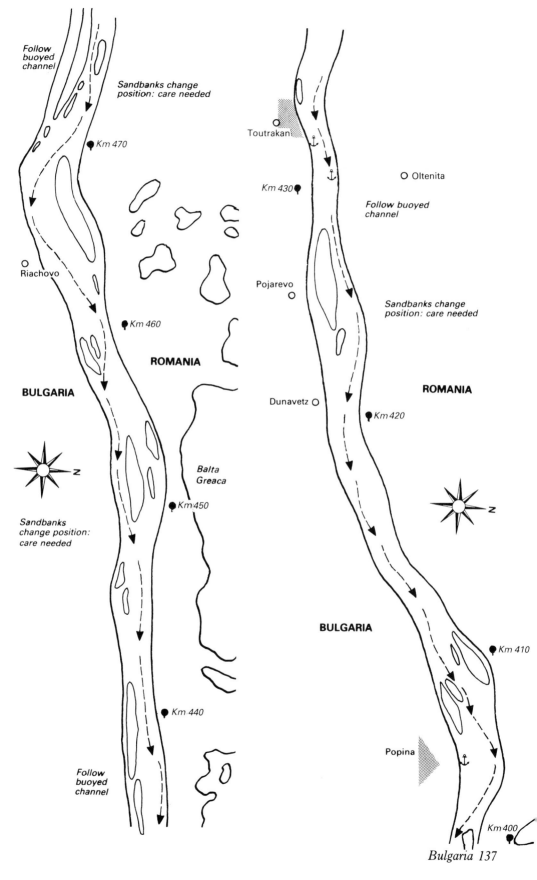

Follow buoyed channel

Sandbanks change position: care needed

Km 470

Riachovo

Km 460

ROMANIA

BULGARIA

N

Sandbanks change position: care needed

Km 450

Balta Greaca

Km 440

Follow buoyed channel

Toutrakan

Oltenita

Km 430

Follow buoyed channel

Pojarevo

Sandbanks change position: care needed

Dunavetz

ROMANIA

Km 420

N

BULGARIA

Km 410

Popina

Km 400

Bulgaria 137

Km 376 – Right bank
Silistra

Formerly a Thracian settlement that was enlarged by the Emperor Trajan into a garrison
town called Durostorum. Little remains except
a Roman tomb, probably late 3rd century AD,
with fine wall paintings. The Turks built a fort
here to guard this corner of the Empire,
though little remains except a tower and some
walls. Silistra is close to the Lake Srebâna Nature Reserve, a marshy region which is a haven
for wading birds, though you must go on a
guided tour to get there.

Km 375 – Right bank
Braţul Ostrov

Border between Bulgaria and Romania.

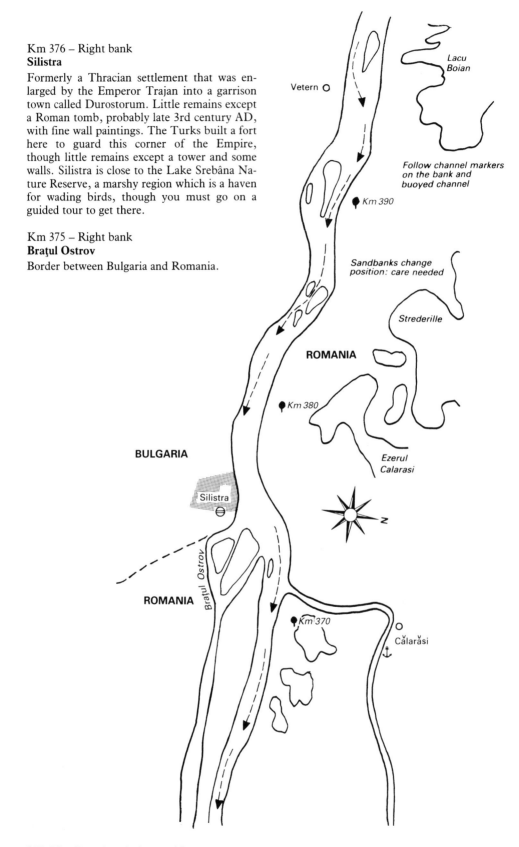

VIII. Romania

BAZIAS TO THE BLACK SEA

Note This chapter covers the left bank of the Danube from part of Yugoslavia through Bulgaria until the Danube turns north into the interior of Romania. The right bank of the Danube opposite Romania is described in the previous two chapters.

Km 1072·8 – Left bank
Bazias
The customs and immigration office for the border with Yugoslavia at km 1075.

Km 1048 – Left bank
Moldova Veche
The old Romanian pilot station for the Iron Gates. It is said that Trajan set out on his campaign against the Dacians here in 101 AD, but this seems out of step with the road along the right bank of the river and the bridge and camp at Turnu Severin. It was apparently later fortified and used by the Turks. When Romania became the Peoples' Republic of Romania the peasants in this savage landscape were not included in the collectivisation programme, their land being considered too poor to be worth aggregating.

On the lower Danube there are small cargo ships as well as barges using the river.

Transylvania To the northeast of the Gorge of Kazan the rugged Carpathians are split by ravines and deep wooded gorges that are shrouded in mist even in the summer, the tops of rocky bluffs have castles on them that look as if they were designed for Disneyland, and small villages appear to have stood still since the Middle Ages. Even from the Danube the appearance of the countryside bordering Transylvania proper produces a feeling of mystery and awe. Anything the geography does to you is amplified by the knowledge that Bram Stoker based his Gothic tale of horror, *Dracula*, on the life of Vlad Dracul or more accurately, Vlad Tepes, Vlad the Impaler, ruler of Transylvania in the 15th century, though Bram Stoker's character takes Vlad, puts him in another century and pours buckets of folk history about werewolves and the 'living dead' into the pages of his novel. The countless films produced in Hollywood about Dracula provide the visual images for Transylvania.

Transylvania is Latin for 'Beyond the Forest', a dark forbidding place considered to be beyond civilization. In 74 BC the Roman general Gaius Scribonius Curio expressed a foreboding about venturing into this land where he was sure evil forces beyond Roman gods and the discipline of the legionnaires would engulf him and his men. Though the Romans conquered a large part of present day Romania, they were always on the defensive against the tribes that populated this area, the Dacians and the Roxolani, eventually retreating to the south side of the Danube. Likewise the Turks, though they dominated the south side of the Danube, had great problems keeping Transylvania under their control.

This is where our friend Vlad Tepes comes in. Vlad Tepes was probably born around 1431 in Sighisoara in Transylvania, but was raised in Wallachia. His father, Vlad Dracul, sent Vlad and his brother Radu as hostages to Anatolia to show good faith to his Turkish masters, but in so doing angered Janos Hunyadi, Prince of Transylvania, who had Vlad Dracul murdered. Vlad junior was released by the Turks and Hunyadi then made him ruler of Wallachia; such were the times that killing off a father or brother was commonplace, and Vlad saw nothing strange in replacing his father under the ruler who had killed him. Hunyadi died shortly afterwards and Vlad, conscious of the power of the Turks, decided to play the vassal and pay a tribute to them while he consolidated his power. To enforce his rule he instituted the death penalty for virtually all crimes and he carried out the penalty by impaling his vic-

tims. The victim was bound, had a stake hammered up his rectum and was then raised aloft until he died. Not surprisingly this public agony had a severe effect on criminals and critics of Vlad's rule. High ranking or powerful local lords were effectively silenced since the size of the stake increased with a person's rank and local lords could expect a stake the size of a telegraph pole for their trouble. In 1459 Vlad eliminated most of the local lords who could challenge him for power by the simple expedient of inviting them all to dinner, and after wining and dining them, had them all impaled. His power increased as he systematically impaled part of his population and the populations of surrounding regions.

His attention now turned to the Turks. His first act was to nail the turbans to the heads of two Turkish emissaries who had refused to doff them in his presence. He then raided Turkish garrisons on both sides of the Danube, killing everyone he found. The Turks retaliated by assembling a large army and crossing the Danube into Wallachia in 1462, only to find the countryside had been stripped of food and the water poisoned. Vlad made guerrilla raids on the Turks and inflicted severe losses, but the worst was still to come for the Turkish army. Before the Turks even reached Transylvania, Vlad had prepared a little surprise for them at Tirgoviste. A forest of stakes, a kilometre wide and three kilometres long, had been prepared and 20,000 Turkish and Bulgarian prisoners impaled on them. The Turks, though well versed in terror and torture, were totally demoralised and turned back from Transylvania. Vlad Tepes was arrested by Matyas Corvinus at the end of 1462 and kept as a hostage until 1475 while his brother Radu reigned. In 1476 he regained the throne, but in the nature of the times was beheaded on the orders of Radu. It is said that his head was sent to the Sultan as a present.

Under President Ceausescu, Vlad was resurrected as an early freedom fighter for Romanian independence. In the valleys and plateaus of Transylvania there is an ethnic mixture of Hungarians, Romanians, Saxons, Romanies and others. Part of Ceausescu's reason for the resurrection of Vlad as a Romanian hero was his policy of destroying the villages of the ethnic minorities who live here and transplanting them to new towns where they are given an apartment in a shiny new tower block. The president for life wanted to create agro-towns where the minorities would be assimilated and in this way control Transylvania where the Romans and the Turks failed. Hungarians have been fleeing from what they

The edge of Transylvania, the land 'Beyond the Forest', in the Iron Gates.

have called 'ethnocide', some 8000 in a three month period in 1988 according to one estimate. The Saxons and Romanies and others are also fleeing the area, sixty a day were reported to try to swim the Danube across to Yugoslavia – thirty were said to make it across without being detained or shot by the Romanian border guards or drowning in the Danube. Once in Yugoslavia their problems were not over as many were returned by the Yugoslav authorities to Romania. The Hungarians have long resented the terms of the Treaty of Trianon that awarded the bulk of Transylvania, they call the region Erdély, to Romania, and accuse the Romanians of trying to wipe out Hungarian culture. The Romanians accuse the Hungarians of doing the same to them when Transylvania belonged to Hungary before the First World War.

Now Ceausescu has gone it is hoped that the persecution of minorities in Transylvania will end. But with the revolution half-finished and old enmities and prejudices surfacing after the euphoria of 1989 and the death of the Ceausescu's, the minorities have suffered near ly as badly as they did in the recent past. Many ethnic Hungarians have fled to Hungary and many of the Saxons to the new united Germany.

Between the arguments the fabric of Transylvania is being ripped apart and although the authorities have restored and opened Vlad's castle at Bran, they may yet destroy the wild country he briefly ruled over.

It is possible to tour around Transylvania either independently or on an organised tour. As elsewhere in Romania, unless you are a hardy independent traveller with a lot of time on your hands, it is best to take an organised tour from Bucharest.

Km 1029 – Left bank
Stenka Corner
Stenka and the mountain range behind is called the Aliberg after a certain Count Ali.

Km 1022·5 – Left bank
Liubcova

Km 1018 – Left bank
Berzasca

Km 1016 – Left bank
Drenkova
A pilot station. In the early days passengers would transfer to a small cutter for the Iron Gates section or go overland to Orsova to pick up a boat there.

Watchtower on the Romanian side of the Danube.

Km 995 – Left bank
Svinita

Km 991 – Left bank
Tri Cule
Three watchtowers were built here to guard against the Turks.

Km 983 – Left bank
Tisovita River

Km 973 – Left bank
Szechenyi Memorial
Before the Iron Gates flooded this area there used to be a tablet here commemorating the achievement of Count Szechenyi in building a road round this side of the gorge. I didn't see the tablet in place on my trip down in *Rozinante* and it may lie buried with his road. Between 1820 and 1834 the Hungarian Count

Szechenyi had a road blasted and bored along the precipitous left bank. However when Romania was given the territory after the First World War, they deliberately let it fall into disrepair. When Bernard Newman cycled down here in 1934 he was deeply saddened by the state of the Szechenyi road – 'It is little short of a scandal that this road, brilliantly conceived and magnificently executed, should be allowed by its present owners to fall into such a state of disrepair'.

Km 972·2 – Left bank
Veterani Cave

In a deep cave here in 1682 the Austrian general Veterani and 400 of his men were trapped by the Turks. For 45 days they held out against the superior force until finally when the last of their food, water and ammunition had run out, they surrendered. In 1788 history was repeated when a smaller group under Lieutenant Colonel Voith again held out for 21 days against the Turks. So impressed were the Turks by their bravery that they were allowed to return to Austria. Although I have not seen the cave, it should still be just above the river as Bernard Newman mentions that he had to scramble up a path to a spot a hundred feet above the Danube to inspect it.

Km 968 – Left bank
Trajan's sundial

Before the valley was flooded there was a sundial here cut into the rock by Trajan. It is supposed to have been rescued to be erected higher up, but I did not spot it from the river.

Km 967 – Left bank
Mraconia River

Km 954 – Left bank
Orsova

Situated at the mouth of the Cerna River, what is now new Orsova takes the name of the old town that was submerged by the river. Originally it was built on the site of a Roman town called Tierna. In the 19th century it was a quarantine station and a pilot station for the Iron Gates. The new town is a mundane place without interest.

Km 954·2 – Left bank
Allion

Under the Habsburgs the Hungarians were often disenchanted and in 1848–49 Lajos Kossuth was one of the leaders of a rebellion against the army of the Double Eagle. It was unsuccessful and Lajos Kossuth escaped east-wards, taking with him the sacred royal crown of Stephen. When he arrived here he buried it rather than risk taking it into Turkey with him. Somehow it was found and the Emperor Franz Josef erected a chapel near the spot where it had been buried.

Km 950 – Left bank
Bachna River

Until 1918 this was the frontier between the Habsburg Empire and Romania.

Km 943
Iron Gates barrage and double lock

When Bernard Newman cycled along the north bank of the Danube in 1934 he hired a local boat to take him across to the island of Ada Kaleh. On the way back the boatman offered to row him down to the Iron Gates and against his better judgement he agreed. On the way down the boat got caught in the current and was soon out of any control that mere rowing could contain:

' 'It is no use', he cried, a touch of anxiety in his voice. 'We shall have to shoot the Gates'.

He jumped to the stern to steer the boat himself. The boy was afraid, and so was I. I had heard too much about these treacherous Iron Gates. In any case there was plenty of evidence of danger around me – the rushing, swirling water, the angry rocks sometimes showing themselves fiercely above the stream, sometimes more cunningly submerged, the numerous wrecks dotted about the river – all this was quite enough to make a mere lands man afraid.

I watched the Turk. Beads of sweat stood out on his swarthy forehead as he swept his oar first to one side and then to another to dodge the rocks which appeared to rush at us. At that moment I felt that disaster was inevitable. I had already taken off my shoes and was prepared to swim for my life. Time after time the rough sides of our crazy boat scraped the jagged rocks. Time after time it seemed that the moment had come. I have never travelled in a boat in such a crazy fashion; it was as if the bed of the river were an inclined plane...I wondered how far down the river my body would be carried.'

Eventually the boat was swooshed out of the Iron Gates and Bernard Newman survived his brush with them. He was relieved to get back on the land again and vowed only to cycle after that.

Romanian fishermen below the Iron Gates.

Km 930 – Left bank
(Dobreta) Turnu Severin

A major Romanian port, famous for the bridge Trajan had built across the Danube. When he wanted to carry his campaign against the Dacians into Transylvania and Wallachia in 103–105AD, Trajan had Apollodor of Damascus design and oversee the construction of a bridge some 1070m (3530ft) long with massive stone supports and wooden beams and planks between them. How it was constructed in the fast flowing river is uncertain, the most likely theory being that the main channel was diverted for a time to allow the stone supports to be built. Trajan established a garrison town at Turnu Severin with fortified towers and walls which were later added to by Severus. The Dacian campaign was halted under Hadrian (117–138) who had the bridge demolished in case the Dacians used it to attack his defences on the south side of the Danube. However under Septimus Severus (222–235) the campaign was resumed and it is possible the bridge was rebuilt. Certainly Severus built new fortifications at Turnu Severin and the ruins of a tower, the Severus Tower, can be found here. All that is left of the bridge are two stone supports on the Romanian side and it is said, though I failed to find it, the remains of a support on the Yugos-

lavian side. There have been reports that the remains of the supports still exist on the river-bed and that at low water they can be seen, but in my trip in *Rozinante* I failed to spot them even though the water level was low.

Old Turnu Severin is a likable place, a little disordered, but much to be preferred to the apartment blocks of the new quarter of Turnu Severin. It is now called Dobreta Turnu Severin after the Dacian settlement of Dobreta that was here before the Romans arrived. Turnu Severin is called the 'City of the Roses' for the numerous parks around it, but on a trip to see a modern Catholic church (a tourist attraction designed to show you that the Romanians both look after their cultural minorities – the Catholics being one – and are a forward looking nation replacing traditional architecture with modern), the best tended park I saw was the football ground where the green grass was almost indecently green under the hot sun. The Romanians are fanatical about their football.

From Turnu Severin you can take a trip to the Baile Herculane in southwest Transylvania. The trip is worth it as much for the spectacular scenery along the way as for the baths themselves which are a little dank though the setting in a steep wooded gorge defies superlatives. The baths were used by the Romans and are said to be able to cure almost anything except times inexorable march.

Km 928
Simian Island

The buildings from Ada Kaleh were to be rebuilt on this island and the Turks resettled here, however little has been done and most of the Turks opted to go to Constanţa or back to Turkey.

Km 876·5 to 860·8
Braţul Gogosi

The Danube separates here with the old channel running around the Romanian shore. The navigable channel follows the Bulgarian side.

Km 794·5 – Left bank
Calafat

An industrial city which, like so many in Romania, pumps noxious fumes into the air and effluent into the Danube. In the 19th century there was a fortress and a substantial shipyard here. It is thought that the name Calafat may be derived from 'kalfatern', the word for caulking a boat whereby caulking cotton is inserted into the seams of the hull with a mixture of white lead to make it watertight.

Swampland

On the Romanian side of the Danube channels and marshy lagoons extend inland for several miles in places. This is a watery land, bedeviled with mosquitoes and midges, thickly overgrown with poplar and willow, a paradise for wading birds which are everywhere. There are few roads through this area with boats used for transport – it is not unusual to see a tarred black hull transporting hay or animals from one island to another. Often you will see a few forlorn looking cows marooned on an island watching boats pass by on the river.

The Danube is now following the southern side of Wallachia and turns up to follow the eastern side of the province. Wallachia was known as a distant outpost of Christendom, mostly Orthodox, until the arrival of the Turks when it was largely forgotten about. Not until the 19th century and the unification of Wallachia with Moldavia in the northeast in 1859, the beginning of modern Romania, did the west slowly begin to look at this forgotten province. For centuries it was a desperately poor area, run much like the *Puszta* by corrupt landowners under a feudal system. Right up into the 20th century things were hardly better and even now there is a poverty in this region amongst the worst in Europe.

Km 697 to 691·5
Copanita Island

Km 631 – Left bank
Corabia

A modern industrial town and river port built after the Second World War. The Danube, slowing down at the Wallachian Plain, often changes its channel. My up-to-date chart of the river showed the channel following the Bulgarian side of the river and not until I got stuck on the tops of a few submerged trees did I realise that the channel now follows the Romanian side.

Km 615 to 605
Calnovat Island

Km 597 – Left bank
Turnu Magurele

A large industrial port with huge fertiliser works pouring acrid fumes into the air and toxic looking effluent into the Danube. There are reports that a large hydroelectric complex is to be built here, but to date nothing has been started.

Romanians

The name, the language and the occupation of Wallachia by the Romans are considered to point to a lineage dating from the Roman occupation. The Daco-Roman continuity theory surmises that during the Roman occupation, Dacians intermarried and adopted the Roman culture and part of the language. This inter-bred culture continued links with the Roman Empire, up to the 5th century it is suggested, and then survived as a piece of Rome marooned in between the Carpathians and the Balkans. Attractive as the theory is – Romanian is often stated to be a language closer to Latin than modern demotic Italian – it has no real evidence to support it. The flat plains of Wallachia were heir to just about every invader going east or west: the Slavs, Huns, Avars, Goths, Bulgars, Vlachs, Magyars, Turks and the Magyars again under the Habsburgs. All of these groups and others had a cultural influence on the region and it would be astounding if a Daco-Roman culture could survive intact through it all.

The importance of the Daco-Roman continuity theory to the Romanians is in establishing their right to the territory Romania now occupies. The Hungarians arguing for their Hungarian minorities in Transylvania, which they say are discriminated against by the Romanians, propose that Romanians and Romanian culture are in fact descended from

Motorised barge number 1772 on the Danube in Romania.

the Vlachs, wandering tribes of herdsmen who who migrated from Macedonia and Bulgaria to Transylvania around the 13th century. Thus the argument goes that the Magyars, who occupied Transylvania in the 9th and 10th centuries, are the rightful heirs to the territory and were it not for the harsh terms of the Treaty of Trianon after the First World War, it would be theirs still. No one seems to mention the poor old Slavs who, it is agreed, were here before both the Vlachs and the Magyars.

The late President Ceausescu propounded the Daco-Roman theory with great vigour as he systematically demolished the villages and towns of Transylvania, a policy which earned him the hatred of every Hungarian. Whatever the merits or not of the Daco-Roman theory, I must confess that at a subjective level I find the Romanians much like a Mediterranean people who have somehow been removed to the oily shores of the Black Sea. There is a spontaneity, a determination to enjoy life despite living under great hardship, and the Romance language itself which delineates Romania from the countries around it.

Km 493 – Left bank
Giurgiu

Unlike Rousse on the opposite shore, Giurgiu is not an attractive place, in fact the part of Giurgiu by the river is purely a river port surrounded by industry. The small town of Giurgiu is about two kilometres away, but it is mostly a dormitory suburb for the port and is a shabby, desperate place.

Romania is not used to small boats arriving on the river and the army, police, customs and immigration were all suspicious. On *Rozinante* we were allotted an armed guard, a young conscript studying forestry, who guided me around the various offices. He fairly bubbled over being able to speak English and quizzed me on anything and everything: on the countries upstream, on England, on London, on the things you can buy in the shops, on *Rozinante* which he persisted in calling a 'playboat swimming in the river'. He turned out to be a friend indeed, whisking me through the various offices, constantly assuring me there was 'no problem', interpreting my replies in the appropriate manner so that the army, police, customs and immigration were all satisfied. He had to do a twelve hour stint before he was relieved by another guard who watched over us through the night. This procedure was to be repeated everywhere in Romania where a guard detail was ordered to watch over the diminutive *Rozinante* twenty-four hours a day. Mostly these young conscripts were amiable lads who would ask for 'souvenirs', *Kent* cigarettes which are an accepted form of barter, real coffee and magazines. I gave the conscript in Giurgiu a *Scientific American* which he immediately buttoned inside his tunic, his face aglow with the anticipated pleasure of a foreign magazine.

Giurgiu is the best place from where to make an excursion to Bucharest. There is a rail service and an irregular bus connection. If you arrive by cruise boat coaches are laid on, and on my second trip it was lucky that two cruise boats were arriving in the night with prearranged excursions to Bucharest the next day. In the morning the Romanian guide was willing, but the American courier was as stony faced and unrelenting as any Romanian bureaucrat. She insisted it was impossible to take us to Bucharest and it was only the intervention of the Romanian tour guide that got us on board.

Bucharest It is often called the 'Paris of the East', but this reputation, gained between the two World Wars, was fast disappearing under President Ceausescu's plan to carpet the city in multi-storey apartment blocks and offices, a habitat he considered suitable for a truly socialist state even if it meant demolishing the old quarters, churches and cobbled squares, even the cathedral. Parts of the old city peep through the new, though so does the effect of a ruined economy: sewerage seeps into alleys, the roads are full of potholes, the electricity is turned off at ten o'clock plunging Bucharest and indeed Romania into darkness, the shop fronts are dressed but inside you will probably find you cannot buy any of the things in the window, in the bars and restaurants the menu is limited unless you can pay in hard currency; the fabric of what was once an elegant city is slowly crumbling. Despite all this there are glimpses that give you an idea of what Bucharest once was and of the almost unquenchable spirit of the Romanians themselves who still manage to enjoy life despite the hardships pressed on them from above.

Bucharest is a difficult place for the independent traveller to get around. Taxis are few and far between, the buses and trams are crammed to overflowing, and often you will arrive to find that what you want to see has just closed for lunch or for the rest of the day. For this reason if you have only a short amount of time in Bucharest I'd recommend a guided tour – I've toured Bucharest as part of a tour group and independently and the former is without doubt the easiest way to see the sights. Doing it independently means you will see more of the real Bucharest and be open to chance encounters with the inhabitants, but you can do that elsewhere as well. While looking around Bucharest independently I met a local who told me a typical self-deprecating joke about Bucharest and life under Ceausescu. A party member was granted permission to go to England for a conference and arrived in London where he wandered about the streets gazing in awe at the shop windows. He was even more astonished to find he could buy anything that was displayed in the shops, that goods of all kinds were freely available. When he returned to Bucharest he was asked about the trip. 'Well,' he said, 'I went into a bakery and I could buy bread; I went into a tailors and I could buy a suit, any suit that I wanted; I went into a bookshop and I could buy books, there were hundreds of books all for sale; I could even buy any sort of car I wanted.' Mouths were agape amongst his fellow comrades until an old party cadré

Rozinante was allotted an armed guard day and night at every port for our stay in Romania.

nodded sagely and said: 'Yes, we were once like that, but you know... those English are twenty years behind the times.'

Km 489
Friendship Bridge

Km 430 – Left bank
Oltenita

The town is three kilometres inland. By the river there is a poor restaurant and an industrial area behind, including a large shipyard. When I arrived a gypsy band was playing for a group of diners here, but with no beer, wine at the equivalent of $20 a bottle, and no food, we opted for a mineral water. Later the waiter strolled up and offered to cook us something for a carton of *Kent*, a ransom I was not prepared to pay. The gypsies, the *tziganes*, were a rough looking lot, playing violent gypsy tunes in drunken disorder. The gypsies in Romania are one of the few minorities the government has trouble getting to conform, partly because of their roving life, but more likely from their ability to procure on the black market, which would probably compromise too many of the police arresting any of them. Everywhere you will be asked by gypsies to 'change money – sell jeans – sell cassette – or *Kent, Kent, Kent.*'

Km 376
Border between Romania and Bulgaria
Silistra on the Bulgarian side of the river marks the border between Romania and Bulgaria. Here the Danube, blocked from continuing eastwards by the low limestone hills of the Dobrudja, is turned north into Romania until it can exit into the northwest corner of the Black Sea.

Km 313 – Right bank
Rasova
Near here Trajan built a defensive line of towers and forts stretching east to the Black Sea since the Danube, now travelling north, no longer provided a natural border between Roman territory and the barbarians.

Km 300 – Right bank
Cernavoda
Cernavoda means 'Black Water' and though the name originally described the peat black water of the Danube, it is ironic that Romania's first nuclear power station is being built nearby on the banks of the new Danube-Black Sea Canal. The power station is to a Canadian design, though being built by Romanians, and given that Ceausescu is alleged to have criticised the amount of concrete recommended by the Canadians for its construction, I have great fears for the safety of the installation. It is scheduled to be operational in 1991.

Cernavoda itself is a dusty poor little place and like so many other towns off the tourist route, there is little to eat or drink in the restaurants and little to buy in the markets and shops. I queued for half an hour to get eggs, another half an hour to get bread, was turned away from a snack bar because it had run out of food, and failed to get hold of any petrol or diesel for the boat despite the advantages of being a tourist and paying in a hard currency.

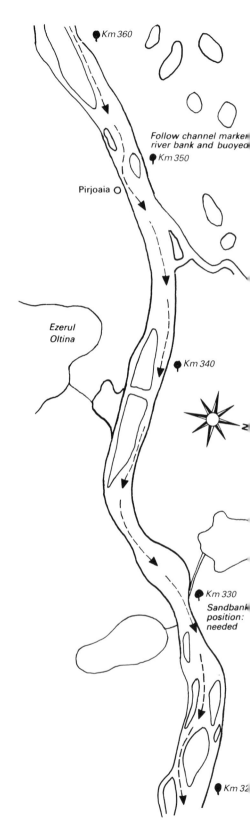

Km 360

Follow channel marker river bank and buoyed
Km 350

Pirjoaia O

Ezerul Oltina

Km 340

Km 330
Sandbank position: needed

Km 33

The rail bridge at Cernavoda, built in 1895 along the lines of the Firth of Forth bridge in Scotland.

The spirit of the people was remarkable given the poverty they lived under in the *epoca Ceausescu*.

The bridge upstream, looking not dissimilar to the bridge across the Firth of Forth in Scotland, was designed and built in 1895 with French capital and was the first bridge to link the European rail network with the Black Sea.

Cernavoda is normally the last stop for cruise boats although some go down to Hirşova and a few continue on to the delta itself.

The Danube-Black Sea Canal At Cernavoda a 60km long canal considerably shortens the distance for cargoes to reach the Black Sea from the Danube. The alternative is another 300km along the winding channel of the Danube to the delta and Sulina. Work on this canal started in 1949 with what amounted to slave labour: peasants who resisted the collectivisation project, minor criminals, critics of the Party and anyone else who could be forced to work under whatever pretext. It is estimated that over a hundred thousand died during the initial construction until it was abandoned in 1953, earning it the title of the *Canalul Mortii*, the 'canal of death'. President Ceausescu resurrected the canal project in 1973, though the route was changed to a more easterly direction so that the canal emerged to the south of Constanţa at Agigea. Here a gigantic port has

Monument to the building of the Danube–Black Sea canal.

been built to accommodate what is hoped will
be the large amount of traffic on the Danube
when the Rhine-Main-Danube canal is completed and it is possible to take a barge train of
international proportions from the Black Sea
to the North Sea. The canal was opened in
1984.

When I traversed the canal there was little
traffic on it. There is a lock at each end,
though the distance I descended was less than
a metre at the Cernavoda end and probably
less than two metres at the Agigea end. When
the Danube is high the descent down the locks
will no doubt be considerably greater. It's possible to take a motorboat tour of the canal
from the Agigea end, though for what reason
other than to marvel at Ceausescu's vision is
uncertain – the canal is a dreary thing cutting
through the equally dreary landscape of the
Drobrudja. The old course of the Danube to
Tulcea and the delta is an infinitely more interesting place to be.

Km 260·5 – Right bank
Ghindăareşti

Km 253 – Right bank
Hirşova

A town largely devoted to fish processing from
the catches in the surrounding lagoons. Although this is not the delta proper, vast
lagoons and marshes are found to the north
where the Danube, nearing the end of its journey to the sea, forms countless channels over
the low-lying land. Hirşova was formerly the
Roman Castrum Carcium and later a Turkish
fortress of which some ruins remain.

Km 238·5
Giurgeni Bridge

The bridge (Giurgeni town itself is just inland
from the left bank) has been built across the
river at an age-old ford where the Vlachs
crossed the river to graze their sheep in the
spring and early summer, the time when the
waters of the lower Danube have not yet swollen with the melting snow from the Alps.

Km 170 – Left bank
Brăila

The town looks Italianate – it has something of
the heavy monumental style that Mussolini so
loved – but in fact its not very old. Its
prosperity and the wealthy buildings were
spawned from the Peace of Adrianople in 1829
soon after which Brăila was created a Free Port
and the large quantities of grain grown on the

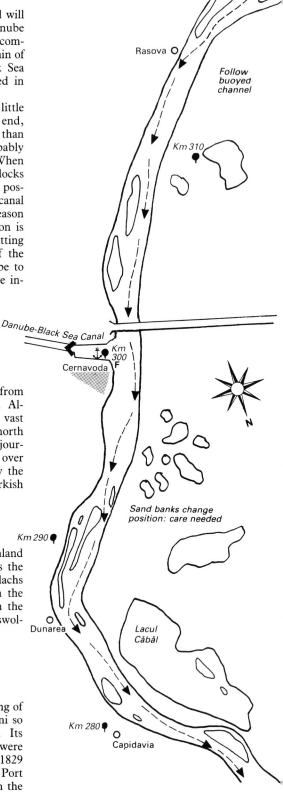

Rasova

Follow
buoyed
channel

Km 310

Danube-Black Sea Canal

Km 300

Cernavoda F

Km 290

Sand banks change
position: care needed

Dunarea

Lacul
Căbăl

Km 280

Capidavia

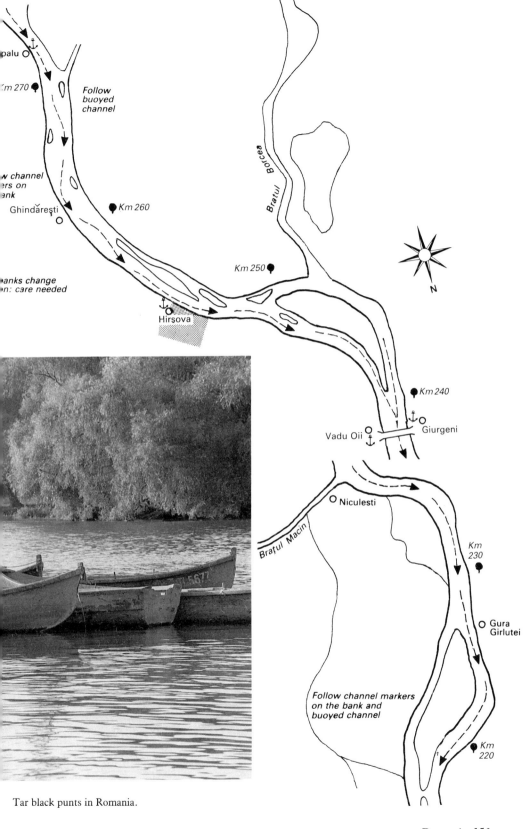

palu

Km 270

Follow
buoyed
channel

channel
ers on
ank

Ghindăreşti

Km 260

Km 250

anks change
n: care needed

Hirşova

Braţul Borcea

N

Km 240

Vadu Oii

Giurgeni

Niculesti

Braţul Macin

Km 230

Gura Girlutei

Follow channel markers
on the bank and
buoyed channel

Km 220

Tar black punts in Romania.

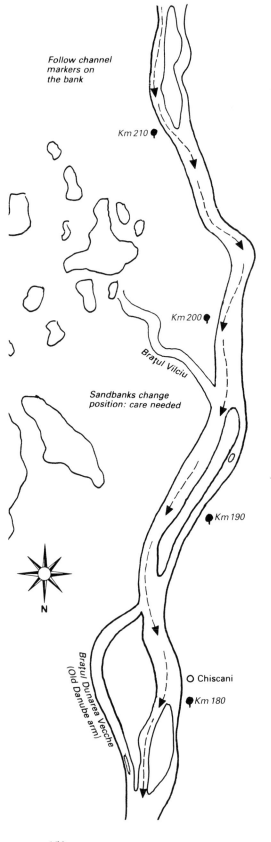

Follow channel markers on the bank

Km 210

Km 200

Bratul Vilciu

Sandbanks change position: care needed

Km 190

N

Bratul Dunarea Vecche (Old Danube arm)

O Chiscani

Km 180

Wallachian Plain were shipped from here. In fact under the Turks before this it had been steadily gaining in prosperity, the treaty simply accelerated the process. In the early part of the 20th century Brăila was known as the 'gypsy capital' of Europe. Up until 1855 there had existed a 'gypsy slavery' and when it was abolished in Wallachia many gypsies migrated to Brăila and the surrounding area to earn their living working at the docks or in domestic service as well as at their time honoured occupation as musicians.

Today industry in the town revolves around the production of cellulose from the abundant reeds that grow all around. It is only comparatively recently in the 1950s that an efficient process was devised to extract cellulose, used in the production of paper and textiles, from the reeds. Prior to this the reeds were burnt off to get scarce grazing land, but now, in the late summer and autumn the reeds, predominantly the genus *Phragmites*, are harvested. In addition to cellulose the reeds can also be processed to obtain glycerin, xylene and alcohol.

Km 155 – Left bank
Siret River

The Siret River and its tributaries drain a large part of Moldavia. This and other rivers emptying into the Danube mean that there is still a substantial current in the river, around three knots in places.

Km 150·5 NM 81 – Left bank
Galati

Situated between the Siret and the Prut Rivers on the banks of the Danube, Galati is Romania's largest port on the Danube. Here the maritime Danube starts so distances are measured in nautical miles, in Romanian *mila*, from here to the mouth on the Black Sea, with Galati at *mila* 81.

Like Brăila, Galati is of comparatively recent origin being established in the 15th century. It prospered in the 19th century when much of the Wallachian wheat was shipped from here and Brăila. In the Second World War it suffered heavy damage from German bombing, but was rebuilt and expanded in the 1960s with the building of Romania's largest iron and steel works. Between the iron and steel works, the huge shipyard and the dormitory suburb built to house the workers, old Galati has been virtually smothered.

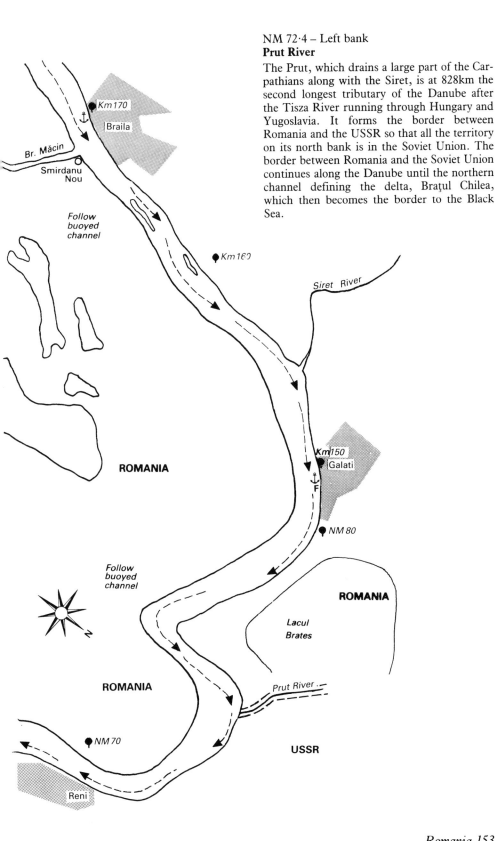

NM 72·4 – Left bank
Prut River

The Prut, which drains a large part of the Carpathians along with the Siret, is at 828km the second longest tributary of the Danube after the Tisza River running through Hungary and Yugoslavia. It forms the border between Romania and the USSR so that all the territory on its north bank is in the Soviet Union. The border between Romania and the Soviet Union continues along the Danube until the northern channel defining the delta, Braţul Chilea, which then becomes the border to the Black Sea.

Km 170
Braila

Br. Măcin

Smirdanu
Nou

*Follow
buoyed
channel*

Km 160

Siret River

ROMANIA

Km 150
Galati

F

NM 80

*Follow
buoyed
channel*

ROMANIA

Lacul
Brates

ROMANIA

Prut River

USSR

NM 70

Reni

Lipovenian house at Mila 23.

The old wooden Lipovenian church at Mila 23.

Towards the end of its journey to the sea the Danube slows and spreads out, to form a huge waterland of channels and islands covered in thick vegetation.

Cherhana at Mila 23.

Lipovenian fishermen, hard characters with an appetite for vodka that leaves lesser men senseless. One Lipovenian joke tells of three fishermen steadily drinking their way through bottles of vodka. Eventually one falls to the floor and the others instruct the barman not to give him any more as he's driving.

Delta boats: Mila 23.

USSR The Russians are not liked in Romania. Like some of its neighbours on the Black Sea, Romania has a historical fear of Russian ambitions in this part of the world – with good reason. Most of the Romanian hatred comes from the Russian ultimatum in 1940, defined in the Ribbentrop-Molotov pact between Stalin and Hitler, which demanded that Bessarabia, the territory north of the Danube delta stretching around to the Dnestr River near Odessa, be handed over to the Soviet Union. Romania had always considered this rich farmland to be a natural part of Greater Romania and indeed many of the inhabitants are Romanian. In June 1941 Romania under Marshal Atonescu, who had proclaimed himself the *Führer* of Romania, joined in the Nazi invasion of Russia and annexed Bessarabia. In 1944 Atonescu was over thrown in a coup and the Romanian partisans helped the Red Army to throw the Nazis out of Romania. Under Soviet influence Romania had little option but to hand back Bessarabia to Russia and the present borders between the two countries were drawn up.

The nationalist backlash against the Soviets essentially got under way in the early 1950s with key Muscovites purged from the party and the nationalist policies of the 'New Course' outlined by Gheorge Gheorghiu-Dej in 1953. Nicolae Ceausescu who came to power in 1965 further pulled away from Soviet ties, pursuing a rampant nationalism. His reputation as an independent (alone in the eastern bloc Romania maintained links with China, Albania and Israel, criticised the Soviet invasion of Czechoslovakia in 1968 and of Afghanistan) earned Ceausescu the gratitude and millions of dollars of aid from western countries, though since the events of 1989 many of the governments formerly friendly to Romania have had to look again at the *epoca Ceausescu* in the light of human rights violations on a massive scale and the programme of disinformation that shielded Ceausescu's despotic rule. Whatever the reasons submerged under the nationalist rhetoric and policies, Romanians have a hatred of the Soviets that is second to none. You will hear no Russian spoken in Romania, and woe betide any visitor who tries out a few words of the despised language!

NM 72·4 – Left bank
Reni
A Soviet oil and ore port.

NM 55·5 – Right bank
Isaccea
A Romanian town built on the site of a Roman settlement, Noviodunum, and renamed by the Turks, Isac-Kioi, the 'Village of Issac' from where it gets its present name.

NM 43
Danube Delta
This huge area of waterland, of swamps and lagoons, low islands and floating islands of reed, of weed-choked and shallow channels, overgrown with willow, poplar and thick reed growing to more than five metres (16ft) high, of manmade canals and canals long forgotten, populated by an estimated 250 species of birds, by Lipovenian fishermen in tar-black boats, breeding ground of the sturgeon and its expensive cargo of caviar, is a region that should be classified as another country on the Danube. It is, as the brochures say, 'all superlatives' – even the dourness of the Romanian bureaucrats who control the delta and the omni-present mosquitoes do not dull it, though they do their best.

In area it covers some 5640 square kilometres, about the size of the county of Dorset, with some 4470 square kilometres in Romanian territory and the rest in the USSR. The delta extends at a rate of 40 metres every so that the Romanians can claim to have the youngest land in Europe. Depending on the time of year and the rainfall over the catchment area of the Danube, every second some 5000 to 9000 cubic metres of water is discharged into the Black Sea. Every year 50 million tons of silt is carried down the Danube and it is this silt, released at the mouth, that causes the astonishing growth of the delta into the Black Sea. The delta can be seen to enlarge over the years and if winter storms and Black Sea currents did not periodically sweep away some of the delta and distribute the silt on the sea-bed and coast away from the mouth, by my calculations it would take a mere 7500 years for the northwest corner of the Black Sea to become silted up from the Danube delta right across to Sevastopol on the Crimean peninsula.

In appearance the delta is more or less a triangle with its base along the Black Sea and its top at Tulcea (NM 38·5). From Tulcea the two sides of the triangle are formed by two old arms of the Danube: the Bratul Chilia running more or less northeast, which forms the border

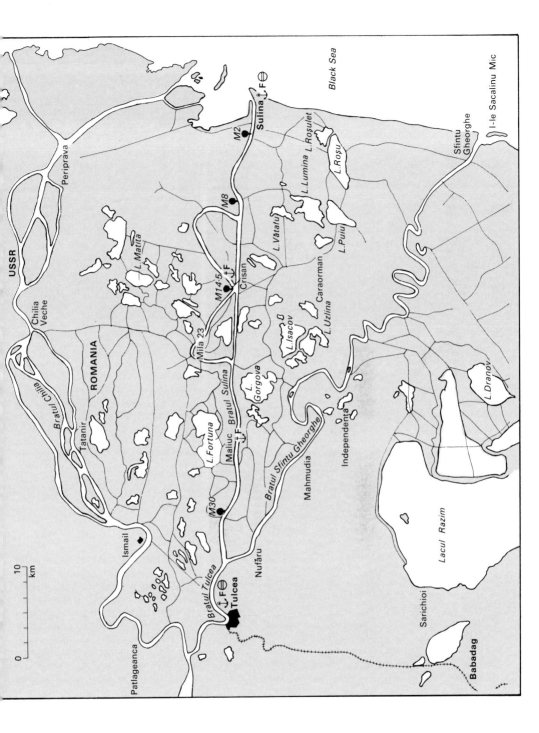

between Romania and the USSR; and the Braţul Sfîntu Gheorghe running southeast. The triangle is bisected in the middle by the Braţul Sulina running east, the main navigable channel for shipping.

Braţul Chilea

This arm is approximately 65 nautical miles (120km) long and is used almost exclusively by the USSR. Only foreign ships loading ore or coal at Ismail will use this branch.

NM 48·5 – Left bank
Ismail

The site of the town is very old. The Greeks established a settlement here called Antifilia and the Romans in turn occupied it until they deserted the delta around the 4th century AD. The Turks occupied this area in the 16th century and called the place Ismail, the name it has retained despite its many changes of ownership. The Russians first captured it in 1770, again in 1790 and 1811, only to lose it to Turkey each time when the various treaties were drawn up to end the fighting between the Russians and the Turks. In 1877 Russia took Ismail again and managed to keep it until 1918 when it was given to Romania. Briefly in 1940 and then finally in 1944 Russia got Ismail back and has managed to keep it. When Bernard Newman stopped here near the end of his cycling tour down the Danube he found it a polyglot place resounding to a jumble of languages.

Danube delta at Crisan NM 14·5.

'...three sailing ships were unloading: they hailed from Italy, France and Egypt, and were being emptied by Rumanian, Russian, Turkish, Bulgar, Greek and gypsy labourers. A Jew did the checking and on the deck of the Italian boat a Chinese cook prepared a meal...Analysing one polyglot sentence which I perpetrated at Ismail, I found that it included five languages.'

Today Ismail is the principal Soviet port on the Danube and as a Danube country, it is entitled to use the river right up into Germany. The powerful black tugs and barges flying the red hammer and sickle can be seen in every country along the river, a powerful force in commerce on the Danube and one that Austria and Germany fear will dominate trade when the Rhine-Main-Danube Canal is opened. Given the history of Ismail you can't say they did not fight long and hard to get a toehold on the Danube.

NM 25·5 – Left bank
Kilija

NM 25·5 – Right bank
Chilia Veche

Until the USSR finally got the northern bank of Braţul Chilia, Chilea Veche was a suburb of Romanian Chilia, now Soviet Kilija, on the opposite bank of the river. It is one of the oldest settlements in the delta, probably founded by the Greeks as Achillea. A Genoese settlement here was known as Licostomo, the 'Two mouths of the Wolf' which was renamed under the Turks as Eski-Kale, the 'Old Castle'. Around the 15th century Chilia, the Moldavian name derived from the original Greek name, was situated some five kilometres from the sea whereas today it is over forty kilometres away due to silting.

NM 13·5 – Right bank
Periprava

A small fishing village on the corner of Braţul Chilea where it curves southwards to the Black Sea. South of Periprava is Letea Island, the

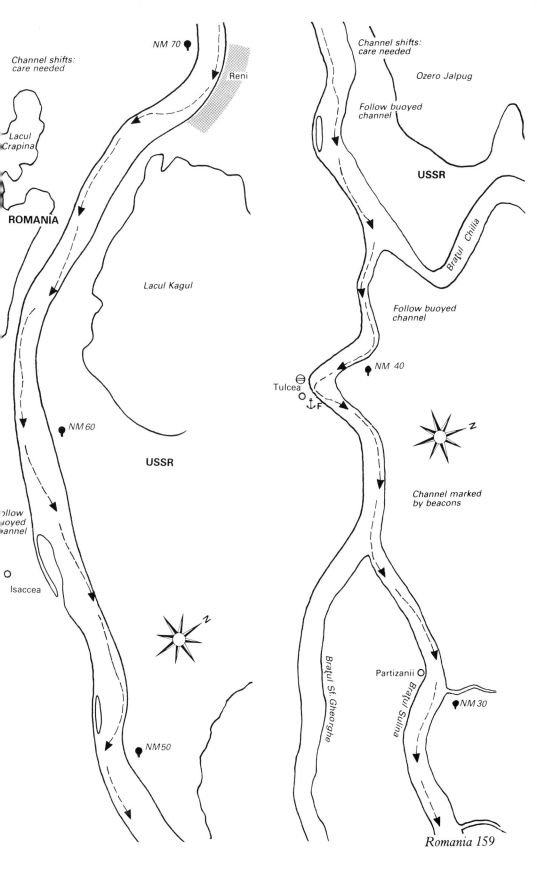

Channel shifts:
care needed

NM 70

Reni

Lacul
Crapina

Lacul Kagul

ROMANIA

NM 60

USSR

ollow
uoyed
annel

Isaccea

NM 50

Channel shifts:
care needed

Ozero Jalpug

Follow buoyed
channel

USSR

Bratul Chilia

Follow buoyed
channel

NM 40

Tulcea

F

Channel marked
by beacons

Bratul Sf. Gheorghe

Bratul Sulina

Partizanii

NM 30

Romania 159

largest sand and silt island in the delta, which has a protected forest of oaks, elms, alders, poplars and willows with many smaller Mediterranean species of plants and creepers under the canopy of the oaks. It is also home to a large number of insect species including the largest European fly, though this is hardly an invitation to visit here. In the forest and the network of lagoons and channels around it there are many species of birds including falcons, sea eagles, owls, egrets, storks and the largest breeding colony of pelicans in Europe.

NM 8 – Left bank
Vilovo

A town situated on Braţul Chilea and an cial channel dredged to the sea; the town was once called the Venice of Bessarabia, though that title could well go to many of the towns in this waterland.

Braţul Tulcea

A short arm running from where the Braţul Chilea divides from the Danube to where the Braţul Sulina and Braţul Sfintu Gheorghe divide at around NM 36.

NM 38·5 – Right bank
Tulcea

Dubbed the 'Gateway to the Delta', from the river it is a scruffy run-down place with ferries and small military hydrofoils churning up the oily water. It is built on a slight hummock in this otherwise flat landscape which immediately confers on it a distinct advantage which the Greeks and the Romans utilised. It is mentioned by Herodotus and under the Romans was called Aegyssus. In the 19th century, like Brăila and Galati, it was an important port for shipping grain from the Wallachian plain, but its fortunes declined in the 20th century. Today, apart from a fish cannery, its importance is as a centre for tourism in the delta. Ferries regularly run down the Sulina Channel taking tourists bussed or flown in on package tours, and for those on a hasty visit this is the best way to view the delta.

In the town there is a Danube Museum, somewhat tucked away behind the town centre, which has excellent displays of the hydrology and history of the delta and an aquarium with some of the species of fish found in the waters. This is the best place to get a view of the sturgeon, the armour-plated carrier of caviar which in the case of the species *Huso huso*, the greater sturgeon, can grow to the size of a large man.

Braţul Sfintu Gheorghe

The southernmost of the arms which runs for a distance of approximately 56M (105km), the exact distance varying with different sources. This is the oldest arm of the Danube, winding lazily to the southeast where it meets the Black Sea at the southern corner of the delta. It is surmised that this is where Jason and the Argonauts anchored off after taking the Golden Fleece from the Colchians. It is generally agreed that Jason and the Argonauts sailed counter-sunwise around the Black Sea and anchored off the mouth of the Danube, the Ister to the Greeks, but of course just where the *Argo* anchored cannot be known because we have no way of knowing what the delta looked like thousands of years ago. Most likely the *Argo* anchored much further inland, perhaps as much as fifteen miles amongst what are now landlocked lagoons.

The channel is not used today for commercial traffic except for cargoes of tourists transported on trips around the delta. This part of the delta is the most accessible by land with a peninsula of the Dobrudja poking into the delta. There are a number of fishing villages along this arm with Sfintu Gheorghe at the end on the Black Sea. At this mouth most of the sturgeon is caught, a state regulated activity that takes the valuable black roe for export. There is none to be had on the delta except on the black market.

Braţul Sulina

The main navigable arm that runs due east for 36M (67km) to Sulina and the buoyed channel into the Black Sea. Although this is the navigable arm, it only carries around 10% of the water of the Danube. It is kept dredged to a depth of 10m for medium sized ships to get up to Galati and Brăila. From Tulcea a ferry and hydrofoil run to Sulina and on its banks are a number of hotels and camping grounds from which you can take an excursion boat or hire a rowing boat to explore the delta.

NM 24 – Left bank
Maliuc

Has a hotel and campsite. A research station was founded here in 1953 to investigate the uses of reeds other than the traditional ones of thatching and wind-breaks. There is a Museum of the Reed Industry which shows the various processes for converting reeds to paper, cardboard, fibre-board, alcohol, glycerin and fertiliser. Little is wasted with the pith left over compressed into briquettes to be used in stoves over the cold winters. The big problem at the moment is not how to use the reeds but

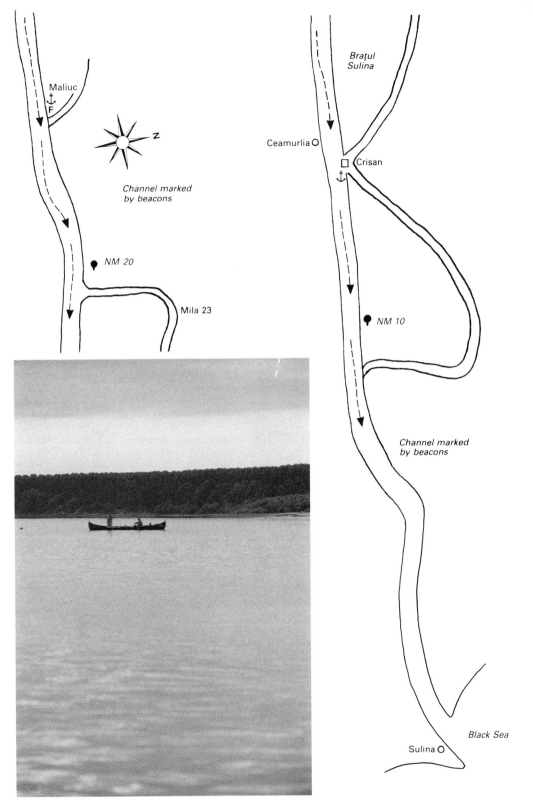

Maliuc

Channel marked
by beacons

NM 20

Mila 23

Bratul
Sulina

Ceamurlia

Crisan

NM 10

Channel marked
by beacons

Black Sea

Sulina

Fishermen on Lacul Lumina in the delta.

The ubiquitous reeds of the delta.

Dalmatian pelicans, glossy ibis, night herons, squacco herons, pygmy cormorants, little egrets, pratincoles, avocets, stilts, storks, white-tailed eagles, Saker falcons, mute swans, snipes, cranes, the list goes on in a catalogue unique in Europe for its diversity and size.

Mila 23 On an old arm of the Danube sits the fishing village of Mila 23, a fishing village rebuilt here after a flood destroyed the original settlement in the 1960s. Most of the population living in the delta are Lipovenians, a strict Russian Orthodox sect that migrated here in the 18th century. In the 17th century Peter the Great introduced sweeping changes to the Orthodox church with new translations of the gospels and changes to church practice. Even worse the Czar was associated with evil new practices, smoking and indecent dress fashions, so the dissenters decided to leave Russia and go to the uttermost part of the world. After crossing the Ukraine where they acquired their name from the lime tree, the *lipo*, they came to the Danube delta. They have dwelt here since that migration, the fishermen of the delta, their religious practices and lifestyle preserved intact. The ginger beards of the old men and the blond haired women stand out amongst the darker Romanians, though now many have inter-married and the restriction on smoking has evidently long disappeared.

Mila 23 is a typical village with reed thatched houses painted predominantly in blues or greens. The old wooden church was falling down when I was there so a new church was being built. The icon inside, transported long ago from Russia, was soon to be transported to the new church, though, for some reason – clearly something to do with the authorities restricting religious activities – the village no longer had a priest. Until an ice factory was built in Tulcea the winter ice on the delta was collected at the beginning of the thaw and stored in a thick reed insulated building, the *cherhana*, where it would stay solid for three to four weeks. The *cherhana* is still here, but not used today. The authorities keep a close check on the number of fish caught; it must now all be turned over to the co-operative, and a police boat accompanies the fishermen to keep an eye on them. Nonetheless a lot of smuggling goes on in full view of the police. I saw bottles of Bulgarian wine, cigarettes and money changing hands for fish that should have been going to the co-operative at Tulcea, all in full view of the police boat some twenty metres away. When I asked how they could get away with it one of

how to harvest them. The reeds are still cut by hand as no satisfactory mechanical harvester has yet been devised that will not ruin the soft ground the reeds need to grow in.

NM 14·5
Crisan

The main tourist hotel on the delta and a campsite. From here trips can be arranged around the channels and lagoons of the delta.

For ornithologists the delta is unique. More than 250 species have been identified, some sources say 300, with 70 of those species normally resident outside Europe. Five important bird migration routes converge at the delta: the Pontic route from the steppes north of the Black Sea; the Sarmatian route from the north of Europe; the littoral route from the Caucasus in the east; the eastern Elbic route from central Europe; and the Carpathian route. Many species of wading birds including some of the only nesting colonies of the glossy ibis and pelicans left in Europe are to be found here. A list of some of the species reads like an ornithologist's dream come true: white and

the fishermen held up two huge calloused hands running with the blood of the fish he was gutting and asked me what I would do if I lived with a lot of rough fishermen in this wilderness – 'Sometimes policemen are drowned,' he said, 'Anyone can have an accident in these waters.' The police, I noted, were studiously looking the other way.

NM 0 – Right bank
Sulina

The end of the Danube. The small port town on the right bank is a sorry looking place with shabby buildings and when I was there, loudspeakers lectured the citizens, no doubt on the thoughts of their president. Most of the population were inside watching a football match. The old lighthouse marking the mouth of the Sulina channel is now a considerable distance from the actual entrance, a reminder of how the delta keeps pushing itself seawards. Most of the silt in fact comes from the Chilia arm that takes around 60% of the water from the Danube, and empties the silt down onto the dredged Sulina channel. When Captain Spratt of the Royal Navy made the first accurate survey of the delta in 1856–7 he recommended

that the Sulina arm not be used because of this problem, and that the Chilia arm be developed as the main navigable channel. The Romanians ignored this advice and developed the Sulina arm which must constantly be dredged to keep it to the required depths. While ships were of comparatively modest size Sulina prospered and expanded as a port, but as ships grew in the 20th century the port and the dredged channel proved insufficient and Sulina stagnated. It had a brief revival after the First World War when it became the headquarters of the International Danube Commission, but after the Second World War when the Danube Commission was moved to Budapest, Sulina once again went downhill and it has never really recovered.

In a way this is a fitting end to the Danube. It doesn't stop abruptly but merges imperceptibly into the Black Sea, losing its identity bit by bit. The horizon between sea and sky is difficult to make out, just as the junction between the river and the sea cannot be clearly identified. There is no certainty that the muddy water is fresh or salt, no movement of waves to identify the sea and no banks to contain the river. It is only the end because a marker says 0·0 nautical miles.

The delta teems with fish, everything from repulsive squat varieties of catfish to silver bream. The bottle of Bulgarian red has just been swapped for a couple of fish.

Appendix

I. HARBOURS, PONTOONS AND ANCHORAGES ON THE DANUBE

The following list details the harbours, pontoons, and anchorages along the Danube that I looked at on my trip in *Rozinante*. I have also included some references from my research and the observations of fellow travellers and residents along the river. Although the list is not complete, it is as exhaustive as I can make it.

It should be remembered that depths in the Danube vary through the year so it is impossible to give depths at pontoons and in basins. In some of the basins a bar forms across the entrance from silt deposited by the river. Sometimes there will be greater depths at one place across the bar than at others, depending on what the current is doing – it is almost impossible to predict where this will be as the current and back-eddies follow no really predictable pattern and you will have to rely on local knowledge. What I have done is to indicate whether a harbour or pontoon is suitable for deeper draught craft of around 2m. Where anchorages are mentioned it is a matter of selecting the depth out of the channel suitable to the craft's draught by slowly motoring into the stream until you determine that the anchorage is suitable – there is a large element of guesswork in it.

Km 2381 – Left bank
Regensburg Motorboot Club. Private pontoons with deep water. Water and electricity. Crane. Fuel, provisions and restaurants nearby.

Km 2377 – Right bank
Regensburg. Pleasure boat pontoon at downstream end of docks. Reasonable depths.

Km 2366 – Left bank
Walhalla. Pontoon used by tripper boats. Deep water.

Km 2354
Ammerworth lock. Small pontoon before and after the lock. Deep water.

Km 2321·5 – Left bank
Straubing. Ferry pontoon with deep water immediately after bridge. Normally only used on Sundays and Wednesdays. Fuel, provisions, and restaurants in Straubing across the bridge.

Km 2321 – Left bank
Straubing. Commercial basin used by small tugs and workboats. Deep water.

Km 2314 – Right bank
Pontoon at the Straubing Watersport club. Shallow.

Km 2289
Pontoon at the Deggendorf Motorboot Club. Clubhouse.

Km 2284 – Left bank
Deggendorf. Donau Yacht Club. Situated in a basin with finger pontoons. Deep water in the basin. Clubhouse. Water. Provisions and restaurants in Deggendorf, a short walk away.

Km 2276 – Left bank
Niederalteich. Ferry pontoon with deep water.

Km 2256·6 – Left bank
Hofkirchen. Small basin. Mostly reasonable depths. Small crane. Water. Provisions and restaurant in the village nearby.

Km 2249
Vilshofen. Pontoons on left (commercial) and right (ferry) bank.

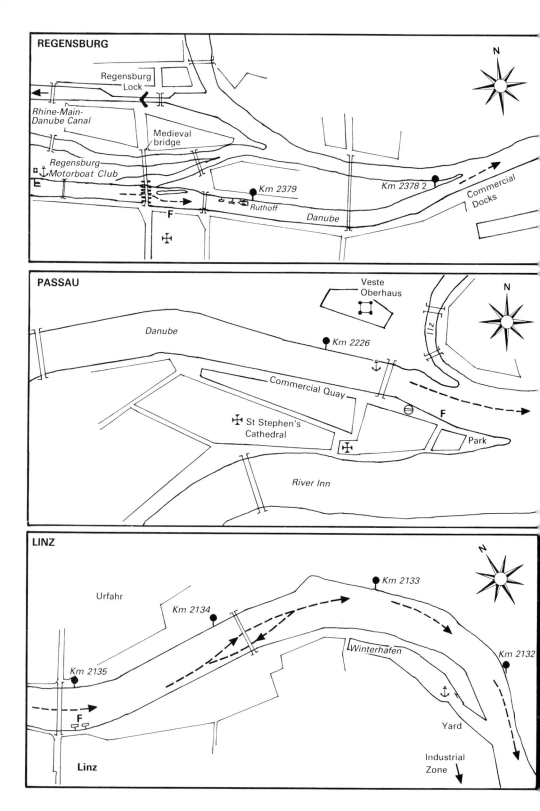

REGENSBURG

N

Regensburg Lock

Rhine-Main-Danube Canal

Medieval bridge

Regensburg Motorboat Club

Km 2379

Ruthoff

Danube

Km 2378 2

Commercial Docks

F

PASSAU

N

Veste Oberhaus

Danube

Km 2226

Ilz

Commercial Quay

St Stephen's Cathedral

F

Park

River Inn

LINZ

N

Urfahr

Km 2134

Km 2133

Km 2135

Winterhafen

Km 2132

F

Yard

Linz

Industrial Zone

Km 2246 – Left bank
Windorf. Ferry pontoon.

Km 2238
Pontoon off a restaurant.

Km 2232·5 – Right bank
Heining Yacht Club. Small basin with reasonable depths. Finger pontoons. Clubhouse. Crane. Water. Provisions and restaurants nearby.

Km 2226 – Left bank
Passau. A low quay under the motorway bridge is reserved for pleasure craft. There is deep water, but the quay is very low and when the river is high it is dangerous to go on here as the wash from ferries and barge-tows will wash you onto it and cause damage. On the right bank you may find a spot to berth for an hour or two, but I was told by a policeman I would get a 'ticket' if I stayed! Provisions and restaurants in the town.

Km 2222 – Left bank
Small commercial basin. A fuel lighter is moored outside it.

Km 2211 – Left bank
Obernzell. Two pleasure craft basins. Reasonable depths. Fuel, water and electricity. Crane and workshop. Showers and toilets. Café. A longish walk into Obernzell itself.

Km 2210 – Left bank
Obernzell. Ferry pontoon and quay. Motorised ferry across the river at the downstream end of quay.

Km 2208·4 – Right bank
Kasten. Pleasure craft basin. Camping ground nearby.

Km 2203
Jochenstein lock. Long quay at downstream end.

Km 2200·6 – Right bank
Engelhartszell. Ferry pontoon.

Km 2198 – Left bank
Small harbour off a restaurant.

Km 2195 – Left bank
Niederanna. Ferry pontoon. A number of private pontoons just downstream.

Km 2193 – Right bank
Wesenufer. Ferry pontoon.

Km 2192
Small pontoon with camping ground nearby.

Km 2187 – Right bank
Schlägen. Large basin with deep water, but there is a shallow muddy bar at the entrance. Moorings and finger pontoons. Clubhouse. Restaurant and camping ground.

Km 2178 – Left bank
Obermühl. Long quay, though it is uncomfortable from the wash of passing craft. Local boats berth on pontoons in the mouth of the Kleine Mühl, though it is not very attractive under an ore-loading dock.

Km 2168 – Left bank
Neuhaus. Small harbour with reasonable depths. Pontoons inside the breakwater. Water. Fuel nearby. Restaurant and provisions nearby.

Km 2161·5 – Left bank
Several pontoons for barges loading timber.

Km 2160 – Left bank
Aschach. Private pleasure craft basin.

Km 2157 – Left bank
Small pleasure boat harbour. Restaurant ashore.

Km 2132·5 – Right bank
Linz Winterhafen. Deep water. Pontoon just inside the entrance for visitors (*gäste*). Water. Crane and workshop. All facilities in Linz about half an hour's walk away. Do not attempt to berth in the river, where there is a strong current and dangerous wash from passing barge-tows. The ferry pontoon is in constant use.

Km 2112·4 – Left bank
Mauthausen. Ferry pontoon.

Km 2108·3 – Left bank
Private pleasure craft pontoon.

Km 2107 – Left bank
Au. Small pleasure craft basin.

Km 2093 – Right bank
Wallsee. Basin in the old arm of the river. It is mostly used by commercial craft but space can be found.

Km 2081 – Left bank
Grein. Basin with deep water. Pontoons. Fuel and water. Provisions and restaurants nearby.

Km 2065·6 – Left bank
Isperdorf. A number of pleasure boat moorings up from the bridge across the River Isper.

Km 2059 Ybbs and Persenbeug. Ferry pontoon on either side of the river.

Km 2050 – Left bank
Marbach Yacht Club. Basin with deep water. Pontoons. Water. Short walk into the village.

Km 2046·5 – Right bank
Pontoon in the mouth of the River Erlaufeinstau.

Km 2036 – Right bank
Melk. There is deep water in the old arm of the Danube, but nowhere to berth for pleasure craft.

Km 2031·8 – Right bank
Schonbühel. Care needs to be taken of a low rocky islet off the castle. Keep to the left side of the river. Just upstream of the castle are several pontoons off a camping ground, very exposed to the current and wash.

Km 2027 – Left bank
Aggsbach. Ferry pontoon.

Km 2019 – Left bank
Spitz. Small pleasure boat harbour with reasonable depths. The approach is tricky and considerable care is needed. Provisions and restaurants in the village.

Km 2009 – Left bank
Dürnstein. Ferry pontoon – always busy.

Km 2004 – Left bank
Fuel pontoon.

Km 2002 – Left bank
Krems Yacht Harbour. Deep water but a low bridge with approximately 4·5m air height. Visitors' berths at the end of the basin at 'Donau Camping'. Water and electricity. Showers and toilets. A short walk into Krems for provisions and restaurants. It is a pleasant walk to Dürnstein to look at the ruins.

Km 2000 – Left bank
Small basin.

Km 1999·4 – Right bank
Small basin.

Km 1998 – Left bank
Krems commercial harbour.

Km 1988·5 – Right bank
Marina Traismauer. Small basin with crane and clubhouse. Visitors' pontoons off the restaurant.

Km 1973 – Right bank
Epersdorf. A breakwater forms a small harbour in a basin. Pontoons. Clubhouse.

Km 1962·3 – Right bank
Tulln Yacht Harbour situated just after the iron girder bridge. Deep water. Visitors' berths at pontoons under the clubhouse. Fuel and water. Crane and workshop. Showers and toilets. Provisions and restaurants in Tulln about 15 minutes walk away.

Km 1957·3 – Left bank
Small pleasure boat basin.

Km 1956 – Right bank
Small pleasure boat harbour. Clubhouse. Crane.

Km 1951·5 – Right bank
Fuel pontoon. Small pleasure boat harbour. Clubhouse. Water.

Km 1945·6 – Right bank
Private pontoons.

Km 1943 – Left bank
Korneuburg commercial harbour.

Km 1939 – Left bank
Weir for the 'Danube Lake'.

Km 1935 – Right bank
Kahlenbergerdörfp. Marina with deep water. Pontoons. Water and electricity. Fuel. Crane and workshop. Chandlers. Several restaurants and *Heuringers*. Provisions at Nusdorf one stop away on the train. Frequent train services into Vienna, about half an hour.

Km 1933 – Right bank
Entrance into the Donau Canal through a lock. *Note* Pleasure craft are not normally allowed to berth in the Donau Canal. Permission may sometimes be granted.

Km 1920·5 – Right bank
Vienna Winterhafen. Predominantly commercial.

Km 1920 – Right bank
Downstream end of Donau Canal.

Km 1917 – Left bank
Lobau commercial tanker harbour.

The *Botel Admiral*, a watersports base at Km 1561.

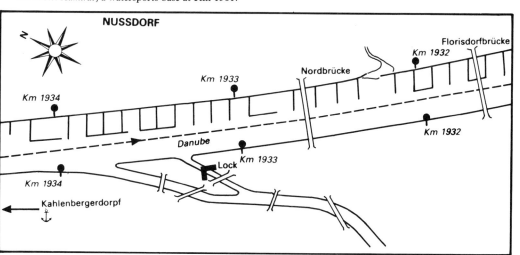

Km 1908·3 – Right bank
Fischamend. Several pontoons in the old arm of the Danube.

Km 1902 – Left bank
Orth pleasure boat harbour.

Km 1895 – Right bank
Wildungsmauer. Pleasure boat moorings in an old arm of the Danube. Mostly shallow water.

Km 1884 – Right bank
Hainburg customs post pontoon. Clear out of Austria for Czechoslovakia here.

Km 1869 – Right bank
Pontoon for clearing into Czechoslovakia. A patrol boat will escort you into here. Care needs to be taken as the pontoon I was escorted to had less than a metre depth alongside. After the necessary formalities have been completed you will be escorted to Bratislava commercial harbour. Procedure may differ now.

Km 1866 – Left bank
Entrance to Bratislava commercial harbour. Deep water. Berth at the end where possible. Water nearby. Provisions and restaurants in

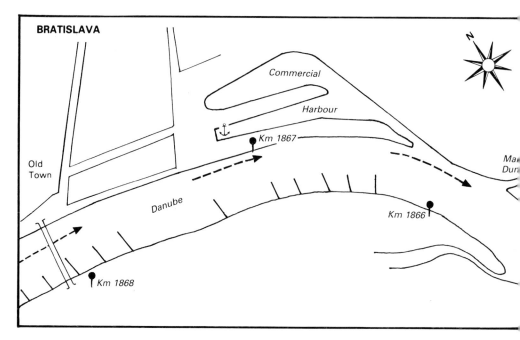

Bratislava a considerable distance away. Clear out with the police at the entrance before proceeding downstream.

Km 1864 – Left bank
New commercial harbour.

Km 1768 – Left bank
Komárno commercial harbour. Deep water. Berth where possible. Clear out for Hungary from the pontoon outside the harbour on the river.

Km 1768 – Right bank
Komárom. Berth on the pontoon outside the offices on the Hungarian side to clear in.

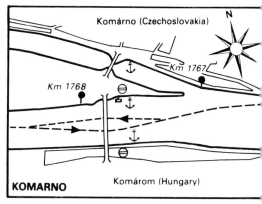

Km 1719 – Right bank
Esztergóm. Berths in an old arm of the Danube. Deep water. Report to the police on the first pontoon inside the arm. Further up there is a pontoon belonging to the hotel nearby. Water nearby. Provisions and restaurants in the town. An excellent fish restaurant further up the old arm.

Km 1688·5 (27·5) – Right bank
Dunabogdany. Pontoon at camping ground. Restaurant.

Km 1680·5 (19·5) – Right bank
Tahitotfalu. Pontoon.

Km 1679·5 – Left bank
Vac. Pontoon.

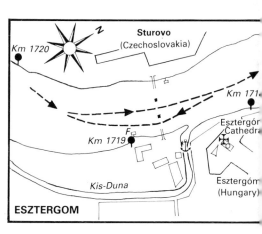

Km 1653 – Left bank
Entrance to commercial harbour.

Km 1651·5 – Right bank
Commercial canal. Deep water. Go alongside where possible. Provisions and restaurants nearby. You have to scramble up the wall to get to the shops nearby, but you are out of the current.

Km 1651 to km 1650
Margaretin Island. You may find a berth at one of the rowing club pontoons. Deep water. Close to the centre of Buda.

Km 1646 – Left bank
Ferry and cruise boat pontoons. You may find a berth somewhere here. Right in the middle of Budapest.

Km 1642 – Right bank
Lagymanyos. A basin with rowing clubs and some old hulks. Deep water. Water. Provisions a short distance away. You are some distance away from the centre of Budpest here.

Km 1640 to 1639 – Left bank
Commercial basins.

Km 1638 – Right bank
Yacht Club. Moorings along the river bank. Close to Budafok.

Km 1586 – Left bank
Old arm of the Danube. The sluice gates controlling the water in the Rackevei arm are about 200m up. Moor by the bank.

Km 1579 – Right bank
Dunaújváros. A large basin runs back up from the river. Deep water. Anchor just before the commercial docks off a small beach. The facilities in Dunaújváros are a considerable distance away.

Km 1561 – Right bank
Dunaföldvár. A watersport club based in the old tug *Botel Admiral* normally has space for visitors. It is a little uncomfortable from the wash of passing barge-tows, but safe enough. Water. Showers and toilets on board. Restaurant on board and in the town. Provisions in the town.

Km 1532 – Right bank
Paks. Pleasure craft pontoon where a berth may be available. Reasonable depths. Uncomfortable from the wash. All facilities in Paks.

Km 1479 – Left bank
Baja. Canal leads off to the town just after the bridge across the Danube. It is difficult to see. Ample berthing opportunities along the way. The signs showing pleasure craft berths lead to a pontoon used by swimmers! Provisions and restaurants in the town.

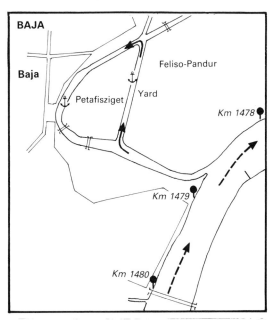

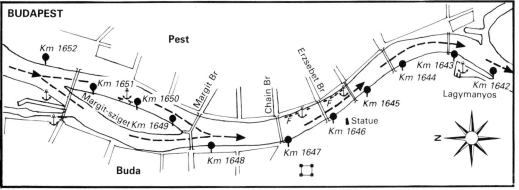

Km 1459 – Right bank
Dunaszekcsö. Private pontoons just past the town.

Km 1447 – Right bank
Mohács. Berth at the pontoon off the offices for clearing out. The Hungarian and Yugoslavian border offices are side by side so you can clear out of Hungary and into Yugoslavia at the same time. By the ferry berths there are several pontoons for pleasure craft where a berth may be found. Provisions and restaurants in Mohács.

Km 1430 to 1360
Numerous anchorages in the waterland just inside Yugoslavia.

Km 1401 – Left bank
Apatin. A channel leads to the commercial port where there are several pontoons for local pleasure craft. Alternatively anchor off the beach closer to the town.

Km 1382·5 – Right bank
Mouth of the Drava River. There are good depths up the river to Osijek where there is a yacht marina with all facilities in the commercial harbour. Berths at finger pontoons. Fuel and water. Crane and workshop. Provisions and restaurants in the town.

Km 1333 – Right bank
Vukovar. Small basin with good depths. Berth where possible. Water. Provisions and restaurants in the town nearby.

Km 1272 – Left bank
Anchorage in a channel off the river.

Km 1261 – Left bank
Novisad Watersports pontoon. Berth where possible. Deep water. Water and a restaurant nearby. A long walk into town.

Km 1258 – Left bank
Watersports pontoon just after the new bridge closer to the centre of Novisad.

Km 1252 – Left bank
Commercial harbour.

Km 1214·5 – Left bank
Mouth of the Tisza River.

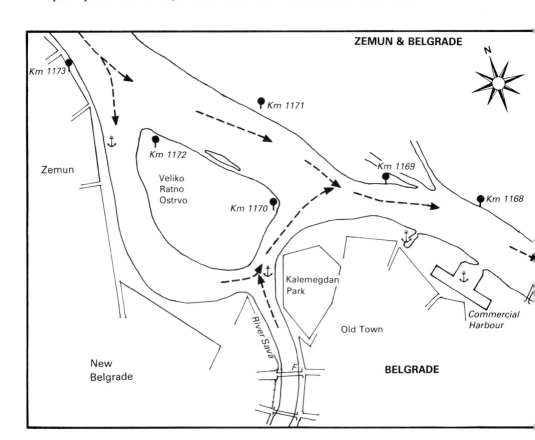

Km 1172·5 – Right bank
Zemun. Moorings off the town at the entrance to the old arm. The old arm has good depths and is navigable to the Sava at Belgrade.

Km 1170 – Right bank
Belgrade. There may be a berth at the ferry and cruise boat pontoons on the Sava.

Km 1169 – Right bank
Marina Doroc. A shallow harbour in a disused commercial basin. There is a bar at the entrance. Water. A short walk to downtown Belgrade.

Km 1167 – Right bank
Belgrade commercial port. There may be a berth available in the commercial basin.

Km 1162 – Right bank
Novi Beograd. Laid moorings and a boatyard.

Km 1154 – Left bank
Pancevo. Two large lighthouses mark the entrance to a canal blocked by sluice gates about 200m up it. Possible mooring in here.

Km 1153 – Left bank
Pancevo commercial harbour.

Km 1116 – Right bank
Smederevo. Berths for small craft with the fishing boats bows-to the sloping quay. The wash from passing barge-tows makes it uncomfortable. Provisions and restaurants in the town.

Km 1078 – Right bank
Ram. Anchor off or go alongside the old barge. Restaurant.

Km 1060 – Right bank
Just before the town Veliko Gradiste an old arm of the Danube has been dammed off creating a basin. Deep water. Anchor in here or go bows-to the sloping concrete wall at the end.

Km 1058 – Right bank
Veliko Gradiste. Go alongside the end of the quay to have your papers checked. Boats crossing to Romania clear out of Yugoslavia here. For pleasure craft it is best to stay in Yugoslavia and proceed on to Bulgaria before finally crossing into Romania from Rousse. It is possible to stay here overnight but it is exposed to the wind and wash from passing craft. The basin upriver affords better shelter. ·

Km 1048 – Left bank
Moldova Veche. Clear into Romania here if necessary.

Km 1042 – Right bank
Near Golubac. Small pleasure boat harbour belonging to a hotel.

Km 993 – Right bank
Donji Milanovac. A lighter moored off the town provides berths for pleasure craft. Deep water. It can be uncomfortable when the wind blows freshly across the 'lake', but is safe enough. Water. Fuel nearby. Provisions and restaurants.

Km 990 – Right bank
Porecka River. There are good depths in the river where anchorage can be obtained with good shelter. Restaurant in the river.

Km 956 – Right bank
Tekjip. A lighter moored off the village provides berths for pleasure craft. Deep water. Water on the lighter. Provisions and restaurants nearby.

Km 943
Iron Gates Lock. Go alongside the quay until entry is allowed. Traffic lights control entry and exit. Sliding bollards. Your papers will be checked.

Km 934 – Right bank
Kladovo. The small harbour here is shallow. A berth can usually be found alongside the floating restaurant. It can be uncomfortable from the wind blowing along the river and from the wash of passing craft. Water and reasonable food at the floating restaurant. Provisions in the town. Customs will want to check your papers.

Km 930 – Left bank
Turnu Severin. Berth at the pontoon off the harbourmaster's office. Craft clearing into Romania will have their paperwork carried out here. Deep water. Restaurants ashore.

Km 864 – Left bank
Prahovo lock. Go alongside the quay until entry is allowed.

Km 861 – Right bank
Prahovo. Berth on the pontoon off the customs office and Duty Free shop. Good depths. There is an old silted harbour just downstream which small craft can get into. There are no facilities locally.

Km 845 – Right bank
A Bulgarian patrol boat moored just across the border, the River Timok, will want to see the boat's papers.

Km 795 – Left bank
Calafat. A pontoon with deep water. Restaurants.

Km 792 – Right bank
Vidin ferry port. The paperwork for clearing in is carried out at the ferry port.

Km 790 – Right bank
Vidin. Hang off one of the pontoons or anchor off the castle. It is uncomfortable here from the current and the wash from passing barge-tows. Deep water. Water tap on the pontoon. Provisions and restaurants nearby.

Km 744 – Right bank
Lom. Pontoon with a few pleasure boats on it in front of the naval R & R building with a watersports mural on it. Reasonable depths. Alternatively anchor off. Water close to the pontoon. Provisions and restaurants in the town.

Km 679 – Left bank
Bechet. Pontoon with deep water.

Km 678 – Right bank
Oriachovo. Commercial quay which is very dirty from coal and ore being loaded. It's better to anchor just down river. Few facilities.

Km 607·5 – Right bank
Somovit. Anchor off the beach just before the town.

Km 597 – Left bank
Turnu Magurele. Several pontoons with deep water. Nearby are several huge factories belching poisonous fumes so the place is best avoided.

Km 597 – Right bank
Nikopol. Hang off the back of one of the pontoons off the town or anchor in a small bight behind a spit at the downstream end of the town. Provisions and restaurants in the town.

Km 554 – Right bank
Svištov. An industrial port where you may find a berth on the quay. Just past the town is an abandoned barge that small craft could go alongside. Alternatively anchor off. Provisions and restaurant.

Km 553·5 – Left bank
Ziminicea. Several pontoons with deep water.

Km 547 – Right bank
An old arm of the Danube with 3–7m winds off with the village of Vardim at the top of the curve. At the junction with the Danube at both ends there is a sand bank where you will have to find the channel through. Anchor off or nose into the bank at Vardim. Some provisions.

Km 495 – Right bank
Rousse. Hang off the back of one of the pontoons. Most boats will be crossing into Romania at Giurgiu from here so must clear out with the relevant authorities. Water on the pontoons. Fuel a considerable distance away but it is worth stocking up by jerry can before Romania. Provisions and restaurants in the town.

Km 493 – Left bank
Giurgiu. Go alongside or hang off the back of one of the pontoons. If entering Romania clear in with the relevant authorities here. Cruise boats stop here for passengers to go on a tour of Bucharest. With luck you may be able to tag along. Otherwise there is a train into Bucharest. Café.

Km 430 – Left bank
Oltenita. Go on the pontoon. There are reasonable depths on the inside as well. Run-down restaurant.

Km 433 – Right bank
Toutrakan. Pontoon off the town.

Km 403 – Right bank
Popina. Pontoon off the town.

Km 375·5 – Right bank
Silistra. Pontoon with deep water. It may be possible to clear out of here for Romania.

Km 370·5 – Left bank
A channel leads off to Călărasi about 6 or 7km upstream. A pontoon and docks.

Km 300 – Right bank
Cernavoda. Pontoon in the entrance to the canal. The procedure and initial paperwork for the Danube-Black Sea canal is carried out here. Water. Some provisions and restaurants. Fuel may be available.

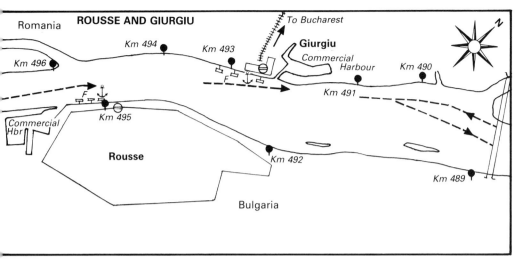

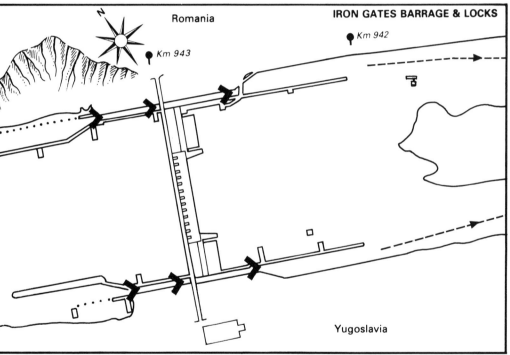

Danube-Black Sea canal At Cernavoda the initial paperwork will be carried out and a pilot allotted. The transit of the canal normally takes a full day. At the seaward end it is best to stay overnight in the canal at Agigea where there is a pontoon. The balance of the paperwork will be done and the canal fees are paid here. Once locked out of the canal proceed through the maze of the vast commercial port before going north to Constanţa about a mile up the coast.

From Cernavoda to the delta there are numerous possibilities for anchoring behind islands and exploring old arms of the Danube.

Km 272 – Right bank
Topalu. Pontoon. Some provisions.

Km 253 – Right bank
Hîrşova. Pontoons. Some provisions and restaurant.

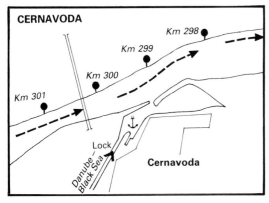

CERNAVODA

Km 298
Km 299
Km 300
Km 301
Lock
Danube–Black Sea
Cernavoda

Km 238 – Left bank
Giurgeni. Pontoon.

Km 183 – Left bank
Chiscani. Pontoon.

Km 171 – Left bank
Brăila. Pontoons. Provisions and restaurants.

Km 151 – Left bank
Galati. Pontoons. Provisions and restaurants.

NM 38·5 – Right bank
Tulcea. Pontoons and docks. Deep water. Provisions and restaurants. Fuel may be available.

NM 23 – Left bank
Sulina channel. Maliuc. Pontoon. Restaurant.

NM 14·5 – Left bank
Sulina channel. Crisan. Pontoon. Restaurant.

NM 0·0 – Right bank
Sulina. Pontoon and docks. The paperwork for clearing out to Constanţa or out of Romania is carried out here. Some provisions. Restaurant.

Note Romanian *Law No. 9/1973* states the following:
Navigation in the Danube Delta with private motor boats is forbidden by law. Use of such craft is allowed only on the Danube.
Art 32 Within the reserves and regarding the monuments of nature, it is forbidden to carry on any activity which might lead to the degradation or modification of the initial aspect of the scenery, of the structure of the fauna and of the flora or of the ecological equilibrium, excepting the cases when the organ designed by law should authorise this kind of activity.
Art 73 The infringement of the provisions of the law regarding the protection of the environment entails disciplinary, material, civil

or penal responsibility, or might be considered an offence.

Constanţa Go alongside the quay inside where there are good depths, 3–4m mostly, and reasonable protection although strong NE–E gales set up a surge. Water. Fuel is difficult to find. Some provisions and restaurants.

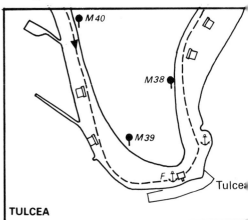

M 40
M38
M 39
Tulcea

TULCEA

GOING UP THE DANUBE

A number of people have asked me about going up the Danube, in effect completing a Grand Tour going down into the Mediterranean and returning to Northern Europe via the Danube and the Rhine. While there is nothing to stop anyone who is determined going up the Danube against the current, it is not the logical route and you must be prepared to take your time over it. The first problem is simply the current you will have to push against. In the lower Danube to the Iron Gates this can be anything between 2–5 knots, though usually around 3–3·5 knots on average. Only in exceptionally dry winters does the rate reduce to the lower figure and then only for the low water period September to October. After the Iron Gates the current is less until around Belgrade, probably 1·5–2·5 knots on average. Through Hungary the rate is normally around 3–5 knots to Budapest. Through Czechoslovakia the rate can be as much as 6–7 knots and likewise through parts of Austria and Germany. Except for planing powerboats, the only real solution to getting up is to get a tow with a barge train. If you do this the whole journey may just turn into a noisy motorised tow through the day and night until you get to the barge train's destination. Frankly this seems to me a waste of time and effort - you will see very little of the countries along the way and experience little of the river apart from the noise and smell of powerful diesels.

II. USEFUL BOOKS

General

World Canals Charles Hadfield. David & Charles. 1986. Some material on the Danube.

The Danube Joseph Wechsberg. Newsweek Books. 1979. Deals mainly with the upper Danube in Germany and Austria. Glossy pictures and some interesting sections.

Travelling on the Danube Johannes Binder. DDSG. Covers Passau to Vienna. Much detailed information and a map of the Danube.

From Vienna to the Black Sea Johannes Binder. DDSG. Covers Vienna to the Black Sea. Complements *Travelling on the Danube* with detailed information and a map of the Danube.

Inland Waterways of Europe Roger Calvert. George, Allen & Unwin. 1963. Has a chapter on the Danube with some interesting information, now fairly dated.

The Danube Bend László Cseke. Pannonia Press. 1977. Covers the Danube bend in Hungary.

The Danube Emil Lengyel. Random House. 1939.

The Danube Erwin Lessner. Doubleday. 1961.

The Danube Julian Popescu. Oxford University Press. 1961.

Narrative

A Thousand Miles in the Rob Roy Canoe on the Rivers and Lakes of Europe John MacGregor. 1st ed. 1870. Classic stuff covering the Danube from Donaueschingen to Ulm.

A Cruise Across Europe Donald Maxwell. Bodley Head. 1906. Amusing tale of a voyage from England to the Black Sea in the 18ft *Walrus*.

Across Europe in a Motorboat Henry C. Rowland. Appleton & Co. 1915. Account of a voyage down the Danube in the motorboat *Beaver*.

Sailing Across Europe Negley Farson. 1926. Reprint by Century 1985. One of the classic accounts of a trip in the yacht *Flame*. Very readable and full of interesting pre-war observations.

The Blue Danube Bernard Newman. Herbert Jenkins. 1935. Readable and interesting account of a cycling journey down the Danube.

A Time of Gifts and *Between the Woods and the Water*. Patrick Leigh Fermor. John Murray 1977 and 1986, available in Penguin paperback. Two volumes (will be three) of a trek down the Danube, with a lot of meandering off to other places, in 1933–34. Peerless travel writing, in a class of its own.

Black Sea and Blue River John Marriner. Rupert Hart-Davis. 1968. Account of a trip **up** the Danube in the motor vessel *September Tide*. Much interesting detail.

Frontiers Adam Nicolson. Weidenfeld & Nicolson. 1985. Covers some of the Danube in a motorcycle trip. Dense impenetrable prose.

The Improbable Voyage Tristan Jones. Bodley Head. 1986. Racy prose and a thrilling read; but your own voyaging on the Danube is unlikely ever to encompass all that Tristan Jones manages to fit in.

Stealing From a Deep Place Brian Hall. Heinemann. 1988. Account of a cycle trip through Hungary, Romania and Bulgaria.

Danube Claudio Magris. Collins Harvill. 1989. A journey down the Danube, as much of an intellectual journey as a straight account of a trip; once you are into it it will tell you more than most of the others.

Gay Bulgaria Stowers Johnson. Travel Book Club. 1964. Intriguing early account touring in a Dormobile.

Romanian Journey Andrew Mackenzie. Robert Hale. 1983. A sop to Ceausescu though it contains some interesting material.

Guidebooks

Michelin: Germany and *Austria*. Usual high standard.

Nagel's Germany Useful.

Berlitz: Vienna and *Hungary*. Compact useful guides.

A Guide To Central Europe Richard Bassett. Viking. 1987. Covers Vienna and environs, Slovakia, Budapest and environs, and Transylvania. Readable stuff.

Czechoslovakia Citbor Rybár. Collets. 1982. Dour official handbook.

Rough Guides to *Eastern Europe – Hungary, Romania, and Bulgaria* (Dan Richardson & Jill Denton) and *Yugoslavia*. Usual excellent down to earth advice characteristic of the series.

Guide to 10 Hungarian Towns István Wellner. Panorama. 1986.

The Two Thousand Years of Budapest Budapest Museum of History.

Hungary István Lázár and András Székely. Fine Arts Publishing. 1986. Glossy photos and a fine text.

Beograd Turistkomerc. 1980. Dour official guide.

Bulgaria: A Short Tourist Guide Collets. 1980. Dour official guide.

Other

The Penguin Guide to Medieval Europe Richard Barber. Penguin. 1984. Very readable guide to medieval monuments.

A History of Europe John Bowle. Pan. Cheap compact volume that paints the wider canvas.

Outside The Empire N H H Sitwell. Paladin. 1986. The outside world the Romans knew, including tribes around the Danube – fascinating stuff.

The Europeans Luigi Barzini. Penguin. 1983. Amusing and enlightening on the Germans, the only Danube nation covered.

The Other Europeans Anton Zischka. MacDonald. 1962. Solid stuff on middle and eastern Europeans.

War and Society in Europe, 1870 – 1970 Brian Bond. Fontana. 1984.

Europe: Grandeur and Decline A J P Taylor. 1950. Penguin 1985. Essays by the master historian.

The Habsburg Monarchy 1809 – 1918 A J P Taylor. 1948. Penguin 1981.

The Blue Danube Tudor Edwards. Robert Hale. 1973. Vienna after Franz Josef.

People of the Puszta Gyula Illyes. Corvina Kiado. 1936/1967. A Hungarian classic.

Balkan Background Bernard Newman. Travel Book Club. 1945. Interesting material by a knowledgeable author – the same one who cycled down the Danube.

Red Horizons Ion Mihai Pacepa. Heinemann. 1988. Account of the machinations in Romania by a spy chief who defected – smacks of American rewriting.

Daco Romania Dumitru Berciu. Nagel. 1978. Academic account of Romanian history.

Dracula Bram Stoker. 1897. Oxford University Press 1986.

Charts and Pilots

The Reise-und Verkehrsverlag maps nos 10 and 11 are useful for the Danube from Donaueschingen to Regensburg.

Carte de Pilotage du Danube 12 volumes covering Regensburg to the Black Sea with a scale of between 1: 10000 to 1: 25000. Commission du Danube Budapest. 1970 to 1976, updated and corrected. The charts are in Russian and French, but charts are charts and they are easily followed. They are not necessary, not always correct, and horrendously expensive.

Kartografiai Vallalat: 3 charts for the Danube in Hungary. Obtainable in Budapest.

A Handbook of the River Danube 1915–1919. Admiralty. OP.

III. USEFUL ADDRESSES

Diplomatic and consular

Austrian Embassy, 18 Belgrave Mews West, London SW1 8HU. ☎ 071-235 3731
Bulgarian Embassy, 188 Queensgate, London SW7. ☎ 071-584 9400
Czechoslovakian Embassy, 25 Kensington Palace Gardens, London W8 4QY. ☎ 071-229 1255
German Embassy, 23 Belgrave Sq, London SW1 8PZ. ☎ 071-235 5033
Hungarian Embassy, 35 Eaton Place, London SW1. ☎ 071-235 4048
Romanian Embassy, 4 Palace Gardens, London W8 4QD. ☎ 071-937 9666
Soviet Embassy, 10 Kensington Palace Gdns, London W8 4QX. ☎ 071-229 3628
Yugoslav Embassy, 5 Lexham Gardens, London W8 5JU. ☎ 071-370 6105

Danube travel and tourism

Tourist Commission of the Danube Countries, Margaretenstrasse 1, A-1040 Wien. ☎ 0222-56 16 66
German Canoe Federation, Rolf Kunze, Friedrich-Beuer-Strabe 42, D-5300, Bonn 3, Germany. ☎ 0228-47 20 40
Danube Travel, 6 Conduit St, London W1. ☎ 071-493 0263
DDSG, A-1020, Wien, Handelskai 265. ☎ 0222-26 65 36
Luftner-Reisen, Reiseburo Dr W Luftner GmbH, A-6020 Innsbruck, Sudtiroler Platz 4, Postfach 509. ☎ 22 423

General travel and tourism

Aeroflot Soviet Airlines, 70 Picadilly, London W1. ☎ 071-493 7436
Balkan and Bulgarian Airlines, 322 Regent St, London W1. ☎ 071-637 7637
Balkan Holidays, 19 Conduit St, London W1. ☎ 071-491 4499
Bulgarian Tourist Office, 18 Princes St, London W1. ☎ 071-499 6988
Czechoslovak Travel Bureau (CEDOK), 17 Old Bond St, London W1. ☎ 071-629 6058
Hungarian Airtours, 3 Heddon St, London W1. ☎ 071-437 1622
Intourist Moscow Ltd, 292 Regent St, London W1. ☎ 071-631 1252
Malev Hungarian Airlines, 10 Vigo St, London W1. ☎ 071-439 0577
Romanian Tourist Office, 29 Thurloe Place, London SW7. ☎ 071-584 8090
Yugoslav National Tourist Office, 143 Regent St, London W1. ☎ 071-734 5243

Other

Collet's International Bookshop, 129 Charing Cross Road, London WC2 ☎ 071-734 0782. (Stocks numerous publications on Eastern Europe.)
Freytag, Berndt und Arteria, Kohlmarkt, 9, A1010 Wien, Austria
Seekarten-n-Material Bucher Christian Bernwieser, Schanzstrasse 15, A1140 Wien, Austria.
School of Slavonic and East European Studies, University of London, Senate House, Malet St, London WC1. ☎ 071-637 4934

Bade & Hornig GmbH, P.O. Box 11,20,45, Stubbenhuk 10, D-2000, Hamburg, Germany
Eckhardt & Messtorff, Rödingsmarkt 16, D-2000, Hamburg, Germany
Geobuch GmbH, Rosental 6, D-8000, Munchen 2, Germany

IV. ROZINANTE ON THE DANUBE

In 1985 I made my first trip down the Danube. Without a plan, but with a substantial amount of research on the Danube rattling around my head, I got a train to Donaueschingen at the source of the Danube in the Black Forest. From there I took a local train down the Danube – luckily the railway track follows the river – stopping off at places along the way and exploring the Danube on foot. At Regensburg I took the ferry to Passau, from there the ferry to Linz and on to Vienna. Here I hoped to hitch a ride on a tug going downstream, but despite the best efforts of my contacts there, it was not possible. I got the hydrofoil to Budapest and from there took a cruise boat, the *Oltenita* down to Cernavoda. From there I took an excursion to the Danube delta where I spent three days before catching the train to Turkey.

It was not enough. I still felt that I needed to explore the Danube in a boat of some sort. In 1987 I bought a small motor-sailer, a Mirror Offshore 19 which had sat neglected on the Thames at Twickenham for a few years. I needed crew and by chance I heard an old friend had thrown in her job in the Caribbean and was at a loose end. I phoned Bridgit and she agreed to do the trip. I made the necessary repairs to the boat I now called *Rozinante* after Don Quixote's horse; he thought the old clumsy nag he rode was the finest charger in the land and I could see definite parallels between the boat I had just bought and my view of what it could and would do; and bought an old, clapped out Rover 3500 to tow it down to the Danube. A friend, Graham, tired of telephones and too many business lunches, agreed to take time off to help us get *Rozinante* to the Danube and to do his best to drive the ailing Rover back to England. It was a project sired on a shoe-string and running on a lot of hope, but it seemed perfectly feasible.

What follows is an abbreviated record of *Rozinante's* journey down the Danube.

16th June

The alarm clock went off at 0630. Time to drive through London's traffic clogged streets to pick up the hired flat-bed trailer in St Albans. A quick run around the North Circular to Tough's boatyard where *Rozinante* is craned onto the trailer. I drive back to Tooting in South London where all the supplies are loaded on. On the lower Danube it will be difficult getting food in some parts of Bulgaria and most parts of Romania, so I have bought enough provisions to see us through this whole stretch of the river.

17th June

The last minute essentials are packed: black pepper and garlic, sellotape and a pencil sharpener, exhaust repair bandage and spare oil. Graham arrives at 1730 and we're off to Dover for the 2330 ferry to Zeebrugge. The trailer wheels are splayed out with the weight of the boat and equipment and provisions, the transmission whines in protest somewhere in the bowels of the Rover, but we make it to Dover.

18th June

0600. Trundling along at 50 mph in Belgium. At 1200 we cross into Germany at Aachen and customs don't even bother to ask about *Rozinante*.

19th June

We arrived in Regensburg at dusk and headed for the docks with a skyline of cranes apparently offering unlimited opportunities to put the boat in the water. It took a kind guard at one of the dock gates to direct us to the Regensburg Motorboot Club on the other side of the river where he thought we might find a crane more suited to our purpose. As I drove down the narrow lane to the club a car coming the other way flashed its lights at us and pulled over. When we stopped the driver got out. 'Hi. I'm Joe. You want the boat in the water. I do it tomorrow. 8·30 OK. Right. You follow me to the club now.' I couldn't get a word in edgeways and was in any case too surprised by the rapid-fire offers that tumbled out of Joe in a thick German-American accent. At the club Joe continued in the same vein. 'You park here. I gonna put you in the water for sure tomorrow morning. We got toilets here. We gotta kitchen in the clubhouse. We got cold beer in the machine there at one deutschmark. White beer, black beer. I don't think you'll like white beer. What the hell. What you like.' We slept in *Rozinante* on the back of the trailer for the night.

20th June

In the morning Joe was as good as his word. German punctuality. In fifteen minutes we were in the water and tied up alongside a pontoon at the club. However, Joe did warn us that the water level was three metres above the norm for the time of year and that we should wait until it went down. It would only take a couple of days to drop two metres, he reckoned – as long as it didn't rain any harder.

23rd June

After three days as Joe and the club members had prophesied, the level of the water was down by two metres. Graham and I had arranged a system of stick markers on the club steps that normally went down to the water's edge and reckoned that when the level got to the second step from the bottom, it was time to go. The medieval bridge just downstream was the first obstacle. It has only two navigable arches, one for going upstream and one for down. As with a lot of things, fear hardly entered into shooting the medieval bridge. I barely had time to line the boat up and gun the small diesel up to full revs before *Rozinante* was sucked through the arch and spat out the other side into a standing wave that covered the boat in spray. Graham was on the downstream side taking the photographs of the event and after picking him up I asked him what it had looked like. I wanted someone to tell me how grand it had looked as all nineteen foot of *Rozinante* was belched through the arch by the Danube. 'Two white faces in a blue boat covered with spray through a shaking viewfinder,' he replied. He was more nervous about the whole thing than we had been and the photographs subsequently showed this – they were so blurred from camera shake that none of them were usable. But he added that the good burghers of Regensburg had looked suitably amazed at the feat and I nursed a picture of their surprised faces for the next thirty kilometres. After nearly sixty kilometres a half-moon bridge and streetlights appeared through the rain-driven dusk. We tied alongside the ferry pontoon and rigged the cockpit tent just before the sky dumped buckets of rain on Straubing.

24 June

In the morning we shopped between rain showers and when *Rozinante* left Straubing we were stocked for a siege. Part of this was a continuous bolstering of the provisions for Bulgaria and Romania where I knew that it was difficult and often impossible to buy food, or much else come to that. We stopped for lunch in Deggendorf. Squat Soviet barge-ships, smartly painted but ugly craft, loaded ore across the river. They are more like small ocean-going ships than barges except the superstructure is kept low so they can pass under bridges.

25 June 1987

Graham had to leave us at Passau to get the train back to Regensburg and drive the ailing Rover and the hired trailer back to England. I turned *Rozinante* into the current near a likely quay and we tied up. A man in a uniform wandered along to tell us a ferry was due in soon. We moved to another vacant space to be told the same thing. Finally we found a space tucked in under the stern of a barge and things looked hopeful. Until a policeman strode up to us and like an imperious traffic warden told us if we didn't

In Baja.

Constanţa.

In Budapest.

In Oltenita.

move in five minutes he would give us a ticket. It was like trying to find a parking space in London. Graham packed his bag and jumped ashore.

26th June

Just past Obermühl there was a sudden clunk that sent a shudder through the boat and stopped the engine dead. I looked over the side to see a water-logged tree trunk drift lazily astern of *Rozinante*, a yellow gash on its top where the propeller had hit it. In Regensburg Joe from the motorboat club had told me to keep a good lookout for bits of lumber and tree trunks in the river. These bits of river flotsam were, he told me, the biggest danger to small boats on the river. He showed me a boat from the club with its propeller shattered after hitting a lump of wood. All the way from Regensburg I had heeded Joe's advice and had carefully zig-zagged around any bits of wood we spotted. Large trees could usually be seen from the branches sticking up out of the water, but water-logged planks and old tree stumps or trunks were more difficult to spot. I re-started the engine, listened carefully to its tune as it beat away, crawled inside and checked the propeller shaft, put the engine into and out of gear. Everything seemed all right. Nothing appeared to have been damaged. A little further on I spotted a small pleasure harbour and nosed *Rozinante* into it. After a walk ashore and a quiet dinner on board I had forgotten about the incident.

29th June

Below Grein there are a series of rapids and standing waves that were long feared on the Danube, though they have now been tamed by the new barrages built since the war. So I had read. The *Schwalleck* was a doddle, but lining *Rozinante* up for the *Strudel* I had to leave room for a pusher tug charging upstream. The wash from the tug and the standing waves of the *Strudel* pushed a wall of water over *Rozinante*. Water poured in around the front hatch drowning bags, books and food. It squeezed in through the windows. Bridgit and I clutching the coamings in the cockpit were soaked. There was no danger. It was the realisation that *Rozinante* was not as waterproof on top as we had thought which shocked us. If we were to take her across the Black Sea into Turkey she needed to be more watertight than this deluge had shown her to be. At Hausstein I concentrated on lining *Rozinante* up into the waves and disturbed water with great care and not a drop came on board. As it turned out, the *Strudel* and the pusher tug provided the worst dousing *Rozinante* encountered. Perhaps old Father Danube had administered a friendly warning.

2nd July

At Stein und Krems I asked a local where to berth in Vienna. He advised me that the best place to be was in the marina at Kahlenbergerdörfp on the outskirts of Vienna. I turned into the river mouth and berthed at a pontoon. In the office I was greeted by Herr Klein – 'Call me Mr Small. You are the small boat out there with the English flag,' he said in thick English, 'Now you want a berth, no,' I nodded. 'Right, there is a nice peaceful berth over there,' he pointed a spot out. 'You are going all the way down the Donau, no – there used to be a few boats going down, now not so many, too many problems in Bulgaria and Romania. You know Romania.' I said I had been there on my earlier trip, by land. 'Then you know,' he continued, 'The poorest country in Europe – really the poorest – you will see poor people like you have never seen before.' Mr Small showed us where to climb under the fence to get in at night, where to catch the train into Vienna, where his office was in case we needed anything, then excused himself and trotted off to tell the crane operator something. Whenever I saw him Mr Small was perpetually out of breath running around the marina, talking breathlessly to everyone who came within earshot. Whenever we walked through the marina to or from the boat Mr Small would appear, call a greeting over his shoulder with a few words of advice – 'You have metal canisters for fuel, no, you need metal as it is against the law in those countries to put fuel in plastic cans' – excuse himself and dash off on an urgent errand.

5th July

Odile arrives to join us for three weeks. Somehow we cram three people into *Rozinante's* crowded interior.

8th July

We left Kahlenbergerdörfp on a sunny Monday morning. Mr Small saw us off – 'You have all the visas. Good. You have enough food for Bulgaria and Romania. Good. You be careful,' – he was still calling advice after us as the Danube picked *Rozinante* up and rocketed us downstream. Around the dock area cruise boats, barges, trip boats and tugs milled about in Vienna's backyard. A large number of barge trains and other boats still use Vienna though the main commercial harbour is downstream of Vienna itself. Several bridges connect the new suburbs on the east bank to old Vienna. The brown waters of the Danube, coloured by the mud and lime picked up from the bottom and discoloured by oil and diesel, are funnelled through the narrowed gap of the new channel past new suburbs and commercial docks that hide Vienna from the river. Hainburg on the border between Austria and Czechoslovakia is nearly 50km from Vienna, but the current whirled us down to it in three hours. I had hoped to spend the night here before going on into Czechoslovakia, but there was nowhere to tie up except at the customs pontoon where we could not stay the night. Customs stamped our passports and with a quizzical look at the overloaded boat wished us what I took to be the Austrian equivalent of *Bon Voyage*.

Before we got to Bratislava an open launch with several soldiers in it came out to motion us into a pontoon on the right bank. They had rifles slung over their shoulders, but the fresh faced boys in uniforms seemed more interested in sneaking sidelong glances at Bridgit and Odile than in threatening any of us. I steered *Rozinante* into the pontoon and it was indicated that we should stay there until the relevant officials were summoned from Bratislava. Three officials turned up after half an hour, greeny khaki uniforms, a few brass stars, peaked hats. The youngest, a pallid young man with a thin moustache, took our passports and went into a little hut by the pontoon to do the paperwork. The other two, a good looking fair haired man in his thirties with a smooth manner I disliked, and a fatter one, breathless and looking a little ill at ease, came on board. They each managed to find somewhere to sit in *Rozinante's* cramped interior and looked around them. The smooth blond picked up a magazine Odile had brought with her, *Actuel*, and began thumbing through it. Suddenly he looked up and I noticed with horror that he had stopped at an article on Stalin in it, old black and white photographs of inmates in the *gulag*, photographs of Stalin meeting world leaders, old posters in bright Soviet realism. 'Do you have any literature on Czechoslovakia?' he asked me. I showed him the few guidebooks on central Europe I had on board. 'No ideology?' he asked. I shook my head wondering just what constituted ideology. He beckoned the fat man over to look at the pictures in the article on Stalin. They pointed to this and that in the photographs, in the way you look over holiday snaps, gesticulating and chattering to each other. One photograph showing labour camp inmates seemed to puzzle them, as if shedding new light on their lives, and they contemplated it silently, finally turning the page after frowning at each other. The fat official looked up and remembered he was supposed to be doing a job. He made a half-hearted effort to search the boat, but the pile of baggage inside eventually defeated him and he sat down with a tired look on his face. He mimed taking a picture with a camera and I pulled out our impressive arsenal of cameras. He mimed a radio and I showed him the radio cassette player. He mimed a rifle and I smiled, 'No'. He jotted down a few details on a scrap of paper and this seemed to exhaust his energy reserves. He resumed looking at the *Actuel* with the colleague who I had decided was the intelligence man. By now they had moved on from the article on Stalin and were discussing the advertisements. Any menace they might have conveyed disappeared in their boyish pleasure at the lingerie advertisements. A cough outside announced that the harassed looking official who had been doing the papers was back; he handed our passports to us and indicated that we should follow the launch to the port in Bratislava.

The launch roared off down the river and though I put *Rozinante* on full ahead it disappeared around a bend. A minute later it was back again as the soldiers realised they would have to idle downstream if they were going to escort us. The buildings of Bratislava appeared and we passed them towards the gantries that picked out the commercial port. The escort launch left us at the entrance and I rattled along inside the huge basin, happy to be out of the current, looking for a place to berth. At the end I saw a large steel yacht tied up with just enough space astern of it to get *Rozinante* into.

10 July

What I hadn't done when we left Bratislava was to report to the patrol base before we left. I assumed that all we had to do was clear into the next port at Komárno and then clear out of Czechoslovakia. We had hardly gone any distance down river before I spotted a patrol boat after us so I slowed down to see what was up. The soldiers in the patrol boat motioned us to go back and I mimed that it was impossible. I turned *Rozinante* around into the current and gave it full throttle. While I could point upstream, *Rozinante* was still going downstream, swept backwards by the strong current, the propeller churning the water. The current in the Danube below Bratislava has to be around seven knots. I motioned helplessly to the soldiers who looked on bewildered – they had orders to get me back but it was evident that this was impossible. While they radioed back to base I was swept gently backwards down river while motoring against it at full speed ahead. The officer in charge finally got permission to check our papers at a pontoon downstream and roared off ahead of us, indicating we should follow. A few kilometres later the patrol boat tied up at a pontoon and I turned *Rozinante* into the current and drifted somewhat violently backwards alongside. The soldiers grabbed the ropes Bridgit threw and we were tied up, though bucking about furiously in the current. It took a minute for the officer to check our papers and with a smile or two from the soldiers we departed.

The patrol boats buzzed us repeatedly as we pottered down the river until I surmised that it was probably the scantily clad bodies of Bridgit and Odile that interested the soldiers rather than our progress in Czechoslovakia. As Odile stepped below she suddenly turned and said, 'There's water in the cabin.'

I handed the helm to Bridgit and jumped below. Water was slopping over the cabin sole. I pulled the engine cover off to discover the engine compartment was awash, the flywheel spraying water everywhere. Bridgit stopped the engine and began pumping. I checked the obvious places first, the inlet for the cooling water, the inlet hose to the engine, the exhaust, the stern gland. Nothing. Once most of the water had been pumped out I restarted the engine and edged over to the side of the river where we anchored in a metre of water. While Bridgit and Odile pumped to keep the water level down I crawled into the bowels of the boat to find the problem. Around the stern tube, which houses the propeller shaft, water was gushing in at the outboard end. It was serious. The little bilge pump needed a hundred strokes every fifteen minutes and there was no way we could keep that up for long. *Rozinante* was sinking. I remembered the log we had hit with the propeller in Austria – it must have damaged the shaft which in turn damaged the stern tube.

Where were all the green patrol boats now I needed one? I reasoned that if I could communicate the problem to the officer on a patrol boat then he would tow *Rozinante* to Komárno which was about twelve kilometres downstream. There I would have to find a way to get the boat hauled out of the water and find someone or somewhere to make repairs. Although I had a back-up outboard engine for *Rozinante*, in the confusion of things to do before leaving I hadn't checked the outboard bracket. When I tried it the bracket crumbled, its wooden pad rotted from the inside out. Bridgit had a few things to say about the preparation for the trip, though thankfully she saved them for later. Eventually a patrol boat came around the bend in the river and I waved frantically for them to come over. After a lot of bumping and bashing the patrol boat was tied alongside and I began a mime show. The boat is sinking. I pumped, drew a picture of *Rozinante* going down, drew a crane hauling the boat out of the water, pointed to Komárno and indicated that we needed a tow to get there. The officer finally understood our problem and radioed to his base. His superior refused permission for the patrol boat to tow us to Komárno, all the officer could do was tow us to the river bank. He was obviously upset about his superior's decision and radioed again. A voluble conversation ensued though the outcome was the same, he was only able to tow us to the bank. The officer raised his two hands palm uppermost in the universal gesture of despair and helplessness; the soldiers nodded in sympathy. I motioned that I would get to Komárno somehow, made a gesture towards the patrol boat's radio that was greeted by sly smiles, and thanked them for their help. There was no way I was going to maroon *Rozinante* in a swamp in Czechoslovakia.

After the patrol boat had departed I started the engine, hauled up the anchor and we drifted downstream. I left the engine in neutral and only put it into gear to line *Rozinante* up for bridges or to avoid a barge train. The current whooshed us down at around six knots and it wasn't long before Komárno came into view. Cranes and gantries gave me some hope that I could find a way to get *Rozinante* hauled out. I swung into the commercial basin and there at the entrance was the patrol boat base complete with a crane for hauling the patrol boats out. It was perfect. I swung around to approach the base and heard a whistle. The guard on duty was waving me away. I came a little closer and tried pointing to the crane and then to *Rozinante*. I pointed to Odile pumping away on the bilge pump. He waved us away pointing back into the Danube and shouting, 'Kontrol, Kontrol.' I needed to do something soon so I pointed to my shoulder, and then ashore, in a gesture I hoped would indicate that I wanted to see a superior officer. The guard pointed to his shoulder, unslung the automatic rifle on his back, and though he did not point it at us, motioned us away from the base in a manner which clearly meant, 'You do not come any closer.' I motored over to where some barges were berthed on the opposite side of the basin, found a space and tied up. While Bridgit and Odile pumped I went ashore to somehow find help.

Halfway along the quay I met a group of seamen on their way back from a run ashore, most of them much the worse for wear after a day on the town. They bantered drunkenly with me while I attempted to find one who spoke English. None did, though one, luckily the only sober one, spoke some German. 'Namen Karol – Charlie, Charlie,' he said. I grabbed his arm and dragged him back to *Rozinante* where in a flash he understood my mime, the girls pumping, and the need to haul the boat out. We tried the dock cranes first and although an operator was willing to do the job, there was nowhere to put *Rozinante* out of the way of the railway wagons being shunted around on either side of the cranes. We went back to Charlie's boat, a huge pusher tug, where he was mate. Telephone calls were made, but with no effect. In the end I went back to *Rozinante*, weary and despondent. Odile, not used to hard physical work, could pump no longer. Her hands were cramped together from holding the bilge pump handle. Bridgit was tiring. In the basin I had noticed a patch of muddy bank that sloped gradually upwards, next to a huge shipyard that built and repaired barges. I decided to run *Rozinante* aground, stern first, in the hope of getting the stern tube into shallower water when there would be less pressure forcing water inside. And at least *Rozinante* would not sink even if she half-filled with water. I explained all this to Charlie and motored over to the bank. Going full astern I drove *Rozinante* up as far as I could, then took a line ashore and using a crude purchase on a pulley block, with the girls heaving waist deep in the water, we got the boat up as far as we could. It seemed to work, there was less water coming in, but still more than enough to require pumping every fifteen minutes.

Charlie appeared an hour later, a smile on his face, 'Morgen, Morgen, Raymond, Raymond,' he said. He held up six fingers, 'Morgen, Morgen,' and pointed at the barge slipway. If I understood Charlie correctly we were going to be hauled out in the shipyard in the morning, at six o'clock. I tried to find out what had happened, who Charlie had contacted, but my German was not up to it.

I sat up the rest of the night and pumped.

11th July

Sometime in the early morning I must have dropped off because Odile woke me to say the boat was filling up with water and her socks were getting wet. I pumped for half an hour and watched the dawn come up with a cup of coffee. At five-thirty workmen began appearing. There were six of them. One of the slipway cradles was lowered and I was motioned to motor *Rozinante* out and back onto it. Bridgit and Odile were desperately hauling clothes on. By the time they were up the boat was out of the water and workmen were examining the propeller and shaft fitting, two of them crawled into the engine compartment and began dismantling the coupling; like magic in the early morning sun *Rozinante* was being taken apart for repairs. Bridgit and Odile were taken away by a man who appeared to be in charge, to a restaurant where they changed money and sat down to breakfast. I stayed to see if I could be of any help to the trio who were doing the work, the *Master*, the *Bulgar* and the *Pharaoh*. I never learnt the names of any of them though I asked several times.

As work progressed it became apparent that more work was needed to put *Rozinante* right than had first been thought. It was impossible to buy spares for the engine in Czechoslovakia and so the *Bulgar* and *Pharaoh* took a pattern off the old coupling and constructed a new one. The propeller shaft was removed and checked to see if it was straight. A new stern tube was made up and threaded on to the old fitting. The stern gland was fibre-glassed into place. With all this work going on I was worried about the cost of it all. I asked the *Bulgar*, who had a smattering of English, how much this was all going to cost. The only reply I got was, 'This is a socialist state – you are our guest – this is a socialist state.' What the hell, I thought, if a bill is presented later that I can't pay, at least *Rozinante* will be afloat rather than at the bottom of the river. Things got more mysterious in the afternoon as the trio toiled on, obviously unhappy at the extent of the work. 'We have been told to stay until the work is finished,' the *Bulgar* said, 'I have to stay here.' I asked who had told him to stay, curious about who had ordered the work. 'My boss, the chief,' the *Bulgar* replied, 'But he has been told to help you'. 'Who told him?' I asked. The *Bulgar* didn't reply and carried on with his work.

In the afternoon two soldiers arrived to ask what was going on. They asked for our passports, the boat papers, then started to interrogate the *Bulgar* and the *Pharaoh*. The exchange was heated. Then the *Master* appeared and with two sharp words shut the soldiers up. I don't know what he said, but it cowed the soldiers who quickly left. The *Bulgar* made an abrupt arm gesture towards the departing soldiers and said, 'They are a big shit for us, they don't work, they have money, I spit on them.' The work was nearing the end and I thought it time to break out the whisky.

By early evening the work was finished. No one appeared to demand payment and the *Bulgar* was still replying with, 'We are a socialist state,' when I enquired how much it was going to cost. Over whisky I gave the trio twenty dollars each which I knew was worth more than a week's wages at black market rates. By late afternoon *Rozinante* was lowered back into the water and though the repairs would not hold up to excessive hammering, they would do. The *Bulgar* advised me to get proper replacements for the bits they had fabricated as soon as I could; as it turned out the repairs had to last until *Rozinante* got to Turkey some 1700 nautical miles later.

12th July

To the Závody Tazkého Strojárstva shipyard in Komárno and to the *Master*, *Pharaoh* and to the *Bulgar* I extend my grateful thanks. I still don't know who ordered the work to be done or why, though I have one or two theories. In the morning we motored over to Charlie's pusher tug and tied alongside. Charlie introduced us to the captain, who spoke English, and we sat down to breakfast. Over thick black coffee I asked the captain whether payment was required. He smiled and said, 'You are a small boat in trouble on the river, Czechoslovakia had to help you.' 'But who ordered the work?' I asked. He didn't know. I pulled out my last bottle of whisky and handed it to Charlie, 'For your help,' I said. He refused to take it. I insisted, but Charlie was having none of it. Then I had a brain wave, 'For the boat,' I said, 'For your boat, for everyone.' Charlie accepted it on behalf of the boat.

I wonder what labyrinthine events the repairs to *Rozinante* set in motion. I hope that there were no recriminations to anyone involved. I felt as if I was defecting from some responsibility I should have sorted out before leaving Czechoslovakia. I also kept looking over my shoulder to see if a patrol boat would speed out to apprehend us before we got to the Hungarian customs post on the other side of the Danube.

13th July

In Esztergóm we put the mast up. The repairs to the stern tube mean we can use the diesel sporadically, but from here we will sail whenever we can. *Rozinante's* mast is so short, about 23ft above water level, we will fit under all the bridges with the exception of the lowest bridge at Novisad in Yugoslavia.

14th July

Arrive in Budapest after sailing most of the way from Esztergóm. I put *Rozinante* into a small commercial canal at the upriver end of Budapest for the night.

15th July

We move to a pontoon for a rowing club at Margaret Island. The caretaker seems a little inebriated but friendly for all that. Too friendly as it turns out. After exploring Budapest we return to *Rozinante* where the caretaker starts to plead with me to 'have one of my women.' I attempt to explain that they are not 'my women', and that neither of them feels like spending the night with an inebriated caretaker. I spent the night sleeping in the cockpit with a hammer beside me while the caretaker stalked the pontoon with a bottle of local firewater and a mournful look on his face.

16th July

We move to a basin at the downstream end of Budapest where we tie up to the pontoon of a rowing club. It is miles from the centre of Budapest, but there are buses and cheap taxis and no prowling caretaker.

17th July

When we leave in the morning we are escorted out by 40 or so kayaks from the club, all waving and cheering and paddling furiously to keep up with us. We anchor for the night in a huge basin at Dunaújváros, swim, and have a leisurely dinner in the cockpit. There is a heat wave killing hundreds in Greece and Turkey and though temperatures are not up to those in the Mediterranean, it is very hot and sticky.

19th July

Paks. Yesterday we stayed in a cheap cabin at a camping ground. Visitors to Hungary are automatically registered with the police at hotels and camping grounds and so our passports were impounded because we had been in Hungary for six days and had not registered. So today I had to bring *Rozinante* to Paks where I was grilled by a plain clothes man, politely but firmly, who eventually handed our passports back after noting down my story.

20th July

Baja. Odile leaves for Paris and I hunt out someone to make up a new outboard bracket. The stern tube repairs in Czechoslovakia are holding up, but will not last for long so I intend to sail and use the outboard, keeping the diesel in reserve for emergencies and for any difficult manoeuvring we have to do. The outboard moves *Rozinante* along at around 2½ knots which with 3 knots or so of current is enough to keep us going at a respectable pace.

24 July

Mohács. We have to clear out of Hungary here so I go up to the customs office. The officer there is a friendly soul who notes down the particulars, then goes back into his office to emerge grasping a telex covering an A4 page. He points to a name: Bertolotti, Odile Marie Susanne. 'Where is she?' he asks. I realise the telex probably details everything known to the Hungarians about us, from my interview in Paks with the plain clothes man. I explain that she has left by train for Paris several days ago. 'No problem,' the amiable customs officer nods, and then takes the telex back to his office. The rest of the paperwork for clearing out is finished quickly – it was only the whereabouts of the third crew member which was worrying him.

25th July

Anchored for the night in the waterland just inside the Yugoslavian border. Just as Bridgit serves the evening meal I notice the sky had changed colour to a greasy grey-black and that lightning is flickering around the horizon. Then I notice a line of white water advancing across the river. The storm hits us before we can get the anchor up properly, the wind blowing *Rozinante* over and waves drenching the boat in spray. The fury and suddenness of it is frightening, all the more so because it is so unexpected on a river. We manage to get the anchor up and in the dusk punctuated by flashes of lightning and to the sound of the wind and waves fly downstream looking for somewhere to shelter. About ten kilometres down river I find a spot tucked in behind an island where we are safe from the waves, now 1½m high with the current, kicked up by the storm off the *Puszta*.

26th July

Vukovar. There is a small harbour where I nose *Rozinante* into the bank. As we are tying up a dark haired man on a racing bike rides up to help. 'You don't remember me,' he says in perfect English, 'You asked me where to get petrol yesterday – on the river.' Now I remember him, idling down the river in a dinghy with a 4hp *Tomos* outboard, and as we were running low on petrol I had asked him where we could get some. I asked Mladen what had happened in the storm. 'We simply kept going,' he said, 'we are used to them.' He went on to tell me how with several friends he had taken his 10 foot dinghy up to the Iron Gates for a holiday. 'In Vukovar,' he said, 'you are not a man without a boat.' I remembered that I had read about this section of the Danube being colonised by Germans who gained a reputation as first class seamen, much in demand on sea-going ships as well as river craft. I asked him if he had a German connection and learnt his grandparents had been German: his grandmother's maiden name was Braun and his grandfather's Haufen. It is surprising this far down the river that there is such a strong and comparatively recent German connection. Not surprisingly the language of the river, right through to Romania, is German. There is another violent storm in the night though *Rozinante* is safe this time tucked up in the harbour.

27th July

Novisad. Just before the town proper there is a Watersport Club with a pontoon and a cheerful caretaker with a single toothed smile helps us tie up. I ask him if there is a *Volvo Penta* agent in the town, but there is no comprehension there. However he leads us over to a smooth-looking man sitting by an expensive motorboat who speaks English. When he understands I have a mechanical problem he motions me into the boat and in an instant we are off at 20 knots down the river to a mechanic he knows. I ask him what he does, intrigued to discover how he owns an expensive Italian motorboat in Socialist Yugoslavia. 'I own a hotel,' he says, 'we are allowed private enterprise here you know.' I do know, I just didn't think it ran to hotels. After racing up and down the river a few times it turns out there is no *Volvo Penta* agent in Novisad, but there is one in Belgrade.

29th July

At the pontoon I take down *Rozinante's* mast so we can pass under the lowest bridge on the Danube after Passau. The bridge at Novisad is a constant problem for barges and cruise boats which either have to dismantle the uppermost bridge deck or on the more modern craft have a hydraulic system to raise and lower the bridge deck.

Belgrade. Finding somewhere to berth in Belgrade is difficult. I pottered down the River Sava to the quay where the trip boats and cruise boats berth, but was waved abruptly away. At the junction of the Danube and the Sava I tried mooring next to some dilapidated hulks which served as a boat club bar and restaurant, but was told to move on. Eventually I found an old commercial basin on the Danube where the amiable club members said I was welcome to stay. The surroundings, a collection of dilapidated buildings, a gravel works and some poisonous looking effluent leaking into the mud, were not the most salubrious, but at least it was safe and close to the centre of Belgrade.

30th July

In Belgrade I manage to track down the *Volvo Penta* agent, but he stocks few parts and doesn't have the flexible coupling I need for the propeller shaft. Belgrade is one of my least favourite cities and this visit does nothing to make me like it any more than on previous visits. Bridgit and I decide we will leave tomorrow. The Danube is slowed down now by the giant dam at the Iron Gates and so there is little current, perhaps a knot at most, helping us on our way.

1st August

We stop in Veliko Gradiste for the night. A good breeze blowing down the river has meant we have sailed all day at speed. The Danube is now over a kilometre wide in places, more like a lake than a river, though it is narrowing all the time as we get closer to the Iron Gates gorge. The people on the river have been unfailingly friendly. The fishermen hunched over their rods wave, the pusher-tug skippers honk their horns, pleasure boat owners scrutinise *Rozinante* with binoculars and then wave wildly, in the harbours the locals want to know where we have come from and where we are going. Moreover they know the river: about the places along the Danube, of the waterland before the Hungarian border teeming with fish and bird life, of the Gorge of Kazan and the Iron Gates dam, about the towns and villages along the way, of where the best *slij-vovitza* comes from and where the best fish restaurants are.

2nd August

With a strong down-river wind *Rozinante* is creaming along. When the Iron Gates dam was completed and the valley flooded, islands in the river were covered by water. But at low water the dead branches of the trees on the islands stick up out of the water, a ghostly forest of branches, and on the section before Golubac we get lost in this dead forest, unsure of where the channel lies, and spend an anxious hour threading our way out until we find the main channel again. That night we anchor at km 1013 behind a small promontory, tied to the branches of a dead tree for added security. It is a lonely place where every sound reverberates off the cliffs and where there seems to be not a soul about.

3rd August

At the Iron Gates dam and locks we wait to lock through. The wind is howling down river and apparently the lock gates cannot be worked.

4th August

The wind is up again and with a reefed main we are flying down river. I had read of the winds and storms of this region, but certainly didn't expect to encounter them in August. At the new dam and lock at km 864 the wind is too strong for the lock gates to be operated so we anchor off and spend an uncomfortable night being buffeted by the waves, up to 2m high, kicked up by the wind.

5th August

At around lunchtime the gates open so we rush to get the anchor up and race over to squeeze into a space at the back of the lock behind a cruise boat, two tugs and barges and a steel Yugoslavian yacht which had been waiting with us. Once out of the lock we hit the current from the weir and only just managed to get across to Prahovo, the Yugoslavian customs post for clearing out of Yugoslavia before Bulgaria.

6th August

Leaving Yugoslavia. The old industrial harbour where I moored *Rozinante* at Prahovo is a grimy silted up place surrounded by cranes and with fume-laden air that hurts your lungs when you breathe it in. I needed petrol and diesel before going into Bulgaria so I wandered ashore with the jerry-cans to fill up. The guard on the harbour gate asked what I wanted and when I had communicated that it was *benzin* I needed, he pointed to the train tracks and said 'Negotin,' holding up eight fingers to presumably show it was eight kilometres away. I started towards the railway tracks to be brought up by his shout of 'nein nein', whereupon he mimed driving a car and pointed to one of the ram-shackle houses shouting 'auto, auto – Ringo'. I went up to the house and was greeted by a dark giant in greasy overalls who pointed at himself and said with a satisfied nod 'Ringo'. I pointed to the jerry-cans and he said 'Ya, benzin, nix problem – Negotin', pointing to his battered Polski Fiat 650 in the garden. '100km to 5 litres,' he said proudly. It didn't look capable of taking Ringo let alone me and two jerry cans as well. We had to push-start it and then jump in while it was still going, something about the clutch or lack of it Ringo had me understand, before we rattled off towards Negotin.

Ringo had worked in Austria and so our conversation was in a bastard German and the English he had picked up from watching sub-titled films on television. He was married to a Romanian woman and had two children on the other side in Romania. He was saving up to pay for them to come over to Yugoslavia, or rather paying for them to get passports to be able to leave. It was difficult, very difficult in Romania he said,

Austria was 'super, extra-prima', Yugoslavia was not bad. As we drove over the rough country roads parts kept dropping off the car and Ringo would stop and pick them up. First an exhaust bracket, then the next exhaust bracket, then the exhaust and silencer, then an unidentified bit and a couple of bolts. By the time we got to Negotin the Fiat sounded like a Sherman tank. I got my petrol and diesel, spent the rest of the *dinar* I had on bread, wine, biscuits, fruit juice, salami, anything I could find. Yugoslavia has an alarming rate of inflation and in a year's time my *dinar* would be worthless. We rattled back to Prahovo and caroomed down to the harbour where I paid Ringo the ten dollars we had agreed on; in hard currency it was a good deal for him, and in any case he was going to spend it on a good cause bribing a Romanian official to speed up his wife and children's passport.

7th August

The border between Bulgaria and Yugoslavia has a fence right to the water's edge and ploughed earth on either side. A Bulgarian fishing boat, poaching on the Yugoslavian side of the river, dispelled some of my fears about our reception in Bulgaria. A little further on a soldier on a Bulgarian gun-boat moored by the bank waves a red flag and motions us to go alongside. Our passports and papers are meticulously checked and then we are told to clear in at Vidin.

On the bank watchtowers with radar on top and the occasional glint of light on binocular lenses tell us we are being watched and our progress monitored. At Vidin I berth at a pontoon and find that we should have cleared in at the ferry harbour two kilometres upstream. However, the kindly old harbourmaster gets the relevant officials to come down to us when I explain it would take *Rozinante* an hour or more to get back upstream against the current, which is up to 3–4 knots again, now we are downstream of the Iron Gates dam.

11 August

Just past Sviŝtov an old arm of the Danube leads off behind a large wooded island. With Bridgit calling the depths I take *Rozinante* down it to the village of Vardim. A police boat asks where we are going and appears unconcerned when I motion towards Vardim, roaring off upriver towards Sviŝtov. The banks of the river and the island are thickly forested, the old channel is like some tropical creek except for the earth coloured houses of Vardim at the top of the curve of the channel. In Vardim there is virtually nothing to buy in the solitary shop and the beer in the one bar tastes like dishwater.

13th August

I clear us out of Rousse but wait an hour before leaving until another of the violent storms which seem to be a feature of the lower Danube has passed over. In Romania at Giurgiu opposite Rousse an armed guard is allotted to us and I begin the long process of clearing in. The 18-year-old conscript who is our guard speaks some English and seems embarrassed that I have to sit around for hours waiting for this or that official. When the harbourmaster starts shouting and waving at me, pushing the boat's papers under my nose, the conscript translates for me that the harbourmaster is upset because the papers do not have my photo on them. 'They are no good,' the harbourmaster shouted, 'you cannot enter Romania.' I tell the conscript that they are normal British boat papers and he nods that he knows, but if I keep quiet and let the harbourmaster have his tantrum then after half an hour it will be all right. Sure enough after half an hour I get the papers stamped. In the customs office I sign a carnet which states that I am not carrying weapons, ammunition, radioactive materials, narcotic and psychotropic drugs, or prohibited records and books amongst other things. After a cursory search of the boat in which the well-stocked food lockers are admired, we eventually get permission to cruise the length of the Danube in Romania.

15th August

I'm happy to leave Giurgiu as the sulphurous fumes from the industry nearby make it difficult to breathe, burning the lungs and making my eyes water. A sulphurous mist hangs over the river for ten kilometres downstream. We stop at Oltenita and wander ashore to a run-down restaurant and bar for a drink. Just as we get there a soldier runs up and orders us back on the boat. After an hour he has apparently radioed his superior who gives us permission to go ashore. The restaurant has run out of food, has no beer, the bottles of wine are $20 each, and the waiter wants a carton of cigarettes, so we go back to the boat for a cup of tea.

Later that night the harbourmaster invites us to his house for a drink. He speaks fluent French so Bridgit translates the bits I miss. He wants to know all about the Rhine-Main-Danube canal and is perplexed when I tell him it is not finished and probably won't be until 1993. He has heard that it is about to open in a months time and has visions of all sorts of craft coming from the North Sea and stopping at Oltenita.

17th August

Cernavoda has to be one of the poorest places we have stopped at in Romania. I queued for half an hour for eggs, Bridgit queued for another half an hour to get bread, there were hardly any vegetables to speak of had we bothered to queue, and the petrol station had been closed for days because it had run out of fuel and none was expected for a few more days. The whole town has a dusty forlorn look to it. Nearby a huge nuclear power station is being built to a Canadian design. Ceausescu criticised the amount of money it was costing and the amount of concrete being used – did orders come from the top to use less concrete? Will Cernavoda be added to the list along with Chernobyl?

18th August

To transit the Danube-Black Sea Canal we must take a pilot, so in the morning Victor turns up, a cocky dark-haired man who immediately makes himself at home on the boat, changing into a pair of swimming trunks, smoking my cigarettes, putting tapes in the cassette player and then choosing a few cassettes for himself, fingering my jeans and examining my camera. When I explain it will take 10 hours or more for *Rozinante* to transit the canal he is aghast. Fortunately for us and for Victor he negotiates a tow alongside a barge in the lock and I forgive him for pocketing our tapes and smoking cigarettes like a train. Tied alongside *Rozinante* is doing 8 knots or more with the hull flexing and cracking under the strain. When the wind gets up on the nose water is sluiced up between the tug and *Rozinante* and in through the fitted windows and the hull and deck joint, distorted from the strain against the tug's side. There is not a lot we can do unless I cast *Rozinante* off, so while Bridgit mops up the water with towels, I'm pumping again.

19th August
Constanţa. The Black Sea.

In Constanţa we waited four days until a northeaster blew itself out. At times the gale was washing solid water right over the top of the breakwater which stands around 20ft high. Though we had any amount of Romanian *lei*, it was a struggle to find anything to spend it on. Even worse was the fact that I could not get hold of petrol or diesel for the 200 mile trip across the Black Sea to the Bosphorus. My plan was to go south down the coast towards the Bulgarian port of Burgas and if there were contrary winds, stop there to find fuel. If the winds were fair for Turkey and the Bosphorus, we would change course without stopping in Bulgaria. We left after the Romanian officials arrived at midday; they had said they would be there by eight in the morning. We left with the warning that we must proceed straight out to sea until we were 10M off the coast be-

fore changing course for Turkey. By the afternoon of the second day we were off Burgas, but as the wind was fair for Turkey I decided not to enter Bulgaria and to continue on towards the Bosphorus. By the middle of that night the wind had dropped and it took us another two days to get to Istanbul. I had just enough fuel left to crank the diesel up and get us into the Bosphorus against a rising head-wind and down to Bebek.

After Romania, Istanbul and Turkey seemed like a paradise, a land of plenty where you could buy food in the shops and dine on dishes in the restaurants that were unimaginable in Romania. On the day after we arrived I found Bridgit had bought four loaves of bread during the day, a reflex action after Romania she said, in case it wasn't available tomorrow. From Istanbul we sailed with the *meltem* down through the Sea of Marmara and down the Aegean to Bodrum. This was home to me, waters I knew well from travels in my yacht *Tetranora*, and despite the diminutive size of *Rozinante* we felt that by now we knew and trusted her, and while larger yachts sheltered from the strong *meltem*, we scudded down the coast in her.

Rozinante has been sold now, to Alvis at the NATO base at Izmir. After over 2500 miles from Regensburg to Bodrum it has to be the most travelled Mirror Offshore 19 in the world. Bridgit went back to New Zealand where she administers a theatre-sport programme. Graham has bought a yacht to sail away from the fleshpots of London. I married Odile and have a map of the Volga pinned to the wall.

V. WATERWAYS SIGNS ON THE DANUBE

(Red band/white border) River bank port hand marker

Red can buoy. Marks port side of channel

Red topmark on torpedo buoy. Marks port side of channel

(Green or black top). River bank starboard hand marker

Green or black conical buoy. Marks starboard side of channel

Green or black topmark on torpedo buoy. Marks starboard side of channel

NOTE Channel is buoyed from seawards. Therefore port hand marks must be left to starboard and starboard hand marks to port when navigating downriver.

Channel forks

Port leading marks

Starboard leading marks

Danger on port hand side

Danger on starboard hand side

Cross to port side

Cross to starboard side

Note Channel buoyed and marked from seawards.

(Yellow diamond) Navigable channel under bridge

(2 yellow diamonds vertical) Navigable channel one way only under bridge

Passage prohibited

Stop

Direction of channel

Sound horn

Vigilance needed

Berthing prohibited

Anchoring prohibited

Berthing permitted

Anchoring permitted

Overtaking prohibited

Crossing the channel and overtaking prohibited

Do not make a wake

Limited height

Limited breadth

Turning area

Depth and breadth of channel indication

End of restrictions

Kilometre board

Mile board (from Galati to Sulina)

Port captain

Customs

Water

Telephone

Typical section of the river showing buoys and channel markers on the river bank.

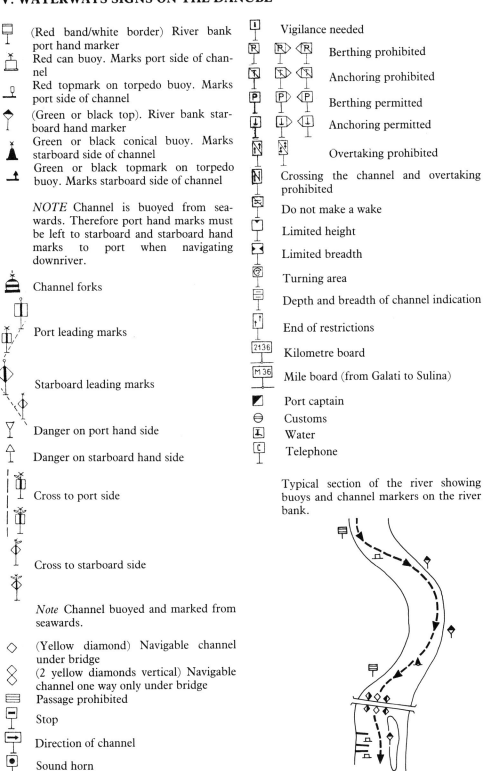

Index